New States in the Modern World

Written under the auspices of the
Center for International Affairs,
Harvard University

New States
in
the Modern World

Edited by Martin Kilson

Harvard University Press, Cambridge, Massachusetts
and London, England
1975

Library of Congress Cataloging in Publication Data

Kilson, Martin.
    New states in the modern world.

    Bibliography: p.
    Includes index.
    1. States, New—Politics and government—Addresses, essays, lec-
tures. 2. Africa—Politics and government—Addresses, essays, lectures.
I. Title.
JF60.K54   320.1'7'096   75-4560
ISBN 0-674-62261-8

Printed in the United States of America

For Rupert Emerson

Contents

Preface

Between 1947 and 1970 over fifty new states entered the world political order. Despite the many distinguishing features among them, they all have in common the colonial relationship to the imperial industrial states of the West. Whether in Africa, Asia, or the Caribbean, the prominent political attributes of the new states have been defined through the colonial experience.[1] An understanding of the contemporary behavior of the new states is, therefore, contingent upon knowledge of the multifaceted influence of the colonial relationships upon them.

No single volume can pretend to treat all the new states and their colonial relationships, so we have chosen to study mainly African states — including one Arab-African state, Egypt. New African states are in many respects ideal for this purpose: virtually every major issue surrounding the formation and development of new states is present in one form or another in these states. For example, ideology has been long recognized as a central factor in the birth and organization of new states, and the Arab-African state of Egypt is a prominent example of the impact of ideology on nation building. The mobilization of modern political forces within Egyptian society, the definition of its political processes, and its international character have all displayed a significant ideological dimension. Indeed, ideology has often appeared to be a political end in itself, satisfying both to important sectors of modern Egyptian society and to traditionalist sectors. No small part of political modernization encompasses the problem of translating the particularistic dimensions of ideology — its symbolic, cathartic, and mythical features — into viable organized categories of political life. Such translation of ideology transforms it into a power and wealth-creating (universalistic) force.[2] This transition, however, is far from easy to make. Few new states have succeeded; India and China are prominent exceptions. Because it is unique in Africa, Egypt's experience in the use of ideology is treated in this volume.

In the black African states, a variety of situations has combined to restrict their power-creating capacity — a capacity that Lucian Pye identifies as the crux of political modernization.[3] In some instances there is

1. See Rupert Emerson, *From Empire to Nation* (Cambridge, Harvard University Press, 1960).
2. Talcott Parsons, *Structure and Process in Modern Societies* (Glencoe, Ill., The Free Press, 1960), pp. 126-128, passim.
3. Lucian Pye, *Aspects of Political Development* (Boston, Little Brown, 1966).

the seemingly simple problem of small-scale political units. Populations are not large in many African states — only several have more than eight million people — and natural resources are sparse. One strategy for surmounting this limitation is the formation of regional groupings. One type involves a fundamental redefinition of sovereignty: federalism. These alternatives, regionalism and federalism, are considered in this volume and their relative efficacy evaluated. Through a case study of the Republic of Cameroon, the attributes of this problem that are unique to new African states receive special attention.

Political modernization is not only complicated by size and limited developmental resources. A variety of cultural and sociopolitical obstacles also hinders the process of modernity. These reveal themselves most prominently in the character of cleavages in African political life. African societies are unique in both the range and intensity of primordial solidarity groupings — kinship, clan, and tribe — and the processes of political modernization, even under the most favorable socioeconomic conditions, have not escaped their influence. More specifically, traditional African solidarity dynamics have distorted the growth of rational patterns of political cleavage, fragmenting the cleavaging process in a manner conducive to high political pathology[4] — corruption, undisciplined opportunism, and especially cleavage convulsion. By convulsive cleavage I mean a centrifugal conflict dynamic. Rather than produce compromise, bargains, trade-offs, and thus a network and hierarchy of competing yet overlapping interest groups, convulsive cleavage emphasizes what might be called the characterological specificity of competing interests. This in turn leaves a distinctive imprint upon the perception of competing interests: the sacred attributes (symbols, heritage, myths, and so on) are accorded a salience equal to and sometimes greater than the secular political attributes. Carried to the extreme, this conflict dynamic stymies any viable political development of African (and other) new states, facilitating what Samuel Huntington has termed political decay.[5] Some dimensions of such political decay are considered in this volume in the chapter on the former Republic of the Congo, now Zaïre, and a case study of cleavage characterized by corruption and undisciplined opportunism is offered in the chapter on Ghana.

The significance of new states extends beyond their internal political characteristics to their position in the world political order. A unique feature in the creation of new states was the direct role of the world political order. Through the United Nations the world political order

4. On pathologies of politics, see Carl J. Friedrich, *Political Pathology* (New York, Atheneum, 1972).

5. Samuel P. Huntington, *Political Order in Changing Societies* (New Haven, Yale University Press, 1968).

actually induced the formation of new states. They found it a satisfactory solution to the conflict stemming from imperialism in international relations. Two dimensions of nation building are studied in this volume: one concerns the conflicts surrounding the intervention of the international system in behalf of the birth of new states; the other concerns the legal-regulatory implications of this conflict for world political order.

Conflict is, in fact, such an enduring feature of new states — both domestically and internationally — that their emergence inevitably poses new burdens upon the institutions of the international political system. Within less than a decade of the birth of independent African states, from 1960 onwards, five major civil wars occurred — in Sudan, Ethiopia, Zaïre, Nigeria, and Chad — and four violent boundary disputes erupted — in Algeria-Morocco, Mauritania-Morocco, Somalia-Kenya-Uganda. The international political machinery, never adequate in its peace-keeping capacity, proved seriously strained in face of these new obligations. The general problem of regulating world political order in the era of new states is, thus, a continuing one. Finally, a theoretical essay on the intrinsic characteristics of the nation-state system, treating especially the sociopsychological impedimenta to viable world order implied in the nation-state stystem, is included.

The range of topics treated in this volume arises essentially from the unique characteristics of new states. But another factor in the choice of topics was their relationship to the intellectual interests of the scholar in whose honor these essays were written — Rupert Emerson. Unlike the typical scholar in the field of international affairs in the last two generations, Rupert Emerson sustained a catholic interest in these subjects. He examined the power structure of colonialism in Indonesia and Malaya, the conditions of representative government in independent Southeast Asia, the impact of nationalism — as a form of modern group mobilization — upon the modern state, and the implications of both the rise and behavior of new states for the international system.[6] The contributors to this volume feel that only a format that embraced all these facets of new states would do justice to the great scholar and humanist here honored.

I should like to express appreciation to the Harvard Center for International Affairs — and especially to its former director, Professor Robert Bowie — for support in the preparation of this volume. Thanks is also due Max Hall, formerly an editor of Harvard University Press, who first suggested that these essays, originally offered to Rupert Emerson in manuscript form upon his retirement, be published.

MK

6. See the bibliography of Rupert Emerson's writings in the appendix.

Part One
Political Dynamics in New States

1. Tradition and Nationalism in Tropical Africa
James S. Coleman

Introduction

The relationship between tradition and nationalism in Tropical Africa is generally regarded as having been a negative and mutually antagonistic one. African tradition has connoted, among other things, conservatism, subservience and dependence, smallness in scale, parochialism, and rule by an illiterate gerontocracy. African nationalism, by contrast, has implied progress, independence, expansion in scale, and leadership by youthful and educated modernists. Whereas elsewhere tradition may have inspired nationalism, in Africa it has tended to be regarded — most militantly by the nationalists themselves — as one of the causes of national humiliation and as the main obstacle to modern nationhood. Divisive tribalism, stagnating customs, and obstructive chieftanships of traditional Africa were considered, along with colonialism itself, as the chief enemies of nationalism. In a word, futurism, not traditionalism, has been the ethos of African nationalism.

This crude characterization of the relationship, although not unreasonable when painting with a broad brush, seriously oversimplifies the complex realities of both African tradition and African nationalism as well as their frequently subtle relationship. Our purpose here is to examine this relationship with special emphasis upon the ways in which tradition was a factor affecting nationalism in the pre-independence period.

The Concept of Tradition

The concept of tradition has acquired a bewildering variety of meanings. It is pointless, therefore, to discuss its relationship to nationalism without some conceptual clarification and precision. At the outset four types of tradition ought to be distinguished:

Typological Tradition. The widespread use of Max Weber's ideal-type construct,[1] together with the equally common use of a simplified transition model[2] and of dichotomous and pattern-variable modes of

---

1. Max Weber, *The Methodology of the Social Sciences* (Glencoe, The Free Press, 1949), pp. 90, 93, in which an ideal-type construct is defined as a "one-sided accentuation . . . by the synthesis of a great many diffuse, discrete, more or less present and occasionally absent *concrete individual* phenomena, which are arranged . . . into a unified analytical construct. In its conceptual purity, this mental construct cannot be found anywhere in reality."
2. For a critique of the transition model widely used in the study of change see Wilbert E. Moore, *Social Change* (Englewood Cliffs, Prentice-Hall, 1963), pp. 40-42.

analysis[3] in the study of change and modernization of whole societies — the emerging preoccupation of most social sciences — have tended
to create or to perpetuate a grossly oversimplified and sterotyped image
of the nature of tradition in the developing areas, and particularly in
Africa. These analytical devices have many advantages.[4] Moreover, the
study of change compels one to specify a baseline, and some concept of
a "traditional society" is understandably the usual baseline used.[5] Also,
when one is making broad sweeping comparisons of a vast array of
complex phenomena a high level of abstraction is probably inevitable.
The end result, however, has been an image of a uniform, homogeneous, and static traditional African society, whose attributes characteristically include a predominance of ascriptive, particularistic and diffuse
patterns, non-legal-rational bases of authority, limited mobility and
differentiation, and so forth. Indeed, one gets the impression that the
trait list of ideal-typical traditionality is derived not from the observation of concrete "traditional societies" but simply from a specifi-
cation of the polar opposites of a trait list of typological modernity
derived from a generalization about contemporary industrialized societies in the West. The extensive and frequently uncritical use of these
analytical devises has contributed no little to confused thinking and
dubious generalizations about the nature of tradition in Africa.

Stereotypical Tradition. This is by far the oldest type of characterization of tradition in Africa. In a brilliant analysis of stereotypes about
Africa Igor Kopytoff has noted:

> The scarcely human beings in the writings of antiquity give way in
> the early Age of Exploration to stable polities ruled by kings and
> nobles. Where Arab travelers saw virtue in relation to Islamic
> influence, the European Enlightenment, alienated from its own social
> order, created the virtuous, because untouched, "noble savage" from
> whom Europe could learn in its quest for regeneration. The later

3. The dichotomies (and their application) of Redfield, Maine, Toennies,
Weber, as well as Parsons' pattern variables, are discussed in Bert F. Hoselitz,
"Main Concepts in the Analysis of the Social Implications of Technical
Change," in Bert F. Hoselitz and Wilbert E. Moore, *Industrialization and
Society* (Geneva, UNESCO, 1963), pp. 11-29.

4. See Francis X. Sutton, "Representation and the Nature of Political Systems," in *Comparative Studies in Society and History*, 2.1 (October 1959).

5. Leonard W. Doob, *Becoming More Civilized: A Psychological Exploration* (New Haven, Yale University Press, 1960). He states (on p. 20), "Without a
baseline changes cannot be sensibly observed. Unless that baseline is cautiously
established, however, the outcome will be no better than that provided by the
snob in modern society who with little encouragement can indicate the characteristics of peoples less civilized than himself."

images are more familiar, for many of them are still with us. Unbridled lawlessness coexisted with robots in the iron grip of unchanging custom, and witch-ridden paranoiacs under tyrannous chiefs vied with happy villagers living in communal harmony. The common thread here is ethnocentrism . . . the universal tendency of all people to perceive other culture patterns through the categories and concerns of their own. The resulting myths may be positive or negative.[6]

One is naturally concerned about the extent to which the ostensibly social scientific formulation of typological tradition discussed above has been influenced by the ethnocentric image of African tradition derived from the highly varied and frequently contradictory stereotypes by which the external world has characterized Africa over the centuries.

Mythopoeic Tradition. This tradition refers to the generalized, and equally ethnocentric, flattering images African nationalists and Afrophiles hold and seek to propagate about African tradition. The images are invariably positive; they frequently are consciously created to counter pejorative stereotypes. Indeed, as nationalistic interpretations of tradition they are themselves expressions of nationalism. They are a near universal accompaniment of nationalism. As Max Radin put it: "In antiquity as in modern times a sense of nationalism may create characteristics not only for persons but for entire groups . . . tradition assists in building a national ideal and therefore helps to create the complex of nationalism. A national ideal usually means a flattering self-portrayal on the part of a people in which certain traits are singled out as especially characteristic."[7]

Empirical Tradition. This tradition is the complex of existential "attitudes, beliefs, conventions and institutions rooted in the experience of the past and exerting an orienting and normative influence on the present."[8] Whether or not a particular tradition exists at a given point in time is an empirical question but one that is admittedly very difficult to answer.

These four distinctions are only analytical, but they are important ones to make. A mythopoeic tradition can become a stereotype and elements in it can even become part of the trait list of a typological tradition. A flattering stereotype regarding African tradition developed

---

6. Igor Kopytoff, "Socialism and Traditional African Societies" in William H. Friedland and Carl G. Rosberg, Jr., *African Socialism* (Stanford, Stanford University Press, 1964), pp. 53-54.

7. Max Radin, "Tradition." *Encyclopedia of the Social Sciences* (New York, Macmillan, 1938), XV, 64.

8. *Webster's Third New International Dictionary* (Springfield, G. & C. Merriam Co., 1961).

externally, can be, and has been, expropriated by African nationalists and made part of their mythopoeic tradition. In any event, we are here primarily concerned with the last three types—with how external pejorative stereotypes of African tradition have reinforced nationalist protest, with how African nationalists have been affected by or have sought to create a mythopoeic tradition, and with how elements in the empirical African tradition affected the rise and pattern of development of African nationalism.

Before turning to these issues, the concept of tradition requires further examination. One point concerns the vexing question of which "experience of the past" is to be regarded as "traditional." The dilemma is put succinctly by Thomas Hodgkin:

> During the first phase [of Africa's interaction with the West] African governments and peoples—in particular those which, like Dahomey, Segu, Samory's military empire, Bornu under Rabeh Zubayr, Mahdist Sudan, were involved in organized and active resistance to European penetration—were naturally concerned to preserve their established institutions, values, and ways of life. These institutions and values cannot properly be described as "traditional," since the nineteenth century was in certain respects a revolutionary period in African history, and the regimes which resisted European aggression most effectively were in many cases either the products of revolutionary upheavals or attempting to carry out policies of internal reform and modernization. Moreover these regimes had already been exposed, in some instances over a long period of time, to Western influences.[9]

Similar uncertainty regarding the "traditional" is created by the new traditions introduced and the old traditions transformed during the colonial period. In former British Africa, for example, efforts were made to introduce the institution of chieftainship among many groups in which it was not indigenous. In many cases these efforts failed; but in some instances the innovation "caught on" and presumably became part of the tradition of the group concerned. Again, the idea of a "Kamerum" nation acquired the power of a tradition as evidenced by its revival after thirty years and subsequent influence upon nationalist development in the two trust territories.

One might argue that the only reasonable position in the face of these confusions is to recognize the ambiguities in Africa's traditions produced by its mixed up precolonial past and arbitrarily to specify that

9. Thomas L. Hodgkin, "The Relevance of 'Western' Ideas for the New African States," in J. Roland Pennock, *Self-government in Modernizing Nations* (Englewood Cliffs, Prentice Hall, 1964), p. 66.

the state of affairs prevailing in African societies at the time of the formal imposition of colonial rule would be regarded as the baseline traditional order.[10] But this overlooks the fact, underscored by Kopytoff, that the institutional framework within which most Africans were operating during the most intensive nationalism — was "a blend of precolonial and postcolonial institutions." He adds that "For the actors in a given social system, the analytical difference between what may be called 'traditional' and other elements may not be relevent, for nontraditional elements have become a part of the present social mythology and shape the expectations of people."[11] Indeed, in many situations it is impossible to distinguish precolonial tradition from the amalgams of tradition emerging out of the experiences and innovations of the colonial period and then specify their respective relationship to nationalism.

A further complicating factor is that contradictory, or at least noncongruent, traditions can exist at different levels or in different aspects of activity of even a single homogeneous society. This fact, Kopytoff notes, is what has made modern anthropology "extremely skeptical of the utility of shorthand descriptions of whole societies," not to mention embryonic nations or whole continents or races.[12] In this same vein Hodgkin has brought out the multivalence of the Islamic tradition in Africa. Whether the conservative authoritarian tradition, or the radical reformative tradition of Islam will be articulated by a given

10. Cf. C. E. Black, *The Dynamics of Modernization* (New York, Harper and Row, 1966), who observes (on p. 8) that "For the societies of Western Europe, the traditional institutions are those of the Middle Ages, and the challenge of modernity to the traditional system occurred between the twelfth and eighteenth centuries. Comparable traditional periods before the challenge of modernity may be discerned in all other societies. In the least developed societies, the traditional period has lasted until well into the twentieth century."

11. Kopytoff, "Socialism and Traditional African Societies," p. 21. As Joseph Ki-Zerbo observed (on p. 274) "Very often the soldier who tries to speak French as it is spoken in Paris will show you the talisman he wore in the fight for the liberation of France. Similarly, during electoral rollcalls, I have often seen candidates call upon both the voice of the people and the intervention of the witch doctors." "African Personality and the New African Society," in The American Society of African Culture, *Pan-Africanism Reconsidered* (Los Angeles, University of California Press, 1962). Peter Lloyd has noted that the sharp dichotomy sometimes made between town and village life (equating it to traditional and European life) is methodologically unsound for Nigeria, where "the educated and town dwelling African is so patently creating a culture that is neither traditional nor European. He is continually adapting his norms and values according to the demands of urban life and salaried employment." On p. 134 in "Tribalism in Nigeria," in A. A. Dubb, ed., *The Multi-Tribal Society* (Lusaka, Rhodes Livingstone Institute, 1962).

12. Kopytoff, "Socialism and Traditional African Societies," p. 57.

movement or institutional arrangement is probably situationally determined. The fact is, of course, that sacred Islamic scripture (like the
Bible) can be interpreted to support either tradition.[13]

A final general point about the concept of tradition is that there is
considerable variation in the responsive and adaptive capability of the
traditions of indigenous African societies. Such diversity in the response
pattern of traditional orders elsewhere is now well established in the
works of Evon Vogt, Herbert Blumer, and others.[14] A traditional order
can reject, tolerate, assimilate, or exploit an innovation, and as well,
elements of tradition can themselves be exploited by a modernizing
movement. This latter phenomenon has been termed a "reinforcing
dualism" by Robert Ward and Danwart Rustow.[15]

The Concept of Nationalism

There is no point to an elaborate definitional exercise on the vexing
concept of "nationalism" and "nation" in the African context; the literature on this issue is already too extensive, the issues and the realities
are fairly well known, and in the final analysis one has to be arbitrary,
as I must be here. In one short sentence Professor Jacob Ajayi illumin-
ates what we mean by nationalism: "In contrast to nineteenth century
Europe where the basic aim of nationalism was to fit people who shared
the same culture and language into a nation state, the fundamental
yearning of African nationalism has been to weld peoples speaking different languages and having different traditional cultures into one
nation state."[16] For our purposes the concept "nationalism" and allied
concepts will be used according to the following schema:[17]

13. The proponents of both traditions were pitted against each other in the
nationalist struggle in Northern Nigeria. See Thomas L. Hodgkin, "A Note on
the Language of African Nationalism," in Kenneth Kirkwood, ed., *African
Affairs* (London, Chatto and Windus, 1961), pp. 26-27.

14. Evon Z. Vogt, "The Navaho," in Edward H. Spicer, ed., *New Perspec-
tives in American Indian Culture Change* (Seattle, University of Washington
Press, 1962); and Herbert Blumer, "Industrialization and the Traditional
Order," in *Sociology and Social Research*, 48 (January 1964), 129-138.

15. Robert E. Ward and Kankwart Rustow, eds., *Political Modernization in
Turkey and Japan* (Princeton, Princeton University Press, 1963). "Reinforcing
Dualism" refers to "the exploitability of traditional institutions, attitudes, and
behavior patterns for modernizing purposes" (p. 466).

16. J. F. A. Ajayi, "The Place of African History and Culture in the Process
of Nation-Building in Africa South of the Sahara," *Journal of Negro Education,*
30.3 (1961), 206.

17. There is nothing novel about this breakdown; it has been used by Rupert
Emerson, Paul Mercier, and others. Rupert Emerson, "Nation-Building in
Africa," in Karl W. Deutsch and William J. Foltz, *Nation-Building* (New York,

Collectivity of Reference	Working Concept for Sentiment and Activity Manifest by/for Collectivity
Race, continent or subcontinent (Negro race, the African continent, Afrique Noire)	Pan-Africanism
Colonial Territory (New State; presumptive new nation: e.g., Ghana, Congo, Kenya, Senegal)	Nationalism
Subterritorial collectivities	
Nationalities	Ethnic nationalisms (ethnicity)
Historic (ethno-linguistic collectivities with previous political unity, e.g., Baganda, Barotse, Bakongo, or without such unity, e.g., Kikuyu, Ewe, Ibo	
Situational (large-scale collectivities acquiring identity and self-consciousness through super-tribalization: Bangala, Baluhya, etc.)	
Tribes (small-scale ethno-linguistic, kinship-defined collectivities)	Tribalism (micro-nationalism)
Regions and Localities	Regionalism or localism
Any collectivity which asserted itself against alien rule prior to the emergence of organized territorial nationalist movements as presumptive successor regime (e.g., primary resistance, nativistic or traditionalistic movements, independent churches, etc.)	Protonationalism

Atherton Press, 1963), on p. 97 notes that there are at least three major levels of social and political community—"the traditional societies of the past, the colonial or colonially-derived structures of the present, and the several Pan-African aspirations." Paul Mercier, "On the Meaning of 'Tribalism' in Black Africa," in Pierre L. van den Berghe, *Africa: Social Problems of Change and Conflict* (San Francisco, Chandler Publishing Co., 1965), p. 484.

These working definitions provoke three observations. One is that by arbitrarily confining the concept of "nationalism" to the colonial territory as the collectivity of reference one makes the negative relationship between tradition and nationalism a function of the definition. This is true, but only in part. In the modern world nationalism is generally regarded as attaching to the nation-state, and with only a few exceptions it has been the artificial colonial territories which have become the new states creating their own nations. The history of postcolonial Africa only serves to reinforce and confirm this historic phenomenon.[18] Second, in broad historical perspective one must recognize the existence of a variety of forms of self-assertion and resistance among the African peoples which were just as "anticolonial" as the more organized forms of territorial nationalism. It was undoubtedly concern over this point — that is, that scholars overlooked or ignored earlier protest movements as a result of how they defined their phenomenon — that led Thomas Hodgkin to include under the rubric of "nationalism" any and all forms of protest from the beginning of colonialism.[19] Recognizing the validity of his argument has led us to include here the category "protonationalism" to cover these earlier phenomena, which were manifestly more closely linked to African "tradition."

A third observation concerns the extraordinary complexity one encounters in defining and classifying subterritorial collectivities and their corresponding modes of self-assertion. The task would be simple if they all fell into the categories either of historic traditional kingdoms (for example, Buganda, Barotse, or the Northern Nigerian emirates) or of such small-scale "traditional tribes" (in the purely anthropological sense) as Colonel Gowon's Birom of Northern Nigeria. The fact is that the overwhelming majority of subterritorial collectivities fall in an indeterminate intermediate category. Some large-scale aggregations had an ethno-linguistic basis for being a distinct identity (for example, Yoruba, Ibo, Hausa, Kikuyu, Luo, and so on), but their self-consciousness as an entity is largely the product of developments during the colonial period, including particularly the rise of territorial nationalisms. Other large-scale aggregations, which had little or no objective

18. See John H. Kautsky, ed., *Political Change in Underdeveloped Countries* (New York, John Wiley, 1965), pp. 34-45, who notes (on p. 38) the general ineffectiveness of unification movements transcending and amalgamating colonial territories, as well as movements of secession and fragmentation within those territories. Cf. C. E. Black, *Dynamics*, and Lucian W. Pye and Sidney Verbe, eds., *Political Culture and Political Development* (Princeton, Princeton University Press, 1965), p. 528.

19. Thomas Hodgkin, *Nationalism in Colonial Africa* (London, Frederick Muller, 1956), p. 23.

ethno-linguistic basis for a distinct identity, acquired a self-consciousness as a result of the phenomenon of "supertribalization" or "ethnic redefinition" described by Wallerstein, Mercier, and Young.[20] Indeed, in some instances, new self-conscious "ethnic" collectivities emerged that were based solely upon artificial administrative units.[21]

The foregoing underscores the fact that a subterritorial ethnic collectivity is not, as Emerson said of a nation, a preordained entity which, "like Sleeping Beauty, needs only the appropriate kiss to bring it to vibrant life."[22] In a large measure, subterritorial "ethnic" consciousness, like nationalism itself is situationally induced and determined and therefore ultimately definable only in subjective terms. As Mercier, drawing on Nadel, put it:

> It is impossible to answer always by "yes" or "no" such questions as: Is the ethnic group defined by the common origin of its members? Is it a culturally homogeneous unit? Is it linguistically homogeneous? Does it have a common way of life? Is it a politically organized unit, or, at least, a whole wherein cooperation between constituent elements is intense and constant? S.F. Nadel concluded that the ethnic reality can never be objectively delineated. An ethnic group is identical with the *theory* which its members have of it.[23]

Given this indetermination it is manifestly difficult to say that a particular ethnic collectivity, or the ethnic consciousness which it expresses, is in any meaningful sense "traditional."[24]

The genesis and the evolution of African nationalism has been significantly affected by, and in turn has affected, at least three different aspects of what we will loosely call African "tradition," namely, traditional ethnic grouping (with all of the qualifications already noted);

20. Immanuel Wallerstein, "Ethnicity and National Integration in West Africa," *Cahiers d'Études Africaines* (October 1960), 129-139; Mercier, "On the Meaning of 'Tribalism,' " pp. 483-501; Crawford Young, *Politics in the Congo* (Princeton, Princeton University Press, 1965), pp. 232-272.

21. Young, *Politics in the Congo*, p. 245, quotes Biebuyck and Douglas that although "administrative units often cut across tribal and linguistic boundaries . . . to some extent their very existence has created solidarities of another kind." He also notes (p. 245) that in the years preceding the urban elections in Leopoldville three of the five major ethnic associations bore the name of administrative divisions rather than tribes.

22. Rupert Emerson, *From Empire to Nation* (Cambridge, Harvard University Press, 1960), p. 91.

23. Mercier, "On the Meaning of 'Tribalism,' " p. 487.

24. This variability determined by the situation makes it necessary to qualify Emerson's observation that in Africa the "natural" boundaries are those of the tribes or other traditional groupings. Rupert Emerson in Deutsch and Foltz, *Nation-Building*, p. 101.

traditional political elites; and traditional political cultures. Viewing African nationalism as the dependent variable, we are primarily concerned here with how these three elements of traditionality affected its development.

Nationalism and Traditional Ethnic Groupings

The Primacy of the Territory as the Nation

The persistence of popular attachments to traditional ethnic groupings has been regarded by most nationalists and their external supporters as antithetical to nationalism.[25] This is so not only because such groupings were by definition subnational but because of the uncritical belief that the continuation of such attachments prevented the development of a positive sense of identification with the territorial nation nationalists were seeking to create. The concept, the feasibility, of multiple loyalties were not recognized. Most nationalists, Jacobinic rather than Burkean in their orientation, were ideologically determined to eliminate all *corps intermédiares*. There were some notable exceptions — Chief Obafemi Awolowo of Nigeria and Joseph Kasavubu of the Congo being cases in point. Awolowo, for example, argued that Nigeria's "ultimate goal" should be an arrangement whereby "each group, however small, is entitled to the same treatment as any other group, however large."[26] Kasavubu and other Abako leaders, Lemarchand notes, "conceived of the Congolese nation as an aggregate of distinctive loyalties based on 'ethnic, linguistic, and historical' affinities . . . [they] favored the maintenance and preservation of all intermediate groups."[27] Both men, be it noted, were leaders simultaneously of a large nationality group (the Yoruba and Bakongo respectively) and of national political parties operating within the framework of the emergent territorial nation. In balance, however, most nationalist leaders were hostile — rhetorically at least — to what they viewed as parochial

25. Pierre van den Berghe has identified six different meanings of the term "tribe," the collective generally used to refer indiscriminately to all traditional groupings. Three of these meanings relate to the scale of the collectivity ("small localized group," a large-scale ethno-linguistic group, and heterogeneous precolonial states); the other three meanings are "rural" as opposed to "urban," "traditional" as opposed to "modern," and simply anything the "opposite of 'national.' " *Africa*, p. 3.

26. Obafemi Awolow, *Path to Nigerian Freedom* (London, Faber and Faber, 1947), p. 54.

27. Rene Lemarchand, "The Bases of Nationalism among the Bakongo," *Africa*, 31.4 (October 1961), 347.

ethnic groupings, to what Tom Mboya has called "negative tribalism."[28]

The African nationalists' animus toward traditional ethnic groupings is understandable once the larger territory became the sole focus for their nation-building efforts. But why did the territories become the focus? The usual explanation has been the manifest unsuitability of Africa's traditional units for modern independent statehood coupled with the strong attraction of nationalists to larger-scale polities. The goals of African nationalists, Professor Ajayi has observed, were "the creation of larger, economically and technologically developed nations able to take their places on a basis of equality with other nations in the world."[29] The key word here is probably "equality." As Ali Mazrui has argued: "Nationalism in Africa is still more egalitarian than libertarian in its ultimate aspirations . . . whereas the Americans proclaimed "equality" in pursuit of independence, the African nationalists have now sought independence in pursuit of equality . . . Perhaps it is useful to coin a term like 'dignitarianism' for such a movement."[30] Others of the "dignitarian" persuasion, such as Margery Perham, attribute the special African passion for equality and racial acceptance to the "sense of humiliation upon realizing their own retarded position among the peoples of the world . . . Denied so many of the things which have given birth and nourishment to nationalism elsewhere, Africans, it seems, are obliged to draw upon [this] one main source."[31] To Thomas Hodgkin such "psychoanalytic" explanations betray a "residual intellectual colonialism" which only serves "to strengthen the common, but mistaken, Western view that Africa is a special case, its revolution unlike other revolutions in human history."[32]

The nationalists' preference for the colonial territory over the traditional ethnic group as the nation-to-be cannot be convincingly ex-

28. Tom Mboya, *Freedom and After* (London, Oxford University Press, 1963), pp. 70-71. Rupert Emerson notes that "tribalism can be dealt with in two fashions — either use of the tribes as the building blocks of the nation or eradication of them as completely as possible, replacing them by a single national solidarity. It is the latter course which is more generally followed." *Nation-Building*, p. 105.

29. Ajayi, "The Place of African History and Culture in the Process of Nation-Building," p. 211.

30. Ali A. Mazrui, "On the Concept 'We Are All Africans,' " *The American Political Science Review*, 57.1 (March 1963), 96.

31. Margery Perham, "The Psychology of African Nationalism," *Optima*, 10.1 (1960), 28. Cf. Lloyd Fallers, "Equality, Modernity and Democracy in the New States," in Clifford Geertz, ed., *Old Societies and New States* (Glencoe, The Free Press, 1963), p. 217.

32. Thomas L. Hodgkin, "The Relevance of 'Western' Ideas for the New African States," pp. 62-63.

plained solely — or even mainly — by their quest to achieve equality and dignity through large-scale polities. If this were so how does one explain the host of micro-states which independent Africa presented to the international community and the willful neglect of unparalleled opportunities to join the modern states system within the framework of such large-scale polities as ex-French Afrique noire (for which a suitable African name could easily have been found), or the Mali or East African federations? Surely there are other, more significant, determinants of their choice. Political necessity was obviously one important factor. The realities of the power structure, as well as the variable colonial policies and practices of the different imperial countries, made it necessary for nationalists to seek independence within the political unit in which fate had placed them, and this was the territory. It was this sheer practical necessity to seek independence within the existing power unit which made the territory the focus, rather than any subterritorial ethnic group *or* supraterritorial entity.

The choice of the territory over the traditional group was further strengthened by the far greater opportunity it presented for rapid upward social mobility and political ascendancy of a rising class of new modernizing elites. Margery Perham's query of 1937 (referring to Nnamdi Azikiwe) underscores the limited career opportunities for the new class available in most traditional African societies: "But what scope . . . can the rudimentary Ibo groups offer to one of the tribe who has spent ten years at American universities accumulating academic qualifications?"[33] Thus, their choice was not simply based on the judgment that traditional groups would not be viable modern states for realizing the collective equality and dignity of the African peoples involved; an equally compelling explanation that such groups patently did not offer the career opportunities and prospect of high status for an aggressive, upwardly mobile, new class in the same way as did the territory. The admittedly atypical case of Buganda — which did offer such upward mobility and thereby deflected the focus of Buganda nationalism from the territory to the traditional kingdom — is the striking exception that confirms the point.[34] In the same vein the history of Zambian nationalism would have been considerably different had the political structure and culture of the Barotse Kingdom provided similar scope and oppor-

33. Margery Perham, *Native Administration in Nigeria* (London, Oxford University Press, 1937), p. 361.

34. See L. A. Fallers, "Despotism, Status Culture and Social Mobility in an African Kingdom," *Comparative Studies in Society and History*, 2.1 (October 1959), 11-32; and David E. Apter, *The Political Kingdom in Uganda* (Princeton, Princeton University Press, 1961).

tunity for individual self-realization of the Lozi members of its rising educated class.[35]

A final point is that analysts have probably tended to underestimate the extent to which territories did acquire a pesonality and an integrity of their own during the relatively brief period of colonialism, and were in fact — and not just aspiration — embryonic nations, despite the accidents of their creation, and the artificiality and irrationality of their boundaries. Identities can be crystallized fairly quickly by situational pressures, vested interests, career calculations and the myriad other forces that operate to differentiate terminal political communities. As Ajayi put it, "As the European administrations became more and more effective, the colonial boundaries, arbitrary as many of them were, began to acquire some significance for the African. Each territorial unit was becoming the focus of some national loyalty of its own."[36]

Variability in the Role of Ethnicity in Nationalism

There have been many factors which have affected the strength and determined the role of ethnicity in the development of territorial nationalism, but at least three variables are particularly significant: the ecology and political structure of traditional societies; the nature of colonial policies regarding traditional ethnic groupings; and the ethnic pattern of the territory. In comparing the phenomenon of "tribalism" in West Africa (particularly Nigeria), on the one hand, and East and Central Africa (Congo excluded) on the other, Peter Lloyd hinted that its manifestation may in part be a function of more highly developed peasant agriculture. The societies in West Africa, he observes, "are peasant societies; many of the farmers grow a crop for export and a very small proportion of the population lives in the modern towns or works as wage labour . . . The rural areas are here better developed with schools and dispensaries. Pride in one's natal area might well grow in Central Africa if rural development is hastened."[37] Assuming the argument regarding differences between the two areas is valid (and there is much evidence that it needs serious qualification), the notion that there is a correlation between vigorous peasantry and extreme localism is a familiar one in the comparative study of nationalisms. One collaborative group of

35. Terrence Ranger, "Tribalism and Nationalism: The Case of Barotseland," unpublished manuscript.

36. Ajayi, "The Place of African History and Culture in the Process of Nation-Building," p. 209.

37. P. C. Lloyd, "Tribalism in Nigeria," in A. A. Dubb, ed., *The Multitribal Society* (Lusaka, Rhodes Livingstone Institute, 1962), p. 133.

scholars put it this way: "Peasants remain completely untouched by the intellectual and political elements of modern nationalism. Their love for the land is love for the locality . . . Thier distinctive dresses and customs are local rather than national; they dislike not only the foreigner but also the men from the next village . . . left to themselves, they will never produce a national movement."[38] This inherent localism of the agrarian peasant may or may not be the basis for an ethnic nationalism in conflict with a territorial nationalism — much would depend upon the size of the ethnic group concerned. However, the problem is more complicated than this, because heightened ethnicity in Africa has tended to be a nonpeasant, mainly urban, phenomenon.

Another proposition is that which postulates a positive correlation between those traditional societies with a history of previous political unity and the assertion of an ethnic nationalism. Hodgkin put the proposition this way: "Ethnic loyalties tend, or have tended, in fact, to be strongest among peoples like the Hausa-Fulani in northern or the Yoruba in western Nigeria, the Ashanti in Ghana, the Moshi in Upper Volta, who had behind them, in the precolonial period, well-developed and powerful states, which were not in any intelligible sense 'tribal.' "[39] The interesting comparative study of Buganda and Ashanti by David Apter provides further support to this line of argument.[40] A related proposition advanced by Parkin and Banton, at first seemingly — but, in fact, not — contradictory to the preceding one, posits a positive correlation between politically uncentralized traditional societies (that is, those which have had no history of political unity or centralization) and the predisposition to form urban ethnic associations.[41] Ian Lewis has challenged this proposition on the basis of other evidence and advances an alternative situational explanation for the variability in the formation of such associations. The crucial factors leading to their formation, he argues, "are less the pre-existing political systems of those concerned than their overall political circumstances at any point in time in the urban situation." In those urban situations where the members of a par-

38. Royal Institute of International Affairs, *Nationalism* (London, Oxford University Press, 1939), p. 274.

39. Thomas Hodgkin, "The New West Africa State System," in Millar Maclure and Douglas Anglin, eds., *Africa: The Political Pattern* (Toronto, University of Toronto Press, 1961), p. 78.

40. David E. Apter, "The Role of Traditionalism in the Political Modernization of Ghana and Uganda," *World Politics,* 13 (1960), 45-68.

41. M. Banton, *West African City: A Study of Tribal Life in Freetown* (London, Oxford University Press, 1957); D. J. Parkin, "Urban Voluntary Associations as Institutions of Adaptation," *Man,* new series, I, 90-95. Banton's study was in Freetown and Parkin's in Kampala.

ticular ethnic group are "treated as outsiders and constitute a sensitive minority, and whose traditional tribal structure — *whatever its type* — is not sufficiently closely associated with the town in which they live to meet their needs satisfactorily," they will form such associations.[42] The fact is that once ethnic oppositions within a territory are aggravated, ethnicity is a phenomenon manifest by all of the interacting collectivities and usually with equal intensity. Indeed, on balance it would be difficult to decide which of two contrasting types of traditional societies, the Ashanti and the Ibo, for example, were more ethnically self-conscious in the development of territorial nationalism in Ghana and Nigeria respectively.

Explanations for the variability in the manifestations of ethnicity in nationalist development usually place considerable weight upon the policies and practices towards ethnic groupings of the colonial powers. Certain general facts are widely recognized and require no discussion, namely: that there were declared differences in policies associated with the concepts of "direct rule" (France), "indirect rule" (Britain), and "quasi-indirect rule" (Belgium and Portugal); that these policies were not uniformly applied nor uniformly successful, and in many instances there was little to differentiate the actual patterns of colonial rule; and that where indirect rule was applied in a thoroughgoing manner (for example, the Buganda and Barotse Kingdoms) there has been greater ethnic self-consciousness among the groups involved than where direct rule (the deliberate effort to extinguish ethnic identity) was practiced. Thus, in general ethnicity is markedly less visible in ex-French Africa than ex-British Africa. Beyond this the only safe generalization one can make is that at most the different colonial policies accentuated or minimized predispositions but were not in themselves the decisive, or necessarily even the most significant, determinant of ethnicity, despite much nationalist rhetoric about "divide and rule."[43]

Ethnicity as a factor in nationalist development in a given territory has been accentuated or attenuated according to the particular patterning of its ethnic groups. This fact underscores once again the role of the situation as both a precipitant and determinant. The effect of ethnic patterns can be analyzed in terms of types of ethnic patterns, ethnic stratification, and the cumulation of ethnic differentiation with other

42. I. M. Lewis, "Nationalism, Urbanism and Tribalism in Contemporary Africa," unpublished manuscript. Italics added.

43. Policies of differentiation by colonial powers (particularly Britain) of major areal clusters of peoples (that is, northern and southern Sudan, northern and southern Nigeria, and to a lesser extent all along the West Coast of Africa) undoubtedly had a major divisive effect in national development.

processes of differentiation. Clifford Geertz has suggested a typology of what he calls "concrete patterns of primordial diversity."[44] Adapting his typology to the African situation, at least five patterns are discernible: the uni-ethnic pattern, represented only by Somalia, Lesotho, and Swaziland, in which the internal divisions are intra-ethnic in character; the bi-ethnic pattern in which one group is dominant over one or more other groups within the territory (for example, the Watutsis in pre-independent Ruanda); the "duopoly" pattern,[45] of which the Matabele and Mashona of Rhodesia are the best example; the tripolar pattern, found in Nigeria (Hausa, Yoruba, and Ibo) and Kenya (Kikuyu, Luo, and the political aggregate of the remaining groups); and the multi-ethnic pattern of which Tanzania, Zambia, and the Congo are illustrative.

Ethnic self-consciousness has tended to be more pronounced, and more prone to escalate, in those situations where the relationship among groups was one of ethnic stratification (the bi-ethnic pattern) rather than ethnic coexistence (the multiethnic pattern).[46] Territories having a pattern of duopoly or a tripolar pattern were, as in all situations of bi- or tri-polarity, vulnerable to the delicate balance of their ethnic duality or plurality suddenly giving way to a polarization into total ethnic bloc opposition and rivalry. Only in the case of the multiethnic pattern have there been opportunities to avoid rigid confrontations, partly because of the absence of actual or threatened domination by one group, but mainly because of the amenability of such situations to ethnic bargaining, shifting ethnic alliances in the classical "balance of power" syndrome, or the shrewd use of ethnic arithmetic by nationalist leaders so disposed.

Ethnic stratification characterized the relationship of many groups throughout Africa at the time of the formal imposition of colonial rule and of the present territorial boundaries. In only a few cases (for example, former Ruanda, Urundi, and Zanzibar) was the system of ethnic stratification coterminous with the territorial boundaries. In all

44. Geertz, *Old Societies and New States*, pp. 117-118.

45. Herbert J. Spiro, "The Rhodesias and Nyasaland," in Gwendolen M. Carter, ed., *Five African States: Responses to Diversity* (Ithaca, Cornell University Press, 1963), pp. 391-392.

46. David Marvin has noted that "tribal rivalry has been greatest in territories in which one or more tribes have acquired a dominant position, either through a tradition of successful conquest over surrounding peoples, through having achieved a more or less centralized government, or through having been in a position to exploit the new economic advantages." "Tribe and Nation in East Africa: Separatism and Regionalism," *The Round Table* (June 1962), p. 255.

other cases it was limited to the relationships among groups in only parts of the territories (for example, northern Nigeria and the Hima kingdoms of Uganda). One of the paradoxes of British colonial policy was the deliberate perpetuation of pre-existing stratifications, while at the same time allowing full scope for the operation of other destratifying influences (education, urbanization, mobility, economic change) which frequently had their greatest impact on grounds in the lower strata of the prevailing stratification systems. Thus, one found in most British territories a dual process at work: on the one hand efforts were made to preserve established systems of ethnic stratification within a context of social change; and, on the other hand, modernizing forces were allowed to spawn new, upwardly mobile, elements pushing aggressively into the top stratum of an emerging territorial stratification system. As these territories entered their nationalist era a massive process of restratification was already in progress — previously dominant ethnic groups confronted or were already caught up in a radical downward "status reversal" while previously subordinate groups had already acquired or had the vision of obtaining high status in the emerging territorial social structure and polity. This juxtaposition of the frustrations of the *nouveaux pauvres* and the aggressiveness of the *nouveaux riches* greatly intensified ethnic self-consciousness and rivalry, which the growth of nationalism only served to exacerbate.

Individuals were, of course, the direct beneficiaries in this process of restratification, but because of the phenomenon of "cumulation," differentiation within the new territorial stratification system tended to fall heavily upon ethnic lines. "The paramount fact," Mercier notes, "is that modern differentiations arising from the degree of economic and educational development, the nature of religious transformations, etc., *cumulates* with traditional differentiations."[47] As is well known, modernizing status-producing influences such as education and the commercialization of land and labor have had an uneven impact upon African societies, and for a variety of reasons (geographical location, cultural receptivity or resistance to innovation, overpopulation, adequacy of the traditional societies to provide scope for new elites, and so

47. Mercier, "On the Meaning of 'Tribalism,' " p. 492. Cumulation of differentiations are not simply vertical. In the development of the Copperbelt in Northern Rhodesia the division between (higher status) Lozi and Nyasa clerks and (lower status) Bemba workers did not reflect "some situation of resurgent tribalism or persistence of loyalties and values stemming from a traditional social order," but rather with the cumulation of the differentiations of an "emerging class structure" and ethnic divisions. Ranger quoting Epstein in "Tribalism and Nationalism," p. 10.

on) differentiation within the new territorial stratification systems has fallen heavily along ethnic lines.[48] This is one important reason why modernizing nationalism, in the short run at least, heightens rather than diminishes intraterritorial ethnic nationalism. As Zolberg notes, "cross-pressures that might inhibit conflict" are weak or nonexistent.[49]

Certain types of ethnic mix, ethnic stratification, and ethnic restratification resulting from cumulation provide the basis for ethnic self-consciousness, but it has been the growth and spread of territorial nationalism itself which, ironically, intensified and escalated ethnic subnationalisms. "Where there is original unity," Emerson notes, "nationalism serves further to unite; where there is felt ethnic diversity, nationalism is no cure."[50] The reasons for the positive correlation between the development of territorial nationalism and the escalation of subterritorial ethnic nationalisms are now fairly well known and documented: ethnic groups provided the most secure political base for territorial "national" leaders, and it was to this base that they almost invariably gravitated in the competitive territorial arena;[51] urban ethnic associations, frequently linked to more comprehensive pan-ethnic movements, provided the original organizational infrastructure of many territorial nationalist movements, and few of the latter were ever able to emancipate themselves from this dependence;[52] as territorial nationalism grew in strength and achieved some of its objectives (universal

48. As I have noted elsewhere, "Uneven acculturation, resulting in part from the uneven tribal acquisition of Western education and the uneven spread of 'status' employment, produced competitive tensions within the educated categories which were powerful stimulants to tribal as well as territorial nationalism." *Nigeria: Background to Nationalism* (Berkeley, University of California Press, 1958), p. 143. Again, for the Ivory Coast, Zolberg has observed that "differentiations between traditional societies have been intensified by the cumulative effect of uneven Western impact and, in recent years, by differential rates of cultural and economic change." Aristide R. Zolberg, *One-Party Government in the Ivory Coast* (Princeton, Princeton University Press, 1964), pp. 47-48.

49. Zolberg, *One-Party Government in the Ivory Coast,* p. 134.

50. Rupert Emerson, "Paradoxes of Asian Nationalism," in Immanuel Wallerstein, ed., *Social Change: The Colonial Situation* (New York, John Wiley, 1966), p. 530.

51. Lewis, "Nationalism, Urbanism and Tribalism," notes (on p. 2), "Politicians who aspire to break down tribal barriers and to erect in their place a new national culture have also, perforce, to utilize the same tribal ties in their search for supporters and power, and to take adequate account of them in their selection of colleagues and allies in governmental and administrative action."

52. The link between urbanization and the growth of ethnic self-consciousness is a familiar syndrome. See Zolberg, *One-Party Government in the Ivory Coast,* p. 143; Immanuel Wallerstein, *Social Change,* pp. 249-300, makes "The Creation of Urban Ethnicity" a major section of his study.

suffrage and, through elections, greater representation and presence in central government; as well as accelerated socioeconomic modernization), these very achievements intensified ethnic nationalisms for the obvious reasons of competition, fear of ultimate domination by one ethnic group, and increased ethnic differentiation through cumulation;[53] and colonial powers frequently aided and abetted ethnic movements and associations as a counterbalance to or disintegrator of territorial nationalism.[54] That this is not a peculiarly African phenomenon, but one generic to all new states in the process of birth is now well established.[55]

These are ways in which ethnic self-consciousness negatively affected and was affected by territorial nationalism. However, there are other ways, as Wallerstein, Mercier, and Sklar have shown, in which ethnicity contributed to national integration and to nationalism. Mercier argues that "Nationalism and tribalism are not always two radically opposed types of movements. In the new states, ethnic identity does not always have a centrifugal effect . . . Ethnic diversity can, in many different ways, contribute to unification or be utilized towards that end."[56] Wallerstein's case in support of this thesis is that urban ethnicity tends to reduce the kinship tie, that urban ethnic groups are instruments for resocialization and keeping the class structure fluid and that they also serve as outlets for political tensions by making it possible for aggrieved individuals to challenge persons rather than the office they occupy.[57] To these integrative functions Zolberg adds the contribution urban ethnicity makes to secularization, and by introducing a secular political loyalty, which inevitably operated to undermine traditional structures and to facilitate the institutionalization of new forms of government.[58] This

53. Emerson observes that it is inevitable that ethnic groups "should seek political expression and be used as built-in constituencies when democratic machinery is introduced," in Deutsch and Foltz, *Nation-Building,* p. 106.

54. This "divide and rule" tactic was used extensively throughout colonial Africa, and currently is being used by the Portuguese in both Angola and Mozambique, and by the South African government in its Bantustan policy. See John A. Davis and James K. Baker, eds., *Southern Africa in Transition* (New York, Praeger, 1966), pp. 15-16, 160-162.

55. "Indonesian regionalism, Malayan racialism, Indian linguism, or Nigerian tribalism are, in their political dimensions, not so much the heritage of colonial divide-and-rule policies as they are products of the replacement of a colonial regime by an independent, domestically anchored, purposeful unitary state." Geertz, *Old Societies and New States,* p. 121.

56. Mercier, "On the Meaning of 'Tribalism,' " p. 486.

57. Immanuel Wallerstein, "Ethnicity and National Integration," *Cahiers d'Études Africaines,* no. 3 (1960), pp. 129-138.

58. Zolberg, *One-Party Government in the Ivory Coast,* p. 144.

latter thesis is not unrelated to Sklar's proposition that Yoruba pan-tribalism, being supratribal and cosmopolitan, was like Jewish Zionism in its innate secularity and capacity to produce "a sense of 'national' identity among peoples who are ethnically or tribally diverse but culturally related."[59] And because Yoruba pan-tribalism provided the main support for a "nationalist" territorial party it thereby contributed to the movement for national independence.

The essence of these arguments would seem to be that both urban ethnicity and pan-tribalism are supratribal and secular, and therefore nontraditional, phenomena. Therefore to the extent that people are emancipated from essentially kinship-defined ethnic groups (the real tribes), and acquire through supertribalization a new secular identity with a larger "nontraditional" aggregate, the bond with traditionalism is thereby weakened or extinguished and those concerned are more open and flexible to new, possibly multiple, and certainly larger-scale affiliations. But the fact remains that the ethnic redefinition that produces such supertribes or self-conscious pan-tribal nationalities is still a subnational phenomenon. And one could argue both logically and from the actual pattern of nationalist development in Africa that it has not been the "ethnic" obstacles to the emergence of territorial "national" identities but the supertribalized collectivities (the Mongo and Bangala in the Congo) or the large-scale and newly self-conscious nationalities (Yoruba, Ibo, Kikuyu, Luo, and so on) that have been the main problem. To elevate, expand, and redefine ethnic identity to larger subterritorial aggregates, no matter what their scale, is still not solving the problem. And, as Zolberg concludes, "from the point of view of participants in the system, the contributions of conflict and ethnicity to national integration are less visible than the obstacles they created."[60]

A second line of argument is Sklar's thesis that ethnicity in the form of communal partisanship contributed to the diffusion of nationalism because the competing communal groups could be manipulated by competing national parties to further the movement for national independence. Traditional communal rivalries were exploited by rival nationalist groups in their effort to cumulate and articulate grievances of any kind and thereby deepen their influence in the countryside. Terrence Ranger has illuminated this same process of nationalization of

59. Richard Sklar, "The Contribution of Tribalism to Nationalism in Western Nigeria," *Journal of Human Relations*, 8 (Spring-Summer 1960), 411.

60. Zolberg, *One-Party Government in the Ivory Coast*, p. 144. He concludes (on p. 285) that few members of the Ivory Coast political elite would accept the validity of the social science hypothesis that racial and tribal pluralism are not incompatible with national integration.

parochialism in his study of the Lozi. Several leading UNIP territorial nationalists in pre-independence Zambia were from the Lozi aristocracy, sons of still prominent personalities in the traditional elite of the Barotse Kingdom who were, during the critical period of the nationalist struggle for independence, in opposition to the then paramount chief. Ranger concludes: "The sweeping victory of U.N.I.P. candidates in the 1962 elections in Barotseland should have come as no surprise. Arthur Wina and Mubiana Nalilungwe . . . offered a traditional form of leadership to the Lozi voters, even though one now in opposition to the paramount rather than in alliance with him."[61] These and numerous other examples of territorial nationalist manipulation and penetration of traditional communal conflict illuminate the way in which traditionalism provided channels for political communication and situations facilitating political mobilization. As Sklar put it: "Millions of tradition-bound people were drawn through the medium of communal partisanship into the mainstream of political activity where they accepted the leadership of progressive nationalists. Therein lies its historic significance . . . Communal partisanship, based on psychological commitments to the traditional values of tribal groups, was utilized by nationalist leaders to mobilize mass support in rural areas and old towns.[62]

Nationalism and Traditional Political Elites

In a discussion of the rise of African nationalism Margery Perham once asked why "almost no traditional authorities have come forward as nationalists . . . [because] it might have been expected that the almost universal and deep-rooted institution of chieftainship would have supplied, as it were, ready-made leaders . . . In most parts of Africa, however, chieftainship [tended] to wither at the first breath of a national movement."[63] Her two explanations are familiar ones, namely, the close association of most chiefs with, even integration within, the ruling power, which thereby tainted them as "imperialist stooges"; and the fact that chiefs were "chiefs of tribes" and therefore are not only symbols but perpetuators of subnational ethnic parochialisms, which territorial nationalism was determined either to domesticate or to suppress.

61. Ranger, "Tribalism and Nationalism," p. 12.
62. Sklar, "The Contribution of Tribalism to Nationalism in Western Nigeria," p. 415. The process of nationalist exploitation of traditional communal conflict was not sheer expediential instrumentalism. Sklar argues (on p. 413) that as a result of the influence of the manipulating radical nationalist leaders "communal participation parties have assimilated nationalistic principles within their codes of traditional values."
63. Perham, "The Psychology of African Nationalism," pp. 179-180.

The hostility of radical nationalism to the traditional political elites was not due simply to the fact that they were perceived to be — and in most places were in fact — part of the colonial administrative establishment nationalists were seeking to overthrow and capture. Rather, it was that chiefs were considered to be positively antinationalist by conviction and by their actions — or inaction. For one thing, the goals of nationalism seemed to be regarded by chiefs as hopeless. As Tom Mboya lamented, chiefs were "convinced through the administrative set-up that the white man's position was indestructible and no amount of agitation was going to move it."[64] More important, however, they frequently openly sided with, or permitted themselves to be used by, the colonial administrations in explicit opposition to nationalism. In former French Africa traditional elites figured prominently in antinationalist "patron-type" parties (in the sense that they supported continuation of the French presence); they were in fact referred to as *partis de l'administration*.[65] In the Ivory Coast in 1951, for example, the chiefs "openly declared themselves against the R.D.A. (Rassemblement Democratique Africaine) and pledged loyalty to France."[66]

In English-speaking Africa the use of chiefs by the colonial authorities as a counterweight to nationalism was even more pronounced, if only because traditional political elites figured more prominently in the British colonial system. Thus, in Tanganyika in 1956 and 1957 the colonial government set up a "convention of chiefs" specifically to oppose the growing popularity of the Tanganyika African National Union (TANU).[67] Colonial government support of the anti-nationalist paramount chiefs and the conservative aristocracy among the Bemba and the Lozi in pre-independent Zambia are other cases in point. However, the most blatant use of traditional elites to frustrate modernizing African nationalism has been in post-UDI Rhodesia and in South Africa's effort to implement the Bantu Authorities Act.[68] Indeed, the examples of colonialism's instrumental exploitation of chiefs are legion. In gener-

64. Mboya, *Freedom and After*, p. 64.

65. Thomas Hodgkin, *Nationalism in Colonial Africa* (London, Frederick Muller, 1956), p. 156. Ruth Schachter Morgenthau has noted that these patron parties were most active and successful in Mali, Niger, Guinea (until 1956), and Mauritania. It was in these territories, she notes, that the struggle against the colonial power barely masked another struggle, most acute in the countryside, between traditionalists and modernizers. "Single-Party Systems in West Africa," *The American Political Science Review*, 55 (1961), 301.

66. Zolberg, *One-Party Government in the Ivory Coast*, p. 120.

67. Cranford Pratt, "East Africa: The Pattern of Political Development," in Maclure and Anglin, *Africa: The Political Pattern*, p. 118.

68. See Thomas Karis, "South Africa," in Carter, *Five African States*, pp. 555-557.

alizing about all the colonial territories which have moved or are moving to independence, Kautsky concluded that "it may in the end be only the colonial government that maintains the old aristocracy in power."[69]

Like most categories and concepts used in generalization about African political developments, the category of "chief" or "traditional elite" tends to be employed in an undifferentiated manner. But, as St. Clair Drake has observed, "There are chiefs and chiefs."[70] At least three categories should be distinguished: village-level local chiefs, who throughout the colonial — as well as early postcolonial — period continued to perform traditional political, familial, and ceremonial functions at the grass-roots level; kings, paramount chiefs, emirs, *grands marabouts,* and other traditional heads of large-scale collectivities and indigenous polities (emirates of Northern Nigeria; the Buganda, Barotse, Ruanda, and Burundi kingdoms, the senior obas in Yorubaland, and so on); and an intermediate category who were sometimes traditional but usually they were "official" creations or clients of the colonial powers. One report described chiefs in this category as owing their recognition "largely to the action of the [colonial] administration, who appointed or recognized influential men of the time and then 'built them up' by giving them legal and moral support."[71] It is mainly this intermediate category which was used instrumentally by colonial administrations to resist nationalism, then subsequently by nationalists (once their ultimate victory was assured), and finally by postcolonial governments of the new African states. A final category includes those educated African nationalists who acquired by various means the honorary title of "chief" or "prince" to enhance their status and legitimacy. This phenomenon was particularly pronounced in southern Nigeria, although it also occurred elsewhere.

The manipulation of the third category of so-called traditional elites — many, be it noted, with little or no "traditional" legitimacy — by whoever was in power, underscores the inherent weakness and extraordinary opportunism of chiefs once nationalism got under way. The oscillations in the loyalties of the chiefs in the Ivory Coast, recounted by

69. Kautsky, *Political Change in Underdeveloped Countries*, p. 42.

70. In H. Passin and K. A. B. Jones-Quartey, *Africa: The Dynamics of Change* (Ibadan, Ibadan University Press, 1963), p. 27.

71. Colonial Office Summer Conference on African Administration, Eighth Session, 27 August-7 September 1957, *The Place of Chiefs in African Administration,* p. 76. See Morgenthau, "Single-Party Systems in West Africa," for a discussion of the nature of the "official chiefs" and their relationship to nationalist parties in former French Africa (pp. 301-302).

Zolberg, provide an excellent case in point. Between 1946 and 1951 most Ivory Coast chiefs belonged to a secular organization founded by Houphouet-Boigny and called Association des Chefs Coutumiers. As he was president of the R.D.A. (Rassemblement Democratique Africaine), the pan-Afrique noire nationalist movement during the last three years of that period, one could say that the chiefs supported the nationalism of the R.D.A. However, when Houphouet fell out with the French in 1951, the association openly sided with the French administration in opposition to the R.D.A., as already noted. Subsequently when Houphouet emerged once again as the heir presumptive to French authority in the Ivory Coast the association became a trade union (Syndicat des Chefs) with Houphouet-Boigny as its honorary president.[72] The same back-and-forth movement has characterized the opportunistic shifts, and the party and government manipulation, of chiefs in Ghana and several other African countries.[73] Thus, the role of traditional elites (genuine or spurious) of this intermediate category in the development of territorial nationalism has been largely a function of their opportunistic calculation of "where power lies"—or is likely to lie—in the evolving political system.

The pattern of development was somewhat different in those territories where genuine traditional elites had retained substantial influence during the colonial period. Indeed, so determinative were they in the development of some West African states, that Post has classified development patterns in West Africa "according to the relationship between the traditional and modern elites during the last decisive decade before independence . . . [because] it was this relationship that determined the nature of the political system which emerged at independence."[74] His four categories, adapted here to illustrate patterns outside West Africa as well, are: countries or regions in which the traditional elite (political or religious) remained relatively powerful (Mauritania, Niger, Northern Nigeria, Burundi); countries in which the influence of traditional elites at a critical point in time was decisive in determining victors among competing nationalist heirs to colonial power (former French Cameroun, Senegal, Dahomey, Federation of Ni-

72. Zolberg, *One-Party Government in the Ivory Coast*, pp. 287-288.

73. The most recent illustration of the sheer opportunism of chiefs and crass manipulation of the chiefly office is found in the revelations of the National Liberation Council of Ghana regarding the Nkrumah regime. During the period 1957-1966 the latter had allegedly promoted a large number of subordinate chiefs to the status of paramount chiefs "without regard to traditions and customs." The NLC was therefore demoting all those chiefs concerned.

74. Ken Post, *The New States of West Africa* (London, Penguin Books, 1964), pp. 54-55.

geria taken as a whole, Uganda, Sudan); countries where the modern nationalist elite found it advantageous to come to terms with, or consciously seek to use, traditional authority (Upper Volta, Gambia, Sierra Leone, Ivory Coast, Western Nigeria, and Congo [Kinshasha]); and those states where residual traditional authority was largely nonexistent or irrelevant (Kenya and Malawi) or where nationalist leadership sought very early, and reasonably successfully, to reduce or to eliminate the power of traditional elites (Ghana, Guinea, Mali, Rwanda, Tanzania, and Zambia). These were the "agitational period" pre-independence patterns. The post-independence syndrome is more singular in character, as evidenced by the respective fates of the Moro Naba, the Emir of Kano, the kabaka of Buganda, and the king of Burundi, to mention the most obvious cases in point.

Although the relationship between traditional elites and modernizing nationalists has tended in general to be marked by distrust and opposition, there have been phases and situations in the development of territorial nationalism when they have made common cause. In most such instances, this occurred as soon as the winds of change convinced the chiefs that ultimate nationalist victory was assured. The "crossing of the carpet" by the chiefs of Tanzania illustrates the power of the bandwagon. Describing the crucial election of 1959 in Tanganyika, Pratt observes that:

> Prior to the election, as TANU's strength grew throughout the country, chief after chief hesitated to court unpopularity by declaring himself against TANU. The fence got very crowded as one chief after another climbed on it. Then, in September 1958, TANU very shrewdly named a leading chief as a candidate in the election. With that, the chiefs en masse began to make their peace with TANU and quietly to demonstrate or at least assert their underlying sympathy with it. In March 1959, at a meeting of the Convention of Chiefs, created by government as a counterbalance to TANU, the political resolutions passed were indistinguishable from the TANU electoral platform. Thus, the political support of the chiefs for the government was lost.[75]

There are instances, however, where chiefs openly sided with nationalists without opportunism being the prime motive. Thus, most chiefs in former Northern Rhodesia and Nyasaland spontaneously joined with modernizing nationalists to oppose the creation of the now defunct Federation of Rhodesia and Nyasaland. This coming together in a common cause has characteristically occurred in those circumstances where the common threat to both categories (traditionalists and

75. Pratt, "East Africa: The Pattern of Political Development," p. 118.

modernists) was so visible and imminent that joint action was inevitable.[76]

There are also instances of nationalists and chiefs collaborating in the early stages of protest. This was particularly true in Ghana and Nigeria,[77] as well as in southern Africa. Ranger has pointed out:

> The fact that the first stirrings of modern politics in Northern Rhodesia occurred through an alliance of the Lozi paramounts with the new educated and through contact with agencies in South Africa and overseas fits neatly enough into a general southern African pattern . . . early political activity in southern Rhodesia centered around the Lobengula family and its "tribal" appeal for a Matabele National Home and . . . the new educated and even "foreign" middle class Africans supported this movement, while Mary Benson has demonstrated that in South Africa the founders of the Congress movement were allied with the paramounts of Zululand, Swaziland and Basutoland, and regarded themselves as much advisors of these royal families as leaders of a supra-tribal political movement.[78]

Thus, although the political outlook of these early centers of protest later became conservative and parochial, the history of African nationalism would be incomplete were it to ignore what Ranger has called this "bridge period between traditional resistance and full scale modern nationalist politics" and the significant role traditional elites with a modernizing bent played in initial nationalist assertion.[79]

Nationalism and Traditional Political Cultures

Variations in the manifestation and development of nationalism in

76. The militant stand taken by Paramount Chief Sabata Dalindyebo of the Tembu tribe in the Transkei against apartheid was identical with that of educated South African nationalists.

77. A West Coast example of this early spirit of collaboration between educated nationalists and traditional elites were the occasional visits made by Chief Ladip Solanke (founder of the West African Students Union) from London to West Africa between 1929 and 1932. Solanke deliberately sought to bring the two elements together. Indeed, Nana Sir Afori Atta of the Gold Coast, and the alake of Abeokuta and emir of Kano were one-time patrons of WASU. See Coleman, *Nigeria,* pp. 206-207.

78. Ranger, "Tribalism and Nationalism," pp. 7-8.

79. One other way in which traditional elites may have facilitated nationalist development is in being scapegoats for unpopular measures and discontent during the critical period of terminal colonialism during which nationalists acquired increasing power over public policy but still had not achieved independence. Thus, in Ghana during this period the C.P.P. encouraged commoners to destool uncooperative chiefs and, according to Drake, destoolment represented one means "by which local and regional discontent is focused on traditional authority rather than upon the new elites."

Africa can also be explained by variations in traditional African political cultures. By the political culture of a particular human group we refer to the ensemble of more or less typical attitudes, beliefs, and values of its members regarding politics and authority. It includes their general orientation toward the political system as well as their political behavioral dispositions.[80] In more familiar language, it refers to the political aspects of "national character." The psychocultural approach to political analysis, of course, remains controversial. It has serious limitations and dangers. It can easily lead to unscientific stereotyping; there are, as well, extraordinarily difficult methodological problems in specifying the political culture of a particular human group. Nevertheless, there is very persuasive evidence that, used with caution and tentativeness, the political cultural variable helps us understand and explain variations in African nationalism that otherwise would remain inexplicable.

In addition to the general limitations to the psychocultural approach, two special problems are encountered in attempting to use it to explain African political phenomena. One is that very few systematic, respectably scientific, psychocultural studies have been made in Africa that are directly pertinent to an understanding of nationalism.[81] Robert LeVine's admirable recent comparative study of the Hausa, Ibo, and Yoruba of Nigeria; Audrey Richard's analysis of the traditional political values of the Baganda; and Ethel Albert's earlier interesting work among the Ruandans and Rundi—these excellent pioneering studies stand out almost alone.[82] The second complicating factor is that

80. The concept is used substantially as defined by Gabriel Almond and Sidney Verba in *The Civic Culture* (Boston, Little Brown, 1965), pp. 12-30; and as further developed by Lucian W. Pye and Sidney Verba in *Political Culture and Political Development* (Princeton, Princeton University Press, 1965).

81. Lystad observes that "Despite the 'psychologizing' that frequently accompanies the analysis of political institutions and processes, and despite the often brilliant insights into psychological, cultural, and value aspects of African politics within individual countries—insights one intuitively feels must have some validity—the study of national character has hardly begun." Robert A. Lystad, "Cultural and Psychological Factors," in Vernon McKay, ed., *African Diplomacy: Studies in the Determinants of Foreign Policy* (New York, Praeger, 1966), p. 104. See also Robert A. LeVine's comprehensive survey of the literature in his chapter on "Africa" in Francis L. K. Hsu, ed., *Psychological Anthropology: Approaches to Culture and Personality* (Homewood, The Dorsey Press, 1961), pp. 48-92.

82. Robert A. LeVine, *Dreams and Deeds: Achievement Motivation in Nigeria* (Chicago, University of Chicago Press, 1966); Audrey I. Richards, "Traditional Values and Current Political Behaviour," in L. A. Fallers, ed., *The King's Men* (London, Oxford University Press, 1964), pp. 256-293; and

because of their great cultural heterogeneity and the relative brevity of their existence as "national" entities, it is difficult to speak meaningfully of the political culture of a new African state as a whole, although Hodgkin and Morgenthau have suggested Mali to be an exception.[83] Our examination of this variable is, therefore, limited to propositions regarding the political culture of traditional African ethnic groups or of the "African people" in general, and how these might have affected the development of territorial nationalisms.

Subterritorial Political Cultures and Territorial Nationalism

My working hypothesis is that there have been significant variations in nationalistic assertiveness among ethnic groups inhabiting a colonial territory, that is, some groups have been more assertive and nationalistic than others, and that these variations are in many instances a function of the differences in the political culture of the ethnic groups concerned. The history of the rise and development of territorial nationalisms in Africa amply supports the fact of marked ethnic disproportionality in both the leadership and mass involvement in radical territorial nationalism. The vanguard role played by particular ethnic groups in the evolution of territorial nationalism in several countries is now well known — the Ibo and Kanuri (and, among the Yoruba, the Ijebu) in Nigeria, the Kikuyu in Kenya, the Bemba in Zambia, the Bamaleke in the Cameroun, and the Ewe in Togo are among the most noteworthy. Moreover, in many instances there was an escalation of territorial nationalism as a result of the defensive reaction of the less assertive ethnic groups to the leadership and prominence of those groups *culturally disposed* to be more assertive and radical. Thus, in such cases, territorial nationalism, paradoxically, was the ultimate

Ethel M. Albert, "Socio-political Organization and Receptivity to Change: Some Differences Between Ruanda and Urundi," *Southwestern Journal of Anthropology,* 16.1 (Spring 1960), 46-74. The discredited study of J. C. Carothers, *The Psychology of Mau Mau* (Nairobi, Government of Kenya, 1964), should be mentioned only to further underscore the inadequacy of our existing knowledge.

83. They argue that modern Mali has an "historically grounded sense of identity, which Professor Ki Zerbo has called Mali's 'tradition étatique,' " which is reinforced "by the continuity of certain types of social institutions." This "statist" element in Mali political culture presumably has minimized tribalism and facilitated the development of Mali's peculiar brand of puritanical nationalism and its monolithic one-party system. Thomas Hodgkin and Ruth Schachter Morgenthau, "Mali," in James S. Coleman and Carl G. Rosberg, Jr., *Political Parties and National Integration in Tropical Africa* (Berkeley, University of California Press, 1965), pp. 220-221.

beneficiary of interethnic rivalry provoked and kept alive by an ethnic imbalance in nationalistic assertiveness.

I am not concerned here with the essentially situational explanations for ethnic variability in nationalistic disposition. Sometimes the situational determinant is the sole explanation; at other times it reinforces a cultural disposition or vice versa. Therefore, it is difficult to disentangle the two and to say with certitude which is the basic and which is the reinforcing factor. Three of the more common situational explanations for ethnic differences in nationalistic assertiveness are : the more protracted and intensive exposure of the vanguard group to exploitative or socially disorganizing influences (for example, the Kikuyu); overpopulation in the ethnic homeland and the consequent disapora abroad (for example, the Ibo, Ewe, and Bamaleke); and earlier and more extensive educational and economic development because of geographic location or better endowment in natural resources resulting in some groups acquiring and retaining a competitive advantage over other groups. These and other situationally determined differentiae have undoubtedly been important, in many instances decisive. For present purposes, however, our concern is with the more enduring "traditional" elements in the political cultures of those ethnic groups which tended to take the leadership in territorial nationalist movements and here I will focus upon two variables: traditional status mobility and the scale and degree of hierarchism of the traditional political system.

My working proposition is that in the historic transformation of Tropical Africa from colonialism to independence ethnic variations in assertiveness and attraction to territorial nationalism, *ceteris paribus*, correlated positively with ethnic variations in achievement motivation, and drawing on LeVine's theory, these latter differences are explained by variations in the traditional status mobility systems of the ethnic groups concerned.[84] Those ethnic groups whose cultures allowed for and encouraged greater status mobility have greater achievement orientation, which is diffuse. As regards the political aspects with which we are concerned, high achievement orientation meant a far greater predisposition to earlier and more emphatic assertiveness of territorial nationalism. The Ibo of Nigeria, who for nearly a decade were the undisputed carriers of Nigerian territorial nationalism, have been regarded as the archetype of this phenomenon. Now, with the results of Robert A. LeVine's systematic social psychological probe, these impressions have social scientific confirmation and explanation. Horton

84. Robert LeVine, *Dreams and Deeds,* pp. 16-21.

has summed up the common impressionistic view of the Ibo people: "renowned in recent years for the value they set on aggressive competition, the struggle for achievement and the willingness to explore new avenues of power and status."[85] Horton explains it by overpopulation; LeVine more convincingly accounts for it in terms of the traditional Ibo status mobility system based on parental values of individualism and specific training of the child in independence and achievement. He summarizes his results and their implications as follows:

> This investigation indicates that associated with well-known regional variations in levels of economic development and Westernization in Nigeria are individual behavioral dispositions of a deep-seated nature which are probably resistant to change . . . [They] . . . are not randomly or uniformly distributed among the three major ethnic groups of Nigeria; they vary significantly, and form a distinctive cluster. The cluster consists of achievement motivation, concern with self-improvement, non-authoritarian ideology, a favorable attitude toward technological innovation, and rapid advancement in Western education and the Western type of occupational hierarchy. The Ibo and, to a lesser extent, the Yoruba are high on all of these dimensions; the Hausa are low . . . One effect of this clustering of dispositions is that those individuals most prepared to occupy the positions of professional, technical, and bureaucratic leadership in the newly formed Nigerian nation are persons . . . [drawn from those ethnic groups culturally more achievement oriented]."[86]

For my purposes the hypothesis derivable from this is that greater assertiveness and leadership in territorial nationalist movements tended to be taken by persons from those ethnic groups having high achievement orientation (associated with an open traditional status mobility system) *in situations where higher status is perceived as being obtainable in a larger territorial status system.* This latter italicized addition to the LeVine hypothesis is required in view of my particular concern with ethnic variations, not in gravitation to ethnic nationalisms, but to territorial nationalism. If the traditional Ibo social and political system, as adapted under colonialism, had provided statuses equal to or higher than the emerging status system of Nigeria, it is just as likely that the Ibo would have confined their aggressive energies to building an ethnic nation-state, with no less passion than that of the Baganda in Uganda. The crux of the matter is surely in Horton's phrase "willingness to

85. Quoted in ibid., p. 83.
86. Ibid., pp. 92-93.

explore new avenues of power and status," and adding thereto "a greater perceptiveness in identifying such avenues."

A second variable that has been used to account for ethnic differences in support of territorial nationalism has been the scale and degree of hierarchism of traditional political systems. Scale and hierarchism are, of course, separate variables, but for present purposes they can be regarded as characteristically associated in the same system. My working proposition is that the smaller the scale of (that is, the greater the decentralization of authority), and the lesser the degree of hierarchism in, the political system of an ethnic group, the more readily and flexibly disposed the members of that group are to join modern associations (such as territorial nationalist parties and trade unions, as well as panethnic associations). This correlation of a disposition for associational formation and activity with a traditional type of political system was suggested by Ken Post in his study of the Nigerian 1959 election:

> It seems that those communities which in the past had no feeling of relationship with one another, sometimes even speaking different dialects of the same language, have been able to come together more effectively in a modern election than those which traditionally had been contained within some larger unity . . . Those societies whose traditional political systems were on a small scale, and least hierarchical, were those which in modern elections were best able to come together in support of a political party . . . where there was a tradition of chieftainship, hierarchical organization, and the association of power with office the way was opened to all sorts of disputes which might be taken up by the parties.[87]

The main thrust of Post's argument (as well as that of Banton)[88] is that the combinational and associational disposition of members of smaller scale, nonhierarchical, societies enabled them to unite more easily than societies of the opposite type when faced with an external challenge. In other words, he suggests that the combinational disposition would be directed ultimately toward greater ethnicity. Our amendment to this proposition is that small-scale nonhierarchical societies do have a greater combinational disposition but that this can be considered separately from the particular aggregate which benefits from it; in a word, it is an "open" or "ethnically neutral" disposition flexibly to combine,

---

87. K. W. J. Post, *The Nigerian Federal Election of 1959* (London, Oxford University Press, 1963), p. 380.

88. M. Banton, *West African City: A Study of Tribal Life in Freetown* (London, Oxford University Press, 1958), pp. 195 ff.

aggregate, and associate, of which either—or simultaneously both—an ethnic group or a nationalist movement of a territory can be beneficiaries.

.The fact that both of my propositions regarding ethnic variability—the disposition for achievement and for combination—are drawn from the modern political behavior of the Ibo raises the questions whether they are *sui generis* to the Ibo or the two are really not ultimately the same thing, namely that an open status system and a decentralized nonhierarchical political system are one and the same phenomenon. Not necessarily so. The Baganda have been achievement oriented but not disposed to combination outside Buganda. Also, in another comparative study, Robert LeVine found that two traditional African societies (the Gusii and the Nuer) possessing the same broad structural patterns did not have similar political cultures.[89] The two societies fall into the same type—stateless segmentary (that is, small-scale, nonhierarchical) societies—according to one of the more common structural typologies of traditional African societies. Yet in political culture (attitudes and orientation toward politics and authority) the two societies are polar opposites, the Gusii being strongly "authoritarian" and the Nuer extremely "egalitarian." This suggests that one cannot necessarily infer political culture from political structure.[90] However, this whole range of issues falls in a category of the unexplored in African political studies. At this stage we cannot and should not generalize except in the most tentative and hypothetical way.

African Political Culture and African Nationalism

We now switch from ethnic variability to ethnic commonality, from particular cultural traits as explanations for differential ethnic assertiveness to generic cultural features as explanations for the distinctive features of a common phenomenon. The actual history of African nationalism has been, of course, the progressive "territorialization" of an original pan-Africanism.[91] So undifferentiated did Lord Hailey consider the phenomenon of self-assertion in Africa that he argued prominence

89. Robert A. LeVine, "The Internationalization of Political Values in Stateless Societies," *Human Organization,* 19.2 (Summer 1960), 51-58.

90. LeVine concludes from his study that "classifying political systems on the basis of their predominant political values, particularly those concerning authority, yields insights into them which cannot be obtained by a scheme based purely on the broad outlines of political structure." Ibid., p. 54.

91. David E. Apter and James S. Coleman, "Nationalism or Pan-Africanism," in AMSAC, ed., *Pan-Africanism Reconsidered* (Berkeley, University of California Press, 1963), pp. 50-75.

be given "to the use of the term 'Africanism' rather than 'nationalism' " because Africans missed "the dynamic influence of the concept of territorial nationalism."[92] It is difficult, however, to make a convincing case that generic African nationalism is distinguishable from other varieties (European, Asian, Latin American) for cultural, rather than situational, reasons. In any event, I neither have the data, nor is this the place, for macroscopic continental comparisons. Here I am concerned only with identifying possible correlations between certain generically distinctive features of African nationalism. This is clearly a realm for wide-open speculation.

Three common characteristics of African territorial nationalisms are the *eclecticism* in the content of a common nationalist language, the pervasive *populism* in the mass appeals made to mobilize the population, and the *futurism* in the nature of the goals of the nationalist movement. Each of these could find a probable situational explanation. Indeed, Hodgkin argues that the existence of a common language of nationalism reflects "a certain kind of historical situation, certain fundamental human problems to be resolved, [which] tend to stimulate a particular way of thinking about the situation and the problems."[93] Each of the characteristics could also find an explanation in the historic pejorative view that Africans have no culture or tradition, or at least none worth preserving. However, I am interested in the third possibility, namely can these common features be explained by generic African culture. Here one must turn to Lloyd Fallers, one of the most competent and perceptive macrosociologists of this generation, who has a penchant and talent for the kind of uninhibited generalization we need. He has suggested the existence of two traits generic to traditional African societies — egalitarianism and political primacy. On egalitarianism he has this to say:

There remained in traditional Africa, even in the larger kingdoms with their elaborate political hierarchies, a kind of egalitarianism that seems to have had two principal roots. One of these was the pattern of kinship and family structure, which over much of the continent rested upon exogamous unilineal descent groups. Although in the structure of the state persons might stand to one another in highly asymmetrical dyadic relationships of economic and political superiority and subordination, every person tended also to belong to one or more extended, solidary descent groups that cut across such hierarchical structures. Exogamy produced in addition, a set of

92. Lord Hailey, *An African Survey* (London, Oxford University Press, 1956), p. 271.
93. Hodgkin in Kirkwood, *African Affairs,* p. 40.

affinal ties knitting descent groups together and inhibiting sub-cultural differentiation among them. At the village level, rights in land characteristically were heavily concentrated in the hands of kin-ship or local groups. Thus, tendencies toward crystallization of rigid horizontal strata were checked, in spite of the frequent concentration of power and wealth in elite hands.[94]

In addition to these considerations, the ethos of egalitarianism has been further strengthened by the absence in Africa of literary religious traditions — by a so-called "high" culture — which, Fallers notes, could have provided the basis for more clearly differentiated elite subcultures. Here we have a traditional cultural explanation for modern egalitarian populism, as well as for the eclectic version of Marxism called African socialism. The ethos of equality involved here, be it noted, is not that which infuses the "dignitarianism" referred to by Ali Mazrui (the passion to be equal with other races); rather it is that egalitarianism defines relationships among the African peoples themselves.

A second generic feature of African culture identified by Fallers is the primacy of the polity:

> In traditional Africa goods and services, both as symbols and as facilities, circulate primarily in terms of political relations, for it is the polity that dominates stratification . . . Traditional African societies . . . have characteristically exhibited patterns of role differentiation in which political specialization has been more prominent than economic. The ambitions of their members have been directed primarily toward attaining authority . . . Although direct cultural continuity may be difficult to achieve, some characteristic features of the traditional systems may perhaps persist and give a distinctly African character to the new independent nations. For example, in the new African nations, as in the old, political structures seem likely to continue to dominate economic ones, and political elites to retain their pre-eminence.[95]

This is not meant to explain, and culturally validate, Kwame Nkrumah's admonition to "seek ye first the Political Kingdom." It does suggest that to the extent that Faller's bold and sweeping proposition is valid, there might be a traditional cultural explanation — supportive of other explanations — for the extraordinary political sensitivity of Africans and for the widespread response to political nationalism and to the leadership of nationalist elites.

---

94. Fallers in Geertz, *Old Societies and New States*, p. 180.

95. Lloyd A. Fallers, "Social Stratification and Economic Processes," in Melville J. Herskovits and Mitchell Harwitz, eds., *Economic Transition in Africa* (Evanston, Northwestern University Press 1964), pp. 126, 129, 130.

2. Egypt's Search for Ideology: The Nasser Era

Nadav Safran

> We, the members of the National Congress of Popular Powers, representing all the sectors in the United Arab Republic and reflecting a popular will marked by unity and solidarity . . . hereby adopt this Charter, proclaiming it as the path leading to the full achievement of the objectives of our Revolution at present and our guide for the future.
>
> We, therefore, thus proclaim our Charter, calling on God to witness our resolve to make it the law of our lives and the rule of our conduct, taking advantage of our utmost capacity to put all its lofty principles into effect.
>
> From the Proclamation of the Charter by the National Congress of Popular Powers (June 30, 1962).

Modern Egyptian thought has been dominated from its genesis nearly a century ago by the problem of evolving a body of ideas, beliefs, values, and modes of thinking to serve as "law of life" and "rule of conduct" for the new Egyptian society that has been in the making since the days of Muhammad Ali. At the root of this problem was the ever more apparent incompatibility between the traditional world view dominated by a particular historically conditioned conception of Islam inherited by Egypt from previous centuries and the conditions and circumstances attending the relentless process of modernization that has embraced ever wider aspects of Egyptian life. In the endeavor to bridge the gulf between the traditional system of belief and the new reality—a gulf that has threatened the stability and well-being of the society—two basic currents of thought emerged at the beginning of the twentieth century. The one sought essentially to reinterpret Islamic doctrine to make it more suitable to the new conditions and thus restore its capacity to be the main guide of life, while the other sought to evolve a new belief system based on the adoption and adaptation of current European ideas, especially those broadly characterizable as Liberal Nationalist. The two currents, initially mutually accommodating and sharing to a substantial extent common sources of inspiration, evolved, under the dynamics of their distinct inner logic and the impact of political, economic, and social events at home and abroad, into mutually hostile

Note: The text of the Charter used throughout is the official English translation, issued by the Information Department, Cairo, U.A.R., n.d. Although the translation is often awkward and sometimes grammatically incorrect, I have preferred to use the official text rather than provide my own translation. Italics are my own throughout.

37

antitheses which succeeded only in paralyzing and distorting one another. The resultant intellectual confusion and intense anomie which moved to their climax in the nineteen forties had a great deal to do with the state of near social dissolution that made revolution both possible and necessary.[1] The new regime was thus confronted with the task of checking the intellectual confusion and then promoting efforts to meet afresh the unresolved ideological problem.

The first part of the task almost took care of itself. The new regime quickly developed comprehensive controls over the traffic of ideas, but these hardly needed to be used in the sphere of intellectual discussion. For the elimination of the politically organized contenders for the Liberal and neo-Muslim trends in the form of political parties and movements and the general uncertainty about the orientation of the new regime were in themselves sufficient to impose a moratorium on the discussion of any basic ideological issues, thus suspending the clashes of the previous decades.

The second part of the task—the promotion of efforts to meet the unresolved ideological problem—proved much more difficult, however. The leaders of the new regime had no particular ideological lead to offer; the famous "six principles"[2] which they enunciated upon assuming power were too vague, too narrow in scope, and not new enough to trigger an intellectual trend. And the intellectuals themselves were by and large divided into the older, Western-educated generation, which had played itself out, and the younger generations, trained in Egypt in the decades of mounting confusion, which lacked the breadth of knowledge and depth of experience needed to strike new paths without guidance.

The prolongation of the moratorium that ensued did not matter much as long as the new regime contented itself with pursuing piecemeal reforms, which it justified by improvising ad hoc principles. But as the regime developed, largely through the chain-reaction effect of the partial reforms, the ambition to effect a total transformation of society, the need for a comprehensive, systematic ideology became increasingly felt both by the more conscious elements of the public, who needed to know where their society was heading, and by the government which needed a means to guide and channel the efforts of the people

1. For a detailed analysis of all the points touched in this paragraph, see my *Egypt in Search of Political Community* (Cambridge, Harvard University Press, 1961).

2. These powers were: the destruction of imperialism; the ending of feudalism; the ending of monopolies; the establishment of social justice; the building of a powerful national army; the establishment of a sound democratic system.

toward the envisaged transformation. The demand for a doctrine, which the public pressed the government to meet and the government pressed the intellectuals, to produce, reached its climax after the decrees of July and September 1961, which socialized the economy and vastly extended the powers of the government.[3] Less than a year later, the Charter was produced at the government's initiative, and was approved by a specially convened National Congress of Popular Powers.

The Charter thus takes its place in the intellectual history of Egypt as a fresh effort to formulate the outline of a comprehensive system of belief to serve as the foundation for a renovated modern Egyptian society after the debacle of Liberal Nationalism and Islamic Reformism; and it will be assessed here from this perspective. It is true that the facts that the Charter is a specific body of thought rather than a general intellectual trend and that it emanates from a government exercising a monopoly over the traffic of ideas rather than from independent intellectuals operating in a free market of ideas make it impossible to equate it with Liberal Nationalism and Islamic Reformism in many crucial respects.[4] But insofar as the Charter purports to fulfill the same function that we have attributed to as the above-mentioned intellectual trends, that is, providing "laws of life" and "rules of conduct" for a modernizing Egyptian society, it does not seem inappropriate to view it as coming in the line of succession to these trends.

The Charter runs to 104 small pages grouped in ten chapters. Its shortness in relation to the subjects it deals with, its many divisions and subdivisions, and its very short paragraphs are designed to give it the

---

3. I recall a radio broadcast of a speech by President Nasser to the National Assembly in late September 1961, in which Nasser chided his listeners for asking: "The doctrine, the doctrine, where is the doctrine?" He said that he could not do all the things he had to do and also produce a doctrine and challenged them to produce one. At the time of writing I could not put my hands on the text of that speech.

4. One of these respects is the extent to which the content of the Charter may be thought to reflect the views of people other than its authors. In the case of Liberal Nationalism, for example, insofar as its ideas were able to withstand the test of competition from alternative ideas and were seen to be reproduced over a substantial period of time, the conclusion could be drawn that they represented a significant current of thought. In the case of the Charter, the absence of competition due to the monopolistic control by the government of the dissemination of ideas makes such a test impossible. Therefore my analysis should be viewed as commentary on a text without commitment as to the extent to which it represents the thoughts of other than its authors or as to the prospects of its acceptance in society at large.

character of a manifesto and a reference document. Traces of multiple authorship are evident particularly in the alternation of styles between the historical parts, with their flowery expressions and their frequent outbursts of passion, and the parts dealing with economic and social principles, written mostly in a matter of fact fashion.

For the purpose of content analysis the ten chapters of the Charter may be grouped into five parts. The first part, consisting of one chapter, touches upon the main themes of the work as it introduces the revolution of 1952 and outlines its unfolding. The second part, comprising three chapters, makes an attempt to put the revolution in the double perspective of contemporary necessity and history and defines its objectives and the circumstances affecting their realization in a general way. The third part, made up of four chapters, elaborates on the main objectives of the revolution and outlines the basic methods and instruments for their realization. It also touches upon some of the problems expected to arise and suggests the lines to be followed in meeting them. The fourth and fifth parts, of one chapter each, deal more specifically with the revolution's approach to Arab unity and with foreign policy. Each of these parts is important for the student of Egyptian and Arab affairs, but only the first and second parts have a direct relevance to the problem of the system of beliefs with which we are concerned. I shall refer to the other parts only to the extent necessary to clarify points raised in the first two.

The most important point in the first part and one which serves as an axis for the entire Charter is the attribution of the authorship of the revolution of 1952 to the Egyptian people as a whole. The *purpose* of this step hardly needs any comment — by attributing to the people the authorship of the revolution the writers of the Charter seek not only to endow the revolution with legitimacy but to facilitate the acceptance of its philosophy and acts as propounded in the Charter. The *manner* in which the attribution of authorship is done, however, requires some attention because it elucidates one of the modes of thinking that characterize the logic of the Charter.

The people are made to be the author of the revolution in two ways. One is simply "by definition." The opening paragraphs, for example, speak as a matter of course of the Egyptian people as having embarked, on July 23, 1952, on a revolutionary experience; as having succeeded in bringing about a basic change in their life; as having turned their backs on bad aspects of their past; and so on (p. 3). this device of taking for granted things which need explanation is encountered not only in this chapter but throughout the Charter. However, for those who read the text carefully, indirect explanations of the grounds for such "definitions" may sometimes be deduced. In the case at hand, the grounds for attributing to the people as a whole what at least appeared to be the action of a few men can be derived from a few paragraphs in the same chapter. The explanation is that the army officers who actually seized power in July 1952, were only the "vanguard" of the people. The people had struggled for the objectives of the revolution and passed these on to the vanguard; and once the vanguard stormed the fortress of the previous regime, the people rushed to their support and instructed them to broaden and deepen the revolution. Thus, after dwelling on the six principles and pointing out how, under the circumstances prevailing at the time of their proclamation, they constituted a remarkable revolutionary act, the writers say: "Those six principles which *the popular struggle passed on to the revolutionary vanguard* mobilized from within the army to serve that struggle and [to] the revolutionary forerunners outside the army who brought their instant and natural support to those principles — were not a complete theory of a revolutionary task" (p. 5). And further on: "The great people who inscribed the six principles in their martyrs' blood . . . the people who rushed the revolutionary vanguard from within and outside the army to face the responsibilities of the revolutionary task . . . these great people endeavored to deepen their fight and broaden its meaning" (p. 6).

Those who are familiar with Nasser's booklet *The Philosophy of the Revolution* will be struck by the contrast in the conception of the role of the people expressed there and in the Charter. There Nasser relates how he had fancied before July 23 that the nation was eager and waiting for the vanguard to storm the wall in order to rush in serried ranks and join the holy advance toward the great objective, and how bitter was his disappointment when, after the vanguard had accomplished its mission, it waited and waited only to be followed by divided mobs and stragglers, by opportunists and sycophants.[5] Nevertheless, the contrast need not be taken as evidence that the Charter's conception is without historical foundations altogether. For it is obvious to the student of Egyptian affairs that the action of July 1952 could not have succeeded so easily had not the people at large been indifferent or hostile to the previous regime. Where the Charter goes beyond plausible historical interpretation is in converting popular discontent into an active will for revolution, and in identifying that will with the specific revolution that has unfolded since 1952. The authors of the Charter go indeed so far in identifying the will of the people with that of the leaders that they

5. See *Falsafat al-Thawrah*, Cairo, n.d. pp. 21-23.

attribute to the people every single tactical move and thought of the leaders. It was thus the people who decided to defy the conventional logic (presumably of Naguib and his supporters) that was inclined to compromise and reform, it was the people who decided to deal a blow to all local monopolies at a time these imagined that the people were in dire need of them, it was the people who refused the dictatorship of one class it was the people who decided to establish new social relations based on new values expressed by a new national culture, and so on (pp. 6-8).

By juxtaposing what seems to be "historical reality" with the conceptions of it in the Charter, the point is not to criticize the writers for engaging in myth-making — all national histories indulge in this kind of activity to a greater or lesser extent. The point is rather to try to arrive at the process of thinking by which the gap between apparent historical reality and interpretation is bridged. In the case at hand, the juxtaposition serves to lay stress on the concept of the vanguard — adapted from Marxist-Leninist thought — and to point out that, as used by the writers of the Charter, the concept involves a *mystical identification* of the leaders with the people whereby the thoughts and actions of the one are viewed as being equally those of the other. It is the presumption of such an identification that makes it possible to project the leaders' will onto the people and convert its discontent into a will to revolution and to convert this will into the sponsorship by the people of every act and thought of the leadership.

A second theme of central importance broached in this chapter is the conception of the revolution as a total one. It is "an overall revolution" comprising "a series of revolutions" (p. 8); it is a movement of national liberation and a political, social, and cultural revolution all at once (pp. 7-8). The writers are aware that this conception of the revolution seems to run counter to historical facts, such as the six principles and the initiatives of the early years, which indicate that the revolutionary leaders had a much narrower view of the scope of their action. But they attempt to reconcile the apparent contradiction by suggesting that the comprehensiveness was latent in the revolution and that the great people, acting as "instructor of the revolutionary vanguard" prompted it to a fuller realization of the latent potentialities. This seems to escape one contradiction in order to fall into another one — that of reversing the role of vanguard and people (the people being the "instructor") — but the new apparent contradiction is resolved by the suggestion that the "instruction" of the people was not through the issuing of any directives to the vanguard, but through inspiring it with "the secrets of their great hopes" (p. 6). Thus, thanks to the "mystical communion" between the people and the leaders, the people remain the authors of the revolution and the prompters of the realization of its potentialities, while the leaders retain their vanguard function in that they read accurately the secrets of the people's hopes and translate them into specific programs and policies.

The assumption that the people entertain certain specific, albeit vaguely articulated hopes, which the leaders of the 1952 revolution have at last fathomed and endeavored to realize is fundamental for an understanding of the Charter and consequently of the image that the leaders of the present regime wish to imprint in the minds of the Egyptian people. This notion, while never expressed in exactly the same terms that I have used here, nevertheless pervades the entire Charter where it is sometimes concealed as unstated assumptions, sometimes revealed in such passages as the following:

> Those people were the great instructor who, in the wake of the revolutionary task on the 23rd of July 1952, undertook two historic operations with far-reaching effects.
>
> (1) First, those people developed and activated the six principles through trial, and correlated them with national history. This progress was leading to detailed programme paving the way before the infinite aims of the Revolution.
>
> (2) Second, those people prompted the revolutionary vanguard with the secrets of their great hopes, widening the scope of that vanguard by feeding it with new elements every day, capable of contributing to shaping their future (p. 6).

A most interesting point touched in this chapter reveals indirectly but unmistakably the general attitude of the writers of the Charter regarding the question of the role of religion in society—an issue that had been at the center of the debate in the modern intellectual history of Egypt up to 1952. The fourth paragraph on the first page reads:

> The devotion of the Egyptian people to the cause of the Revolution, the clarity of their vision and their undying struggle against all challenges have enabled them to produce a wonderful example of the *national Revolution which is the contemporary phase of the free man's struggle throughout history for a better life,* free of the chains of exploitation and underdevelopment in all their material and moral forms (p. 3).

The italicized lines seem to imply clearly a theory of history which may be made to spell out something like the following: history is the story of man's struggle for a better life; this struggle has assumed diverse forms depending on the circumstances under which it unfolded; at one time, for example, it assumed the form of striving to make religion prevail; at present, it takes the form of national revolution—which is therefore the latest phase of that struggle.

It may seem at first sight that this reconstruction attempts to read too much into the quoted lines. But this impression would be dispelled if two points are kept in mind. The first is the writers' conception of the revolution. *Every* revolution is viewed as an organic whole aiming potentially at the reconstruction of the totality of social life, though not every revolution realizes its potentialities. The revolution of 1952 occupies a special place in the history of revolutions in that it has quickly unfolded its potentialities and proceeded to transform the whole of Egyptian life.[6] Thus, in terms of its scope at least, the revolution is as comprehensive as the most comprehensive of all religions.

The second point to keep in mind is the writers' understanding of religion as it is expressed in various places in the Charter. This understanding is one typical of the modernists, who consider the main function of religion to be the promotion of the happiness and well-being of individuals and societies and who stress faith in a supreme moral being in the same proportion as they minimize the importance of specific dogmas and laws and blur the distinctions between various religions. Thus the Charter says:

The freedom of religious belief must be regarded as sacred in our new life.

The eternal spiritual values derived from religions are capable of guiding man, of lighting a candle of faith in his life and of bestowing unlimited capacities for serving truth, good and love. *In their essence, all divine messages constituted human revolutions (to) reinstate man's dignity and his happiness . . .*

The essence of religious messages does not conflict with the facts of our life; the conflict arises only in certain situations as a result of attempts made by reactionary elements to exploit religion—against its nature and its spirit—to impede *progress . . .*

The essence of all religions is to assert man's right to life and to freedom (p. 75).

If religions are "in their essence" revolutions for life, dignity, progress,

---

6. The notion that every revolution is viewed as aiming at a total reconstruction is clearly expressed in these lines: "A revolution is . . . the action of a whole people mustering their strength in a determined attempt to remove all obstacles and barriers standing in [the progress of] 'the way of life' they conceive as desirable. It is also a jump across the gulf of economic and social underdevelopment with the intention of making up for what was lost and of realizing the great aspirations which form part of what the people ideally want for future generations" (p. 33). The special place of the Egyptian revolution in the history of revolutions is expressed in pp. 7, 9, 35, among other places.

and freedom, it is easy to see how the national revolution with its equally noble aims but more practical and better adapted ways can be conceived as the later and higher phase of the eternal struggle which religion once led.

One last point needs to be mentioned, and this is the effort made to link the revolution with Arabism. The question is worth pondering even from the perspective of intellectual history because it pertains to the definition of the identity of the Egyptian people that the Charter seeks to promote.

The Egyptian people are linked to the Arab nation by two means. One is by assertion—the qualifier "Arab" is simply added periodically when the people of Egypt are mentioned. The other is by arguing the existence of an organic connection between the Egyptian revolution and the Arab awakening: "The Revolution of the Egyptian people awakened the possibilities of revolution in the entire Arab world. There is no doubt that this awakening was one of the main factors leading to the success of the Revolution in Egypt" (p. 9). This interaction is seen as a confirmation of the unity of the peoples of the Arab world and the conclusion is drawn from it that "the Egyptian people are called upon to place their victory at the service of the overall revolution in the rest of the Arab world" (p. 10).

The treatment of the link between Egypt and Arabism here reflects its ultimate treatment in the special chapter devoted to the subject. An effort is made in the preceding chapters to integrate the Arab aspect into the discussion, but the effort is less than successful. In the end, the special chapter reverts to making the link rest on present existential grounds, after making a general reference to the unity of language and unity of history:

> The Arab Nation is no more in need of giving evidence of the unity binding its peoples.
>
> Unity has passed this stage and is identified with the Arab existence itself. Suffice it that the Arab nation has a unity of language, forming the unity of mind and thought.
>
> Suffice it that the Arab Nation is characterized by the unity of history creating unity of conscience and sentiments.
>
> Suffice it that the Arab Nation enjoys a unity of hope, the basis of the unity of future and fate (p. 91).

The second part begins with a chapter which proceeds to argue that "experience has shown, and ever confirms the fact that revolution is the only course which the Arab struggle can take to head for a better future." It is "the only means by which the Arab Nation can free itself of its shackles, and rid itself of the dark heritage which burdened it. For the elements of suppression and exploitation which long dominated the Arab Nation and seized its wealth will never willingly submit." Revolution is also "the only way to overcome underdevelopment, forced on the Arab Nation through suppression and exploitation"; it is "the only way to face the big challenge . . . offered by the astounding scientific discoveries, which help widen the gap of development between one country and another" (p. 11).

Although the chapter deals mostly with other issues, it is clear that the definition of the role of revolution in the Arab destinies is the most important point in the mind of the authors as is evident from the title they gave to the chapter: "The Necessity of Revolution." Equally clear is the reason for the importance of this issue: by arguing that revolution is "the only bridge which the Arab Nation can cross to reach the future it aspires to" (p. 11), the authors seek to meet from the perspective of "logic" the problem of legitimizing the seizure of power by the revolutionary leaders. All revolutions must face this problem; and most of them resort to a "transvaluation of values" which puts the onus of illegitimacy on the opponents, who are accused of conspiring to obstruct normal evolution or to suppress the "natural" rights of the people. The writers of the Charter conform to this pattern when they argue that the obstinate "forces of suppression and exploitation" which would not submit easily make revolution inevitable. The "forces of suppression and exploitation" include reaction, feudalism, capitalism, and imperialism and its stooges and allies—all real enough, perhaps. But there are also hints that advanced nations, simply by advancing and developing science, somehow conspire against Egypt by widening the gap between them and it—hints that accord with the tendency of all revolutions to assume a conspiratorial view of the world.

After thus arguing briefly the necessity of the revolution, the writers go on to define in general terms what might be called the "mode of thinking" of the revolution, its objectives, and the circumstances affecting their realization.

The mode of thinking is summed up in three points, oddly characterized as "powers," which should enable the revolution "to realize its aims and destroy all its enemies" (p. 11). These are: "consciousness based on scientific conviction arising from enlightened thought and free discussion, unaffected by the forces of fanaticism and terror"; "free movement that adapts itself to the changing circumstances of the Arab struggle"; and "clarity of perception of the objectives . . . which avoids being swept away by emotion and diverted from the high road of the national struggle" (p. 11). It will be agreed that the three points amount essentially to matching means to ends on the basis of an "objective" assessment of the situation, free of prejudice, dogmatism, and emotionalism—hardly a revolutionary prescription in itself. Its exaltation to the level of "powers" expected to accomplish miracles reflects undoubtedly the novelty of the prescription in the context of the history of Egyptian intellectual and practical thought, which has been greatly distorted by the negatives mentioned in the formula. But it also reflects an intellectual bent of the makers of the revolution and the men who surround them, which is crucial for a correct assessment of the Charter and the orientation of the regime. This bent may be characterized as enthusiasm for "positivism" in the Comtean sense of the term.

The mention of a few general manifestations of the "positivist" inclination of the regime and its men and a comment on the social origins and professional background of the men should indicate that orientation:

The adulation of science evident throughout the Charter.

The implicit belief in the capacity of science to arrive at definite "laws" of society and a consequent unbounded faith in planning and "social engineering."

The recognition of the existence of class antagonisms but the belief in the possibility of so organizing society as to neutralize these antagonisms and to substitute for the exploitation of man by man the common effort of all to exploit nature (see p. 43).

The indifference toward metaphysical and theological issues implicit in the neglect of these subjects in a document that purports to outline comprehensively the principles of thought and action of the whole society.

The thorough social conception of the "essence" of religion which is very reminiscent of the Saint Simonean-Comtean "religion of humanity."[7]

In speaking of the "positivist" bent of the Charter I do not necessarily imply a conscious option on the part of men of the present regime for the specific philosophies of Comte or Saint Simon, even though works of Comte were translated or summarized long before 1952 and even though the Saint Simoneans have had a long association with Egypt from the days of Muhammad Ali through the reign of Ismail. The

7. It is interesting that the Saint Simoneans and Comte thought that Islam was the closest of all historical religions to their conception of the "religion of humanity." The Saint Simoneans actually searched in the Muslim East for a "prophetess" for their new religion!

probability is that the governing men of the present regime have acquired their "positivist" bent by being what they are—soldiers, scientists, technicians, and administrators not belonging to an aristocratic or an entrepreneurial class—since the Saint Simonean-Comtean vision has become long ago the unconscious common heritage of men of the same occupations and social origins everywhere. A glimpse at the values and mode of thinking implicit in any work of the "scientific management" school or of prominent public administrators should suffice to prove the point.[8]

The ends of the revolution are defined as freedom, socialism, unity. In the chapter these goals are defined further only slightly, but the elaborations provided in the third part of the Charter (not considered otherwise here) may be drawn upon for comment. Freedom is further defined as "freedom of the country and freedom of the citizen" (p. 12). Freedom of the country, it becomes clear in other contexts, is understood as independence of the entire Arab homeland. Freedom of the citizen, which is mentioned without any qualification, turns out in subsequent discussion to have quite a different meaning from what might be supposed on first sight.

In the first place, it transpires that not all citizens are citizens; feudalists, reactionaries, and exploiters are excluded from the fold of citizenry.[9] In the second place, it becomes clear that freedom is understood in a combination of the Athenian, Rousseauean, and Soviet senses of the term to mean freedom of participation rather than in the Western liberal sense of freedom of choice and opposition. The argument is essentially that freedom of choice and opposition is worse than meaningless when economic and social opportunity is unequal. Such freedom becomes then a deceptive facade ensuring the domination of the economically privileged classes. But if economic and social opportunity is equalized—which can only be done through depriving the exploiting classes of the means of exploitation—it becomes unnecessary to have formally organized choice and opposition. The antagonisms, as distinguished from clashes, that remain among social groups can then be resolved peacefully within the frame of a single union of the forces of society properly conceived (see pp. 36-45).

8. For a good discussion of the administration's way of thinking, see Dwight Waldo, *The Administrative State* (New York, 1948), esp. pt. 2.

9. The Charter actually says only that "it is indispensable that the Revolution should liquidate the force of reaction, deprive it of all its weapons and prevent it from making any attempt to return to power and subject the state machinery to the service of its own interests" (p. 42). However in practice, this was translated into expropriation and denial of citizenship rights.

The same line of reasoning is applied to specific civil liberties. Freedom of the press in the conventional Western sense, for example, is viewed as a deception hiding its very opposite. Because of technical requirements, publishing has become big business requiring vast amounts of capital which ipso facto places it in the hands of big capitalists and out of reach of the people. Moreover, because the big publishers are bound with other big businesses by a community of interest, they are impelled to reflect their views to the exclusion of those of the people and to serve as instruments for their political domination. Consequently, by striking at the privileged classes generally and expropriating for the benefit of the public the means of publication specifically, freedom of the press is automatically placed on the most secure foundations (see pp. 45-46). In the third place, since political freedom in the sense just explained is made dependent on economic and social equality of opportunity, the full realization of political democracy must await a substantial realization of social democracy (see pp. 42 ff.).[10]

Socialism is defined in the present chapter as being "both a means and an end, namely sufficiency and justice" (p. 12). In another chapter, sufficiency is explained as meaning a high level of production, and justice is defined as "acceding to the lawful rights of the working people" (p. 49). The two are viewed as the mutually dependent supports of social freedom, just as social freedom is considered the necessary foundation of political freedom. The realization of a high level of production requires "the people's control over all the tools of production and (the) directing (of) the surplus according to a definite plan" (p. 51). The realization of justice "calls for programmes for social action . . . that enable the popular working people to reap the benefits of economic action and create the welfare society to which they aspire" (p. 51). This whole conception is called "scientific socialism," and its adoption by Egypt is viewed as "inevitable."

It is quite clear from the context of the discussion that by "scientific socialism" the authors understand simply socialism that uses science rather than socialism whose principles are *derived* from the discovery of "the laws of motion of history" and economic laws, as Engels argued in his *Socialism, Scientific and Utopian*. In any case, it is obvious that the authors have no objective criterion for determining "the lawful rights of the working people" and their share in the fruits of economic action, as

10. "Only when a citizen possesses these three guarantees (freedom from exploitation in all its forms, an equal opportunity to have a fair share of the national wealth, and freedom from anxiety) can he be said to have political freedom, and can take part by means of his vote, in shaping the authority of the state he aspires to have" (p. 42).

the Marxists have in the labor theory of value and the concept of surplus value. Justice, one of the two pillars of the Charter's socialism, is left to the subjective determination of the political leadership in competition with the requirements of "sufficiency."

With regard to the notion of the "inevitability" of socialism for Egypt, the writers do have the outline of a theory of economic development to support it. Economic development, they argue, has taken place in the advanced countries in one of three ways: through looting the wealth of the colonies; through the exploitation of the working class by capitalists; through the sacrifice of whole living generations for the sake of others still unborn. The first way is out of the question for Egypt morally and practically; the second way is not only unjust but leads local capitalism, in its inability to compete with advanced countries, to relate itself to the movements of world monopolies and become their appendage "dragging the whole country to doom"; as for the third way, "the nature of the age no longer allows such things." There remains, therefore, only one way: development through socialist planning (see pp. 49-51).

Unity is interpreted in this chapter as consisting of "the restoration of the natural order of a nation, torn apart by its enemies against its own will and interests (p. 12). Since I have already commented on this subject, I shall confine myself here to pointing out that just as the word "restoration" harks back to the historical argument, the words "natural order" probably mean the interaction and community of fate mentioned above. In other words, natural is used in the sense of necessary rather than in the sense of prescribed by some transcendental authority.

The reader will have noticed that the writers of the Charter have borrowed generously from the Marxist literature in their elaboration of the goals of freedom and socialism. This tendency prevails throughout the Charter though it is heavier in the contexts reviewed. The borrowings may be classified under three types. The first consists of the borrowing of isolated terms, such as "vanguard," "scientific socialism," "inevitability," and so on, which are given an entirely new meaning. This is the least important kind though it is by no means meaningless, since it reflects a mounting general intellectual orientation toward Bolshevik literary sources. The second type consists of substantive concepts, such as the class struggle, economic determinism, finance capitalism, and so on, which are adapted in greater or lesser degrees but still retain significant traces of their original meaning and use. This type of borrowing is obviously quite important; however, care should be taken not to exaggerate the extent to which the concepts themselves have determined the thought of the writers. Clearly they saw in them useful instruments for interpreting important aspects of Egyptian reality and they did not hesitate to tamper with them in order to make them more usable. The third type of borrowing is rather difficult to define precisely, yet it is the most important of the three because it affects the process of thinking itself. It includes such phenomena as proclaiming the principle of the freedom of the citizen and then whittling it down by means of definitions; or of arguing in the face of a reality well known to those who make the argument that the press was never freer than since it came under total ownership of "the people." This "new scholasticism," this method of arguing by definition, this "double think" technique characteristic of Bolshevik political literature at its worst, can do more damage to Egyptian thought in the long run than the combined evils of prejudice, dogmatism, and emotionalism against which the Charter inveighs.

Freedom, socialism, and unity are asserted by the writers of the Charter to "have always been the slogans of the Arab struggle"; it is only the method of their pursuit which is new, being "imposed by the changing circumstances particularly those far-reaching changes which occurred in the world after the Second World War" (p. 13). These changes are summed up as the spectacular strengthening of the force of the nationalist movements in Asia, Africa, and Latin America; "the emergence of the communist camp as an enormous force, with steadily increasing material and moral weight and effectiveness in facing the capitalist camp"; the great scientific and technological advances, including the development of the means of production, of mass destruction weapons and the balance of terror, the revolution in transport and communications; finally, the increasing weight of moral forces in the world reflected in the United Nations, the non-aligned states, and world opinion (pp. 13-14).

These changes have affected the means of achieving the three objectives in important ways. Their interaction has made it possible to attain freedom by means of national revolutions and made it unnecessary to placate the imperialists or bargain with them. The progress in the means of production, the development of nationalist and labor movements, and the tendency to peace in the world have obviated the need "to observe literally laws formulated in the 19th century" and opened new prospects and new conditions for the realization of socialist experiments (p. 15). The same changes make impossible the repetition of the German and Italian methods of achieving national unity and call for peaceful means and unanimous approval of the people as the only possible way to achieve Arab unity (p. 15).

Leaving aside the claim that freedom, socialism, and unity have always been the slogan of the Arab struggle, the assessment of world circumstances and their implications for the pursuit of the three goals is very clear, realistic, and frank and calls for no comment beyond pointing out that the Charter is at its best when it deals with issues of diplomacy and strategy, reflecting probably the dominant interest of the top leadership of the regime. One may also point out, incidentally, that the listing of the emergence of the communist camp and its effectiveness in facing the capitalist as a positive development from the point of view of the pursuit of the Arab goals shows the extent to which the Western powers deluded themselves when they sought until very recently to use that very rise in power as an argument to press the Arabs and Egypt in particular to align themselves with the West.

Chapter 3 "The Roots of the Egyptian Revolution," is probably the most interesting for the historian. The primary object of the chapter is to endow the revolution with legitimacy by reference to its past, just as the previous chapter, "On the Necessity of the Revolution," sought to bestow on it legitimacy by reference to its mission. In pursuing this object, the writers suggest an outline of Egypt's history as they wish it to be written, which contains interpretations of specific episodes and periods that are even more relevant to the interest of the student of ideas than the main theme itself.

The main theme of the chapter may be summarized as follows: the history of Egypt is the story of the revolutionary struggles of its people to achieve liberty, justice, and unity with the region surrounding it. In its struggle, this valiant people was occasionally overwhelmed and more often deceived by suppressors and betrayed from within. However, its revolutionary zeal in the pursuit of its goals was never extinguished; and after each setback it flared up again with renewed vigor, until it achieved a decisive victory in 1952, which secured for good the way to the realization of its long-sought objectives.

This interpretation of Egyptian history not only endeavors to give the goals of the revolution the legitimacy of duration and tradition but seeks also to give further substantiation to the claim of the leaders of the revolution to be the "vanguard." For the idea of vanguard presupposes a main army seeking to move in the direction taken by the advanced unit. For example, in the Bolshevik literature, from which the idea is borrowed, the main army of which the Communist party is the vanguard is considered to be the working class, which is alleged by definition to be "spoiling for a fight" with capitalism. In the case at hand, by depicting the Egyptian people as ever struggling to achieve freedom, justice, and unity, the makers of the 1952 revolution become automatically the instruments of the main army of the people — its vanguard.

Of the specific theses adopted in the course of the presentation of the historical outline, the following — not all pertinent to the main theme — seem to be most interesting:

1. Ever since Pharaonic times there has been an organic interconnection between Egypt and the area around it now inhabited by the Arab nation. In this interconnection, Egypt normally assumed grave responsibilities for the whole region in the political, military and cultural spheres (p. 17).

2. The Pharaonic heritage of Egypt is acknowledged with pride. Pharaonic history is referred to as "the maker of Egyptian civilization and the first civilization of man" (p. 17). This is significant in view of the debate that has raged over this issue for half a century, in which all the traditionalist and some of the modern intellectual leaders vigorously opposed the inclusion of the heathen and remote Pharaonic heritage in Egypt's cultural self-image. It is also significant in view of Egypt's present Arab vocation. Opponents of the present regime in other Arab countries, for example, have used the acknowledgment of the Pharaonic heritage in order to embarrass the present Egyptian leadership as recently as a year ago.

3. The Ottoman period is viewed as a period of total darkness and reaction, of weakness and disintegration "imposed by the Ottoman Caliphate in the name of religion, while in fact religion is incompatible with such factors" (pp. 17-18). The Charter thus repudiates the principle of community based on religion — the concept of the *ummah* — which had been at the root of a very real and widespread loyalty to the Ottoman regime up to its very end. It also repudiates the thesis propounded by some Arab nationalist spokesmen which views the breakdown of the Ottoman Empire as the breakdown of the last historical manifestation of real Arab unity.[11] The total repudiation of the Ottoman period seems all the more remarkable when contrasted with the proud acknowledgment of the Pharaonic heritage. The principle underlying both operations is the same: the primacy of the nationalist perspective over any other. Variants of this principle are also seen in the following points.

4. The crusades are seen as "the first wave of European colonialism, taking cover behind the Cross of Jesus, while in fact colonialism and the message of that great teacher are poles apart" (p. 17). Here too there is

11. See, for instance, F. Sayegh, *Arab Unity: Hope and Fulfillment* (New York, 1958), passim.

a very interesting reversal of perspective: generations of writers since Jamal al-Din alAfghani have viewed modern Western encroachments upon the lands of Islam as a continuation of the crusades under the guise of secular colonialism; now the crusades themselves are viewed as secular colonialism under the guise of religious enterprise. Incidentally, for those who are interested in "mentalities," the tendency evident here to view things from a single perspective, to search for a single explanation of historical processes, offers ample room for speculation.

5. Al-Azhar is viewed with pride as a stronghold against Ottoman obscurantist-reactionary-colonialist thought and as a guardian of the heritage and wealth of Arab civilization (pp. 17-18). The device used here of appropriating elements of the Egyptian heritage which do not quite accord with the philosophy of the regime by giving them a nationalist or revolutionary "angle" is common in this chapter and will be encountered again below.

6. "It was not the French campaign against Egypt that led to the Egyptian awakening . . . as some historians claim. For when the French campaign (expedition) came to Egypt, it found Al-Azhar simmering with new trends which had their impact on life throughout Egypt . . . the French campaign, however, brought in a new supply of revolutionary energy for the Egyptian people at that time" (p. 18). This interpretation of the role of the French expedition sets the tone for the interpretation of subsequent historical episodes which seeks to view the Egyptian awakening as self-induced and popular rather than as the result of a foreign impact or an imposition from above. Thus:

7. "The popular awakening was the driving force behind the reign of Muhammad Aly. It is almost unanimously assumed that Muhammad Aly laid the foundation of modern Egypt. Yet the tragedy of that age was that Muhammad Aly believed in the popular movement only as a springboard for him to reach his ambitions" (p. 18). Muhammad Ali drove Egypt to futile adventures which impeded the movement of the Egyptian awakening and brought a setback with grievous damage. "This setback widely opened the gate to foreign interference in Egypt, while the people had previously foiled continuous attempts [at] invasion, the latest at that time being Frazer's campaign against Rosetta" (p. 19).

8. The period leading up to the Orabi revolution (1882) is seen as characterized by imperialist machinations in collusion with princes of the Muhammad Ali dynasty on the one hand, and of swelling popular revolutionary energy on the other hand (pp. 19-20). The revolutionary energy was released by the youth sent to Europe for their education in the flourishing days of the reign of Muhammad Ali; these youths produced upon their return a flourishing new culture and "made of

Egypt in the second half of the 19th century a platform for thought in
the Arab world, a stage for its art, and a rallying ground for all Arab
revolutionaries crossing artificial and illusory boundaries" (p. 20). The
cultural revival issued in its turn into a revolutionary battle against the
alien Muhammad Ali dynasty which reached its culmination in the
Orabi revolution. This interpretation involves a modification of chro-
nology which gives the cultural contribution of Egyptians temporal and
causal priority over the contribution of Syrian émigrés; it completely
fuses cultural activity and political agitation to make the Orabi
revolution an "organic" outgrowth; and, for the same reason, it projects
some post-Orabi trends back to the pre-Orabi period.

9. The writers do not deal specifically with the military campaign
that ushered in the British occupation; but while speaking in another
context, they hint that the defeat of the Egyptian army was due to
betrayal: "Hardly had . . . the noise of the battle fought by the valiant
Egyptians who were betrayed at Tal-el Kebir faded when new voices
were heard . . . expressing the brave people's eternal will to live and the
awakening which neither difficulties nor disaster could put out" (pp.
20-21).

10. The period between 1882 and 1919 is seen as another period of
revolutionary fermentation before the explosion that occurred in 1919.
This period, which imperialism and those who collaborated with it
thought to be a period of stagnation, was one of the richest periods in
the history of Egypt in its searching into the depths of its soul and its
mustering anew its revolutionary impulses" (p. 21). During this period,
Muhammad Abduh called for religious reform, Lutfi al-Sayyid "stressed
that Egypt should belong to the Egyptians," Qasim Amin called for the
emancipation of women. "These calls heralded a new revolutionary
wave which was soon to rise in 1919" (p. 21). This interpretation of the
period is interesting on several scores.

From the point of view of the main theme of the chapter and from
that of the philosophy of the regime in general, Abduh, al-Sayyid, and
Amin should not qualify as national heroes. All three of them happened
to have favored "collaboration" with the British and were opposed to
the intransigent nationalism of Mustafa Kamil. None of them had
much of a notion about socialism. And one of them, Lutfi al-Sayyid,
explicitly rejected pan-Arabism while the other two were silent on the
issue. It is of course easy to think that the admission of these three men
to the national pantheon for the contributions mentioned as just
another example of the tendency to use anything as grist for the nationalist mill regardless of consistency. But to dismiss the subject with this
view would be to miss the real point, which is that in the minds of the
writers a revolution is not a limited uprising for the sake of correcting

specific evils, but is *in principle* a movement seeking total renovation. Such a movement rarely fulfills its potentialities but this should not detract from the fact that all contributions, however partial, are sparks from the larger flame. This conception is even more evident in the interpretation of the 1919 revolution.

11. The revolution of 1919 — conceived as a process extending up to 1952 — receives special attention and occupies the remaining part of this chapter and the whole of the next. As the latest — and for once incontrovertible — revolutionary expression of the Egyptian people, this revolution is quite important to the writers' effort to link the 1952 revolution to the past struggles. But there is the problem that the 1919 revolution was clearly limited to political objectives and was local Egyptian in its orientation, contrary to the main theme and purpose of the historical analysis.

The solution adopted by the writers to at least one aspect of the problem can be easily anticipated by now. In principle, and as far as the people were concerned, that revolution was comprehensive in its aims, but the leadership "overlooked" the social aspects for which the people had arisen. This oversight is at the root of the total undoing of the revolution. It isolated the revolutionary leaders from the people, leading to the government's fall under the control of the big landowners, exploitative capitalists and their hirelings. Democracy became a sham and a facade; and the residual leadership of the revolution found itself at the mercy of the palace and completely incapable of resisting the British. They ended up by surrendering to the latter in the 1936 treaty and "selling their souls to the devil" by seeking to gain office from the palace at any price.[12]

This formula meets the problem of the scope of the 1919 revolution, but it does not answer the problem of its purely Egyptian orientation. Except for suggesting that the leaders "overlooked" the Arab dimension as a result of failing to read correctly the lessons of history, the authors fail to reconcile the thesis that unity has ever been a slogan of the national struggle with the facts of 1919 and just leave it hanging.

The notion that the revolution of 1919 failed to achieve even its limited objectives because its leadership betrayed its broader, social, and economic goals, whatever its merits as history and as political analysis, reflects an important element of the thinking of its proponents. It suggests that for the leaders of the revolution of 1952, sweeping social and economic transformations for the benefit of the people are not only national and moral imperatives but are also dictated by the requisites of their own political survival.

12. The Charter's interpretation of the 1919 revolution and its "betrayal" is found on pp. 21-26.

3. Nationalism and Separatism in Africa

M. Crawford Young

A scholar of unusual wisdom, Rupert Emerson, has remarked that one of the paradoxes of nationalism is that its very success in binding men together has as its counterpart "its intensification of their sense of separation from those on the other side."[1] Normally we assume this sense of separation to refer to persons and groups politically organized in a different state, having a different flag, a different diplomatic corps, and a separate vote in the United Nations. This, however, is not always the case; historically, the nation and the state have not always been identical, and, as Emerson also points out, nowhere in the contemporary world is the gap wider than it is in Africa between the territorial state, born of the colonial partition, and the matrix of factors producing nationalism.[2]

The answer to this discordance, of course, is nation building. The state exists, now graced with international sovereignty since the achievement of independence by most of Africa. For independent Africa to prosper and develop, nationalism must cohere about the existing territorial entities. The state must legitimize itself through generating the overriding loyalty to itself as a human community which we usually understand by nationalism. African elites and students of African politics are in full consensus on this point.

Yet the bases for political solidarity are not always easily susceptible to manipulation, either by Africa's leaders or its analysts. Nation building has its antithesis in fragmentation, or what French-speaking African intellectuals stigmatized as "balkanization." Several examples of this occurred in the controlled circumstances of the decolonization process. In the very different environment of postcolonial politics, we have already two important specimens, in Senegal's withdrawal from the Mali Federation, and Katanga's abortive (but not necessarily final) secession effort 1960-1963. A full understanding of the requirements of nation building supposes an adequate appreciation of contrary forces. Accordingly, I propose in this brief essay to seek out the serpent of separatism which lurks in the gardens of African nationalism.

To begin with, I must clarify the sense in which I employ the term "nationalism" in this discussion. The specific environment in which African self-assertion has emerged has spawned some particular definitions of the term nationalism in African politics. James Coleman, for example, tends to link his definition of nationalism to the assertion of

1. Rupert Emerson, *From Empire to Nation* (Cambridge, Harvard University Press, 1960), p. 329.
2. America Assembly, *The United States and Africa* (1958), pp. 14-15.

the right to self-government within the territorial framework of the colonial entity.[3] Thomas Hodgkin, on the other hand, suggests nationalism should be used "to describe any organization or group that explicitly asserts the rights, claims, and aspirations of a given African society . . . in opposition to European authority."[4] Lord Hailey proposes the substitution of the term "Africanism" for "nationalism," situating the phenomenon as a racial reaction to European rule.[5] These classic definitions, however, and many which fell between them have become obsolete after the great year of African independence, 1960. Nationalism can no longer be defined in terms of the largely achieved goal of independence. One postcolonial definition of nationalism might be the assertion by a self-conscious group of the will to constitute an autonomous political community, whether or not the group coincides with a recognized state; this will be the sense in which the term is used in this discussion. In many instances, perhaps to an increasing degree, this does coincide with the established territorial framework; no one can deny the potency of Ghanaian, Guinean, Malien, Algerian, Tanzanian, or Nigerian nationalism. In other instances, however, nationalism so defined involves a group lesser than the state (Baganda, Mongo, Northern Nigeria, Kabylia), or one overlapping two or more states (Somali, Lunda, Bakongo, Ewe, Fang); it is with these latter categories that we are presently concerned.

The colonial period, in retrospect, was peculiarly favorable to the development of a territorial form of nationalism. In the first place, the territory was held firmly together by the instruments of colonial force. Until the time came to begin negotiating the terms of power transfer, no separatist movement against the forces of colonial authority had the slightest chance of success. Gestures in this direction in Buganda, and in Kivu, Katanga, and Lower Zaïre in Zaïre, were easily stifled by the colonizer. Similarly, the struggle to terminate European rule made of territorial unity an overriding imperative. Self-government, as a practical matter, could only be achieved through acceptance of the colonial territory as the basis for political organization. Establishment of a clear claim to representativity in negotiating with the colonial ruler entailed mobilizing all or most of the territory's population in support of power transfer to an African government, either within a single

3. James S. Coleman, "Nationalism in Tropical Africa," *American Political Science Review*, 48.2 (June 1954), 404-426.

4. Thomas Hodgkin, *Nationalism in Colonial Africa* (London, Frederick Muller Ltd., 1956), p. 23.

5. Lord Hailey, *An African Survey, Revised 1956* (London, Oxford University Press, 1957), pp. 251-254.

movement, or in any event through a coalition of several, united on the issue of independence. Overt assertion of self-rule demands by nonterritorial movements was sharply inhibited by the tactical fact that there was no prospect of success and that such action played into the hands of the divide-and-rule, "they're-not-ready-yet" factions in colonial administrations.

The very success of African nationalism in its pre-independence phase transformed its environment in several fundamental ways. First and most obviously, the powerful unifying impulse of ending direct European rule has been removed. Although the reality of "neo-colonialism" in a number of African states can hardly be denied, this more diffuse threat to African independence is a pale substitute for its predecessor as an imperative for unity. A number of African states, such as Ghana, Guinea, Mali, Ivory Coast, Tunisia, Tanzania, and Malawi, had forged in the independence struggle the potent unifying weapons of the mass, single-party, and the charismatic national leader, which at least in the initial postcolonial period served well as instruments of territorial integration. The new African rulers also inherited the coercive instruments of the colonial state, supplemented in the case of many of the former French colonies by detachments of metropolitan troops, also a significant deterrent to separatist movements. But the colonizer himself had at least apparently disappeared.

Further, important new stimuli to fragmentation emerged. A concomitant of rapid modernization, especially the extension of mass primary education programs in many areas, was the enlargement of the potential arena of active political participants. Historically, culturally plural states have been subjected to great strains by the advent of mass politics. The breakdown of Austro-Hungary was made inevitable by the transmission of political consciousness in the form of nationalism to middle class and peasant strata of the "subject minorities."[6] The rise of Irish nationalism coincides with the extension of suffrage and parliamentary representation to rural Ireland. Linguistic nationalism in India, a serious threat to the very survival of the political community, arises only with the advent of mass political participation.[7] Thus states that possessed several major, self-conscious ethnic groups could well anticipate serious fissiparous pressures.

6. Royal Institute of International Affairs, *Nationalism* (New York, Oxford University Press, 1939), pp. 81-84; Hans Kohn, *The Idea of Nationalism* (New York, Macmillan Co., 1945), p. 432, 527-534.

7. See the interesting analyses of linguistic nationalism in India, Naresh Chandra Roy, *Federalism and Linguistic States* (Calcutta, Firma K. L. Mukhopadhyay, 1962). Selig S. Harrison, *India: The Most Dangerous Decades* (Princeton, Princeton University Press, 1960).

Massive Africanization of the senior civil service, armies, and public corporations has come more swiftly in most countries than was thought prudent or likely before independence. This has often heightened regional and ethnic tensions which easily decant into separatism. In most African states, we scarcely exaggerate in suggesting that these several thousand top positions are the crucial resource being allocated by the political system to its most conscious members in the early post-independence phase. The whole process takes place with high visibility; a veritable illuminated ethnic scoreboard often exists, and the losers are unlikely to accept defeat with equanimity. This has been most conspicuous in Nigeria and Zaïre but has been present nearly everywhere.[8]

Sources of Separatism

Fragmentation, then, has become a possible option for discontented groups. The pre-independence inhibitions are in good part removed. Modernization itself, although necessary to broaden loyalties toward the state, may also reinforce other patterns of conscious solidarity. The race against artificiality is engaged throughout the continent. The question then arises as to what sorts of factors breed separatism in active form.

The most frequent type of fragmenting movement is ethnic; here we encounter what is usually advertised as "tribalism." Although the common theme of an ethnic label for the loyalty network appears to suggest a single phenomenon, closer examination reveals that rather diverse elements are present here.[9] The loyalty may focus upon a traditional state, such as the Hausa-Fulani emirates in Northern Nigeria, or the Kuba kingdom in central Zaïre. It may be to a group with a long history of cultural identity and perhaps centralized institutions, such as the Bakongo, Yoruba, or Baganda. Or it may relate to entirely novel groupings, artifacts of "supertribalism" in the new cities, without any history of a collective psyche, such as the "Bangala" in Kinshasa — and to a certain extent the Mongo in the central Zaïre basin and Ibo of Eastern Nigeria.[10]

8. See, for example, "Tribe and Nation in East Africa," *Round Table,* 52 (June 1962), 252-258.

9. For further exploration on this important theme, see Paul Mercier, "Remarques sur le signification du tribalisme actuel en Afrique noire," *Cahiers Internationaux de Sociologie,* 31 (1961), pp. 61-80; Immanuel Wallerstein, "Ethnicity and National Integration," *Cahiers d' Études Africaines,* no. 3 (October 1960); Max Gluckman, "Tribalism in Modern British Central Africa," *Cahiers d' Études Africaines,* 1 (January 1960), pp. 55-70; J. Clyde Mitchell, *The Kalela Dance* (Manchester, Manchester University Press, 1956); Philip Mayer, *Townsmen or Tribesmen* (Capetown, Oxford University Press, 1961).

10. For further exploration of this point, see my chapter on "The Politics of

The common thread, then, in this form of nationalism is its identification by an ethnic label and the fact that, with the exceptions of Lesotho and Swaziland, this form of loyalty does not coincide with the territorial state. Even where ethnic nationalism is pronounced, it should be at once emphasized that it is never the sole determinant of political behavior. Most individuals belong to several indentifiable solidarity units, based on extended family, lineage, and clan; social differentiation; occupation and racial reflex, to name but the most obvious. However, the postcolonial environment tends to greatly reduce the occasions when the individual relates himself to the political situation simply as an African. The visible symbols of European domination — discrimination of various sorts, exclusive European clubs and residential quarters — tend to disappear, or at least to be carefully camouflaged, along with formal European rule.

Meanwhile, the full implications of the widespread fact of differential acculturation become fully evident, both to the successful and unsuccessful. During the colonial period in most areas, there had been important differences both in access to the modernization process and receptivity toward it. On the opportunity side, there were such variables as location near a major zone of urbanization, early extension of missions and therefore schools, situation on a major communications axis, and a dense population which attracted labor recruiters as well as missionaries. On the propensity to modernity side, one may mention the nature of the traditional social systems and adaptibility of its value system, its degree of success in resisting colonial occupation and penetration of the area by the accoutrements of modernization, its degree of cohesion or dislocation at the moment of colonial conquest, and the nature of the customary economy.

Accordingly, a situation had been created where social stratification, particularly in urban centers, frequently tended to overlap ethnic identification. The intertwining of these twin sources of group conflict is capable of engendering violent tensions. An ethnic vocabulary is substituted for the perceived social differentiation; in Kananga, for example, "have" and "have-not" became "Baluba" and "Lulua." The successful attribute their advance to industry, frugality, and superior intellect, frequently citing as academic support for their stereotypes the research of European travelers, administrators, and anthropologists.[11] The un-

Ethnicity," in *Politics in the Congo: Decolonization and Independence* (Princeton, Princeton University Press, 1965).

11. See for the genesis of many such stereotypes, Philip D. Curtin, *The Image of Africa* (Madison, University of Wisconsin Press, 1964), pp. 388-413 and passim. To cite a more modern example, see the enthusiastic citation of the

successful, once conscious of their disadvantage, tend to blame neglect by the colonizer, an unholy alliance between Europeans and favored groups, and discrimination for their retard.

The prospect of African self-rule adds new dimensions to ethnic conflict. In situations where it had developed, and especially where the independence movement had been plural, acute sensitivity arises as to who rules. Electoral competition can easily be perceived in terms of hegemony aspirations by one or more groups; in Kenya, KANU was alleged by its rivals to be the instrument of Kikuyu-Luo domination. In Nigeria, the NCNC was accused of serving Ibo ends, the Action Group (and subsequently the UPP and NNDP) was an alleged agency of Yorubadom, and the NPC the political arm of the Hausa-Fulani emirates. In Zaïre, the Abako was seen as an avowed engine of Bakongo domination in Kinshasa, and the Balubakat and Conakat as advancing the competing claims of Shaba (former Katanga) Baluba and Lunda-southern Shaba groupings in Lobumbashi. In Rwanda, UNAR was the fifth column of the deposed Watutsi monarchy and aristocracy, while Parmahutu defended the liberation of the long-oppressed Bahutu. The list need not be further extended.

With independence come important policy options which often seem to work to the particular benefit of one or another group. The successful adapters have a crucial advantage when the hour of Africanization of the civil service sounds; they have many more educated sons who can benefit from even the objective application of an entrance examination. Also, decisions about the siting of major new industries or development projects, or universities, can readily take on overtones of ethnic favoritism.

Territorial contiguity is an obvious but fundamental prerequisite for separatism to seem a practical policy. For the Bahutu in Rwanda, living in a symbiosis of subjugation to the Watutsi, separation was impossible; the only alternative to Watutsi domination was revolt. If, then, the ethnic group is geographically compact, large in number, politically organized, and comes to feel a systematic deprivation within the framework of the existing state, the ingredients for an ethnic separatist movement are at hand. Because, in Deutschian terms, an ethnic nationality grouping has the potential for an intense level of social communication, and a large number of tangential points within the group, this form of

favorable judgment on the adaptability of the Bakongo by Georges Balandier in *Sociologie actuelle de l' Afrique noire* (Paris, Presses Universitaires de France, 1955), quoted in *Abako, 1950-1960* (Brussels, C.R.I.S.P., 1962), p. 105.

separatist nationalism probably poses the most acute threat to the integrity of the existing African states.[12]

Partially overlapping the ethnic factor is that of regional solidarities, related to an administrative division, or a recognizable geographic area which may not have any formal legal status. For a sharp sense of deprivation to occur on this basis, remoteness from the capital seems to be a necessary condition. Often the self-awareness takes a regional rather than an ethnic form because the zone is a mosaic of ethnic groups, no one of which is large or cohesive enough to implant its own stamp on the movement. Distance from the capital, both before and after independence, has often brought a relative neglect. The area may have very few of its sons resident in the capital, or represented in the higher ranks of the civil service or even the political leadership. Colonial neglect meant fewer schools and was thus a serious handicap toward effective representation of the region's viewpoint. The region is less well equipped to enforce its claims to attention on the central government than zones closer to the capital, where disaffection would pose a more immediate threat and which possess large contingents of native sons in the capital population, constituting a potent pressure group. In these circumstances, separation may come to seem an efficacious remedy for prolonged neglect or at least an ultimate threat if some more satisfactory distributive justice is not secured. The problem has been closest to the surface in Zaïre, where the entire eastern half of the country has been sharply dissatisfied with Kinshasa's allocation of centrally distributed resources. In Chad, nearly one third of the Territorial Assembly members signed a petition for separation of the Muslim north in 1959.[13] This cleavage, however, is also clearly visible, whether or not separation has been openly mooted, in Casamance (Senegal), the northern reaches of most West African states, whose capitals are nearly all along the coast, in northern and western Uganda, in southern Sudan and Ethiopia.

A concentration of wealth in a clearly defined region may also produce a regional separatism. Those of the region, once conscious of their relative well-being, can be easily persuaded that their situation could be further improved by reducing their tax liability to support of poorer regions and can concentrate on developing their own area. Where the disparity in productive resources is pronounced, there can be no doubt in the short run that the wealthy region pays a very disproportionate

12. Karl Deutsch, *Nationalism and Social Communication* (Cambridge, MIT Press, 1953), pp. 60-80.
13. Jacques le Cornec, *Histoire politique du Tchad de 1900 à 1962* (Paris, Librairie Generale de Droit et de Jurisprudence, 1963), p. 235.

share of the costs of the territory. This was undeniable in the case of Shaba in Zaïre, and Ivory Coast in the former Afrique occidentale française federation.[14] In both these cases the motivations for separation were more complex than a simple rich province situation, but this factor played a major role. Gabon's eagerness to dissociate itself from the old Equatorial federation sprang largely from similar considerations.

Related to the general problem of regionalism are the special strains existing for the states which have more than one major pole of urbanization and economic growth. A great urban center tends to create its own social and political universe. Its institutions of higher education produce a local elite, rooted in the populations and problems of the city's human hinterland. Social communications over a large surrounding area are oriented around the major city. "Going to town" for sons of the village means almost always following the well-marked trail into their adjoining urban agglomeration. Roads and railways drain into it; news of political life in the country and the world outside arrives filtered through this screen. Many African states have only one major urban center, which is also the capital; they are accordingly spared this fragmenting strain. But countries which do face this challenge, with Zaïre the most dramatic example, are subjected to a chronic centrifugal force. The Kinshasa-Lobumbashi duality would be in the best of circumstances a difficult obstacle to preservation of the polity; in the event, it has already given rise to one secession, and the possibility of a repetition can by no means be precluded. One may speculate that in an Africanized Southern Rhodesia, the Bulawayo-Salisbury tandem might have political relevance, and in a more distant future, Johannesburg and Capetown might pull a nonracial South Africa in different directions.

Two other factors which have been important in Asia in the fragmentation equation, but not yet in Africa, are religion and language. In Asia, the rise of nationalism itself was closely associated with religious movements in its early phases, and subsequently religious solidarity became a motor factor in a series of dissident or separatist movements, from Karen Christian insurgents in Burma, to Darul Islam in Indonesia.[15] In North Africa, Islam made some contribution in the early phases of nationalism, as a focal point for resistance to assimiliationist seductions, but the territorial nationalist movements which led

14. J. Gérard-Libois, *Sécession au Katanga* (Brussels, C.R.I.S.P., 1963), pp. 7-8; Elliot J. Berg, "The Economic Basis of Political Choice," *American Political Science Review*, 54.2 (June 1960), 391-405.

15. Fred R. von der Mehden, *Religion and Nationalism in Southeast Asia* (Madison, University of Wisconsin Press, 1963).

the independence drive were predominantly secular. Islam also played some role in Sudanese and Somali nationalism. Elsewhere, Muslim marabouts and emirs by and large accommodated themselves to colonial rule at an early date. Generally speaking, Muslim areas were those least affected by the ferment of social change. The alliance with traditional elites with the colonizer at the summit ensured the docility of the mass. The schools which trained the future nationalist elites in sub-Saharan Africa were first built by Christian missions outside the Islamic zones; thus, the leaders of anti-colonial movements were for the most part not differentiated religiously from the colonizer. The relatively secondary role religion per se,[16] particularly Islam, has played as a basis for colonial resistance perhaps explains the absence of aggressive religious chauvinism in most African states. The coexistence of Christianity and Islam in the numerous African states with large numbers of both has so far been much less uneasy than, say, in Lebanon. The major exception is the southern Sudan, distinguished from the north by ethnic-cultural distinctiveness, regional remoteness from the center of national life, and religious differentiation from the Arab-Islamic culture which dominates the country and especially its elite.[17] To a certain extent, the Islam-Christianity dichotomy overlaps the savanna-coast duality in West African states, and has played some part in sacralizing Somali irredentism in Kenya and Ethiopia.

Language historically is perhaps the most powerful single factor in facilitating intensive social communication and creating a basis for instant recognition. In Europe, nationalism largely followed language lines; the emergence of vernaculars as languages of administration was a major step toward the splintering of dynastic states like the Hapsburg empire in favor of national states. In Quebec and Flanders today, militant separatist movements are fueled by the grievance of second-class status for their own languages and those that speak them. It would be logical to expect, then, that the existence of linguistic pluralism would be a major source of fragmentation potential in Africa.

Aside from the Arab tier of states, only Somalia, Rwanda, Burundi, Lesotho, Botswana and Swaziland have linguistic unity. Nine other

---

16. This ignores the rich vein of social history embodied in the syncretic, messianic, millennarian, or separatist churches in Africa. In many instances, these sprang from the same sources of frustration and insecurity which in other circumstances gave birth to nationalism. But their role was quite different from that, say, of the Muslim League in India, Sarekat Islam in Indonesia, or the Young Men's Buddhist Association in Burma.

17. The case is detailed by Joseph Oduho and William Deng, *The Problem of the Southern Sudan* (London, Oxford University Press, 1963).

states have a single dominant African language (Kenya, Tanzania, Zambia, Southern Rhodesia, Malawi, Senegal, Upper Volta, Mali, and Gabon).[18] The rest have at least several and often dozens of significant languages. In these cases, the option to date has been retention of the European language of colonial administration. Inadequate as this solution is from many points of view—beginning with the proposition that democracy is meaningless when government is carried on in a language not understood by the humbler strata of citizens—Asian experience would strongly suggest that the alternative of trying to impose one of the major vernaculars as a national language would have a far more explosive fragmenting effect. The Indian example is perhaps relevant for a number of African states; in 1947 the decision was made to adopt Hindi in principle as the national language over a period of time. Hindi was spoken by 47 percent of the population and was by far the leading candidate for elevation to national language status if any single language other than English were to be utilized. But hostility to Hindi rapidly crystallized, especially in the Tamil and Telugu areas of the south; if a language other than English was chosen, it was argued, other regional languages should have equal status. Pushing hard on Hindi risked exacerbating linguistic tensions to an intolerable point. Granting equal status to regional languages would in time create an India whose regional elites were unable to communicate with one another. Faced with these cruel dilemmas, English has been granted a respite, which some suspect may become permanent.[19]

In a few states, a vehicular language not closely associated with any particular group and widely spoken throughout the territory, is available. Thus is the case with Swahili in Tanzania, and to a lesser extent Kenya, and Nyanja in Malawi. It is interesting that Tanzania and Malawi are notable for the relative absence of ethnic nationalism (the African-Shirazi racial nationalism on Zanzibar was qualitatively different); the linguistic unity is beyond doubt a key factor.

Catalysts for Separatism

These, then, are the primary factors leading to emergence of separatist movements in a polity. But the existence of one or several of them need not lead immediately to the emergence of fragmentation demands. There are also certain specific types of situations which seem to

18. An interesting survey of this factor was made by Pierre Alexandre, "Problèmes linguistiques des états négro-africains à l' heure de l' indépendence," *Cahiers d' Études Africaines*, 2.1 (1961), pp. 177-195.

19. Roy, *Federalism*, pp. 240-260.

catylyze separatist potential, to actualize latent fragmenting forces. The perspectives of the potential separatists must comprehend the fragmenting act as within the realm of feasible political action. Separation, in short, must have not only sociological logic, but practical application.

Distance from the center is a first obvious consideration. Traditionally, areas on the periphery of precolonial African states could regard separation as a political option whenever a weakening of the center provided the opportunity. Those close to the royal court could only hope to change the ruler at the center. Similarly, in a large state like Zaïre, outlying areas like Shaba can envisage withdrawal from the system as an option which is simply not available for an area in the central part of the country, however disaffected the latter may be.[20]

Possession of minimum political resources permits the separating area to envisage independent status with some confidence.[21] Political factors would be more important than economic, in the first instance; an economic sacrifice is not difficult to envisage, if the political compensations are substantial. Thus Malawi quite possibly suffered a short-run economic loss in removing itself from the now-defunct Federation of Rhodesia and Nyasaland. Yet the incentive to separate from what was seen to be a settler-controlled mechanism was so powerful that the economic loss was cheerfully borne. Likewise, Rwanda may well have made some economic sacrifice by choosing separate political status over continuation of the Rwanda-Burundi association; but the political arguments were compelling, and no serious consideration was given to economic aspects of the argument. One of the prices for expanded autonomy for Northern Nigeria in the Nigerian Federation was acceptance of the derivation principle of distribution of export tax receipts, clearly to the financial advantage of the southern Regions.

There are in the lives of states occasional cataclysmic moments when what appear to be decisive and perhaps definitive options are made. At the apocalypse, the latent separatist must suddenly make his choice; the circumstances which led up to the fundamental reappraisal of the basis of political community may well provide the occasion for attempting to opt out, in the knowledge that another chance to act may never come.

This situation frequently occurs during the negotiations with the departing colonizer over the terms of power transfer. For the kingdom of

20. Internal withdrawal is another option; for all practical purposes, the Bakuba kingdom has withdrawn from the Congo for a period in the early 60's, by simply removing from their lands "strangers" who had settled during the colonial period and quietly ceasing to recognize the writ of Kinshasa or the provincial authorities.

21. In the sense suggested by Robert A. Dahl, *Who Governs?* (New Haven, Yale University Press, 1961).

Buganda, for example, the prolonged pre-independence dickering involved deciding once and for all whether coexistence with non-Ganda areas in the frame of a single state was compatible with the interests of the kingdom, and if so, on what minimum terms. The traditional rulers of Barotseland well understood that their special treaty relationship with the British crown, which conferred some privileges and exemptions during the colonial period, could hardly continue in the same form in an independent Zambia. The Somalis in northeastern Kenya, more or less quiescent under colonial administration, saw passing under the control of an African government as an entirely different affair and the signal for insurrection. Rwanda and Burundi, although never reticent toward colonial overrule within a single territorial framework, saw self-rule in such a context as mutually unacceptable.

In the immediate post-independence period, the short-lived Mali Federation faced its moment of truth. In August 1960 Leopold Senghor and his associates were confronted with an imminent coup by Modiba Keita and his collaborators, which would have transformed the Federation into a unitary state and displaced much of the Senegalese leadership. The choice was clear; either secession had to be immediately undertaken, or the very basis of the polity would have been totally transformed, probably permanently. Separation was the immediate consequence.

In the case of Zaïre, a somewhat differently structured judgment day also followed hard on the heels of independence. Political polarization between the radical, unitarian nationalism of the late Prime Minister Patrice Lumumba and the autonomy aspirations of the southern Shaba leadership, symbolized by Moise Tshombe, had reached a point where both believed that the success of the other was incompatible with his own survival. Lumumba would have had to crush Tshombe to realize his unitarian goals; Tshombe could never be assured of the leeway for Shaba necessary to fully benefit from its geologic good fortune as long as the unitarian sword of Damocles hung overhead. Thus the occasion of central confusion, created by the mutiny of the *Force Publique* and the subsequent panic flight of the senior European civil servants and officers, was eagerly seized to pronounce withdrawal from Zaïre.

Unusual opportunities for separation occur when the former state falls into general disrepute, and the stigma of illegitimacy is widely attached to the parent unit. Although separatism is in principle objectionable in the mainstream of African nationalism, those who propose to withdraw from a polity which fails to pass the test of genuine African rule may find general support for their initiative. No African nationalist voice was raised against the withdrawal of Malawi and

Zambia from the late Federation of Rhodesia and Nyasaland. The Federation bore the stigma of European domination, and accordingly Dr. Hastings Banda's act was as virtuous as Tshombe's was reprehensible. Similarly, African states have launched a major offensive to pry Southwest Africa Namibia from South African tutelage; the position would no doubt be very different if one-man, one-vote democracy prevailed instead of doctrinaire apartheid in the Republic. Tshombe's claim to self-determination, however, could not even secure a hearing; here a genuine African state was being splintered, rather than the zone of African rule being enlarged. However, in 1964-1965, had a portion of the eastern Zaïre, invoking the Lumumbist heritage and symbols and slogans of radical African nationalism, proclaimed its independence from a Kinshasa regime heavily marked at that time by American associations and Tshombe's leadership, there would have been a real possibility of African recognition. In the case of Rwanda and Burundi, strong African pressure, channeled through the United Nations, was exerted to avoid the inevitable rupture between the two.

The very process of carefully considering the possibility of fragmenting a state generates an upsurge in ethnic and regional nationalism. In Nigeria, the act of dispatching a Commission to Enquire into the Fears of Minorities and the Means of Allaying Them led minority groups in the three Regions to give redoubled consideration to the extent of their grievances in preparing their testimony to the commission.[22] In Zaïre, tacit acceptance of representation at the various round table conferences in early 1961 by self-designated "provinces" initiated a dialectic of fragmentation which broke the six original provinces into 21, largely based on ethnic criteria.[23] The very process of serious consideration of the desirability of new provinces created irresistable pressures from a dozen fragmenting groups which came forward to claim the right to regional self-rule; the act of posing the question created the answer. A similar sequence of events can be found in India, the creation of a States Reorganization Commission in December 1953 unleashed a flood of linguistic special pleading. The decisive moment to advance linguistic claims was at hand; the existence of a public agency to receive particularist memorials sufficed to set linguistic nationalists up and down the subcontinent to work preparing them. The commission had no fewer than 152,250 documents submitted to it.[24]

22. *Report,* H.M.S.O., Cmnd. 505 (London, 1958).
23. Young, *Politics in the Congo,* Chap. 18, "The New Provinces"; Benoit Verhaegen; "Présentation morphologique des nouvelles provinces," *Études Congolaises,* 5.7 (August-September 1963), 22-36.
24. Roy, *Federalism,* pp. 202-203.

Tactics for Separators

If we examine the evidence which the history of decolonization and initial independence offers us, we may discern several variations on the separatist theme. There is more than one way in which the will to achieve separate or at least autonomous political community can be gratified by nationalist groups whose boundaries do not coincide with a territorial state. Tactics of the separators have ranged from complete severance of political ties with the former territory, to the mere invocation of the separation alternative as a negotiating lever to obtain certain advantages within the existing framework.

The most successful form of withdrawal, from the fragmenters' point of view, involves the negotiated dismanteling of the colonial entity in cooperation with the colonial power before independence is achieved. This avoids the serious complications of enforcing the decision and securing recognition for it; separation is an irreversible *fait accompli* at the moment of formal accession to the prerogatives of international sovereignty. This has happened in the instances of the old Afrique occidentale française and Afrique equatoriale française groupings, Rwanda and Burundi, the three members of the defunct Federation of Rhodesia and Nyasaland, and Sudan (with relation to Egypt). It is true that in the case of AOF and AEF, the administrative integration of the component territories had never been complete. The sequence of political evolution had produced an African leadership whose roots were territorial rather than federation-wide. These territorial elites then insisted on power transfer to the territories instead of to the federations; the protests of the radical intellectual groups against "balkanization" were entirely ineffectual. The act of withdrawal from an independent and sovereign AOF or AEF would have been an entirely different operation, with serious international complications and success uncertain. Sudan had been under Egyptian rule before the Anglo-Egyptian "condominium" was established. Sudanese political leaders were careful to engineer themselves out from under both the Egyptian and the British overrule when independence was won in 1956.

Post-colonial secession is a more difficult undertaking, in its unadulterated form. To date, there have been only three examples where a separate government actually established itself, Senegal's withdrawal from the Mali Federation, Katanga's adventure in separate existence, and the Biafra episode in Nigeria. In the first instance, the secession was made possible by the brevity of life span of the political entity and the support of the overwhelming majority of the seceding community's political elite. Mali had been formed out of the wreckage of the old AOF

Federation only 18 months earlier, and thus had not yet become a fully integrated administrative and political unit. At the critical moment, Senghor had the support of the key leaders from all parts of Senegal, and Mali lacked both the military capacity and necessary international support — and perhaps the desire — to perpetuate the union by force. In the Katanga case, however, hostility in most of Africa and much of the rest of the world was so sharp that the two states which had some sympathy with Katanga, Congo-Brazzaville and Madagascar, dared not risk recognition. The parallel development of United Nations intervention in Zaïre, with a mandate to preserve the integrity of the territory, made international hostility singularly operative, as the dominant military forces present were those of the international community. A second fatal flaw was the absence of support from nearly half of the seceding unit for this act; had the secession been limited to the southern portion of Katanga, where Tshombe's Conakat party was dominant, he could have showed a far more convincing popular mandate for his act, and made far more difficult the United Nations' decision to terminate the secession ultimately by force. In the case of Biafra, the disparity of force was again crucial. Although four African states recognized Biafra, federal forces had far greater access to arms and manpower. The Biafran cause was further weakened by the lack of support from non-Ibo groups.

A more practical alternative in terms of obtaining at least some external support for secession aspirations exists for groups which could attach themselves to an adjoining state. In this way, the emptiness of the international sovereignty claim without recognition is avoided. At the same time, existing armed forces can be brought in to protect against reconquest. The former parent state is unlikely to willingly accept this territorial deprivation, if it is in a position to resist by force. Thus Ethiopia and Kenya have both reinforced border regions inhabited by Somali groups, some of which would clearly prefer to rally to a greater Somalia; open intervention to roll back the frontier by the Somali army would definitely bring war, as it has already brought sporadic skirmishes on the Ethiopian-Somali frontier.[25]

Leaders of Ubangi province in northwestern Congo in early 1961 opened furtive negotiations with the Central African Republic, with a view to escaping the disorder and discouraging prospects of the Congo

---

25. A. A. Castagno, "The Somali-Kenyan Controversy," *Journal of Modern Africa Studies*, 2.2 (July 1964), 165-188; Mesjin Wolle Mariam, "The Ethio-Somalian Boundary Dispute," ibid., pp. 189-219; John Drysdale, *The Somali Dispute* (London, Pall Mall Press, 1964).

by joining their northern neighbors. Two important ethnic groups, the Banda and Ngbaka, are found on both sides of the frontier, and the Ubangi River could as easily unite as it now divides. At that point, neither Kinshasa nor Kisangani (ex-Stanleyville) could have effectively resisted such a scheme, had it been swiftly executed. However, the Central African Republic did not give real encouragement to the overtures, and they were quietly dropped. But, it is perhaps not without significance that the political party established by the Ubangi provincial leaders in September 1963 assumed the name of Mouvement pour l'Evolution Democratique de l'Afrique (MEDA), consciously modeled on the title of the ruling party in Central African Republic (MEDAN).

Such an option may exist in the future in a larger number of states. Ethnic or cultural affinities across the border are probably a necessary prerequisite, and perhaps disruption at the center of the territory being truncated, diminishing its capacity to react effectively militarily or diplomatically. There was before and immediately after Ghana independence a significant movement in Eweland and reunification with Togo, and in 1958-1959 and again in 1962 some dissident activity by Moroccan-backed Moorish irregulars in northern Mauretania seeking incorporation in Morocco.

Federalism is a popular constitutional creed among potential separators, who see little prospect of or even advantage in a total rupture of links with the colonial territory to which colonial partition assigned them. The demand for a "federal" constitution frequently arises in the process of decolonization; nonterritorial nationalisms find in this formula the widest protection of their interests which they are likely to be able to get. This was the case of the Ashanti-backed National Liberation Movement in Ghana in the terminal colonial epoch. Federalism also found its advocates in Nigeria, Zaïre, Libya, and Uganda, where they were at least partly successful, and Kenya, where they were not.[26]

Another variation on the separatist theme is achievement of autonomy for the putative political community through internal fragmentation of an existing state. This occurred in 1962-1965 in Zaïre with the wholesale creation of new provinces. With the de facto breakdown of centralized controls in 1960, a considerable degree of autonomy was available simply through recognition as a new province. This neatly

26. Libya in 1963 abandoned federalism for a unitary structure, a symptom in this case of a growing acceptance of Libya as a political community by the initially suspicious components, Cyreneica, Tripolitonia, and Fezzan. This listing excludes federalism imposed by joining of territories separately administered in the colonial period, as in Cameroun.

avoided the multifold complications of total separation; no international recognition was necessary. The end was achieved through internal negotiation between the fragmenting movements and the central office-holders, and accordingly no military confrontation was involved. But the sweeping internal restructuring of the country which accompanied the break-down of six provinces into 21 went far beyond a mere administrative reorganization. The new provinces were self-constituted areas, for the most part; the exceptions were the inevitable left-over zones, after the self-conscious ethnic and regional nationalist movements had asserted their claim to provincial status. The newly homogeneous units were better able to exercise provincial autonomy than the badly divided six old provinces. After the advent of the Mobutu regime, the process was reversed, and the number of provinces reduced to eight. A similar process began in Nigeria, when a Midwest Region was carved out of the Western Region in 1963. The military regime sought to break the power of the three largest ethnic groups in 1967 through the division of the four Regions into 12.

The final variant in separatism is its invocation as a threat in reinforcement of political demands within the system. In Nigeria, the Northern Peoples Congress (NPC) has on a number of occasions threatened secession if unable to obtain satisfactory arrangements within the federation. Northern Premier Sir Ahmadu Bello put the matter quite bluntly in his autobiography, stating: "A sudden grouping of the Eastern and Western parties (with a few members from the North opposed to our party) might take power and so endanger the North. This would, of course, be utterly disastrous . . . it would therefore force us to take measures to meet the need. What such measures would have to be is outside my reckoning at the moment, but God would provide a way."[27] In Uganda, the Kabaka and his Baganda associates made no secret of the limits to their willingness to continue within a Ugandan framework. In Libya, the independence negotiations and early years in Libya were marked by the threats to Cyreneica to contemplate alternative options if its demands were not met.[28] In Zaïre, Bakongo leaders had in successive negotiations over composition of central governments before 1965 implied their commitment to remain within the country was contingent not only on autonomy for their region but also on possession of key central positions. Their first leader, Joseph

27. Sir Admadu Bello, *My Life* (London, Cambridge University Press, 1962), p. 229.

28. Majid Khadduri, *Modern Libya* (Baltimore, Johns Hopkins Press, 1963), p. 168.

Kasavubu, became chief of state, and the finance ministry had always been occupied by one of their members until the Mobutu regime came to power.

Separatism has thus far been kept in check by a broad consensus amongst African leaders that the genie of boundary revision had to be kept firmly in the bottle. Any general revision of frontiers could have devastating effects on the often precarious political balance in many countries; no infallible standard for guiding a rationalization of boundaries exists, in any case. It is indeed remarkable that so little of the fragmentation potential has become activated. But neither has it disappeared. Although with each passing year, the matrix of loyalties built around the existing territorial states ramifies, there can be no assurance that other patterns of loyalty will not simultaneously deepen. If the history of nationalism has any lessons, these are surely that there is no single linear progression. Time and social change have not in all circumstances produced the convergence of state and nation which could finally lay to rest the spector of separatism. Fragmentation is and will remain a crucial challenge to statecraft in Africa.

4. Cleavage Management in African Politics: The Ghana Case

Martin Kilson

Nature of Tensions in the C.P.P.: An Overview

During the period of authoritarian one-party rule by the Convention People's Party (C.P.P.), political tensions were characterized by a perplexing interplay of what may be termed horizontal and vertical forces. The horizontal forces were, of course, those associated with class, status, economic and related functional interests or allegiances. The vertical forces were regional, tribal, traditional or neotraditional in nature. But these were not polar opposites, in the sense that some sectors under the regime functioned largely along horizontal lines and other sectors mainly along vertical lines. Although some political groups or clusters were identified as mainly horizontal or vertical in orientation, in practice most groups constituted an amalgam of both orientations. In this coexistence of both orientations within a given group lay the source of a not insignificant tension under the C.P.P.'s single-party state.

The C.P.P. itself was at the center of the horizontal forces in Ghanaian politics in the post-independence period. The party's organs lambasted regionalist, tribalist, and traditional aspects of Ghanaian society. From 1957 onwards the C.P.P. government curbed the official status of chiefs in the political system, relegating them largely to ceremonial roles. The government also enacted legislation like the Avoidance of Discrimination Act (1957) which outlawed all parties of a regional, tribal, or subcultural nature; and similar legislation, for example, the Ashanti Pioneer Control Act (1961), placed newspapers with a regionalist bent under government censorship.

Yet not even the C.P.P. government, overly self-conscious of its horizontal orientation, could escape the influence of vertical forces in Ghanaian society. Prominent C.P.P. leaders like Krobo Edusei succumbed to the awe in which some Ghanaians hold chiefly office and used their influence to help their kin secure such posts. When convenient or necessary, the government lifted its official ban against chiefs having a major political role in local or national politics. Furthermore, the national leadership of the C.P.P. was markedly

Note: I am indebted to the Ford Foundation's Foreign Area Training Program, to Robert Bowie and Samuel Huntington of the Harvard Center for International Affairs, and to Thomas Hodgkin, formerly director of the Institute of African Studies, University of Ghana, for funds which enabled me to research in Ghana in fall 1960, summer 1962, academic year 1964-65, and summer 1968.

weighted in favor of tribal groups in southern Ghana (for example, Fanti, Ewe, Akwapim and Nzima), and businessmen, lawyers, doctors, educators, and administrators from these tribes claimed more than a fair share of government-party favors, contracts, appointments, and largesse. Indeed, by the end of the C.P.P. regime the Nzima, Kwame Nkrumah's own tribe, were especially favored in these respects.

It is, then, precisely the coexistence--indeed, the symbiotic overlap--of both horizontal and vertical forces and orientations within political groups in African politics that gives this politics its particular form of tension and cleavage. Although not unique to African politics, this situation acquires a special form in African systems. More specifically, the vertical lines of political allegiance, so close to their primordial roots and reinforced during the colonial era by the politics of indirect local administration — regardless whether colonial administration was British, French, or Portuguese — are at a primary stage of transformation. They have yet to be recast in more politically functional terms. Such functional recasting of vertical allegiances in African politics is, in fact, another way of conceiving what political modernization is about in African systems.[1]

Class Alignments in C.P.P.: Context of Tensions

The pattern of class or interest alignments within the C.P.P. was not at all simple.[2] Leadership roles at the national level of the system were divided between two sets of new elites. One set, the dominant group, comprised self-made men who possessing meager social background (for example, their parents were illiterate or at best semi-literate), acquired some variant of middle-class status, a rather low one, in the modern sector of Ghanaian society. A few of these men obtained higher education in Western countries but most of them gained little more than upper-primary or middle-school education. Before entering politics they were occupied as primary-school teachers, clerks, cocoa brokers, hawkers of patent medicines, middle-sized traders, and the like.[3] Thus

1. Cf. Martin Kilson, *Political Change in a West African State* (Cambridge, Harvard University Press, 1966), passim.
2. Cf. Bob Fitch and Mary Oppenheimer, *Ghana: End of an Illusion* (New York, Monthly Review Press, 1967). This monograph suffers from a vulgar application of Marxist analysis to the nature and role of stratification under C.P.P. rule. This is unfortunate because Marxist concepts and method, cleverly employed, have much to contribute to the analysis of political modernization in Africa.
3. For a more detailed treatment of the political role of these elements

at Ghana's independence in 1957, the occupations represented among the 72 C.P.P. legislators included 36 percent traders, 20 percent clerks, and 27 percent teachers. Only 5 legislators (or 7 percent), all ministers as well, had obtained full-fledged professional education.[4] Men of similar meager backgrounds also predominated at the local level of the party structure and thousands of others were available for local party roles, waiting anxiously in the wings at the periphery of the party for the opportunity to move closer to the center or near-center of party influence.

The other set of new elites who shared leadership in the C.P.P. was fundamentally different from the first set in social and educational background, as well as style. A few were the second generation to obtain higher education, others were from prominent white-collar and merchant families, and still others were sons of educated and wealthy chiefs. At independence, only a small number of such persons held leading or influential positions in the C.P.P. government. For example, Archie Casely Hayford, a lawyer and son of a prominent Fanti lawyer and early Gold Coast nationalist personality, was minister of Agriculture — E. O. Asafu-Adjaye, a lawyer and son of a wealthy Ashanti merchant who belonged to a traditional ruling clan in Kumasi, was minister of Local Government; and Aaron Ofori Atta, also a lawyer and son of an educated and wealthy Akan (Akim Abuakwa) chief who was knighted by the British Crown, was minister of Justice. Moreover, as the C.P.P. came to grips with national government in developing society, it required more and more persons of upper-level elite attributes.

How to absorb and control those Ghanaians of upper-level elite attributes became a perpetual source of tension down to the military seizure of power in February 1966. Inasmuch as the C.P.P. was officially a party of radical, quasi-Marxist persuasion the absorption of persons of high bourgeois background, style and orientation was *prima facie* a difficult undertaking. Much ideological dispute within the C.P.P. in the period of single-party rule, 1960-1966, centered on this issue.[5] After all, the very rise of the C.P.P. as a major Ghanaian political force

among African new elites, see Martin Kilson, "The Emergent Elites of Black Africa 1900-1960," in L. H. Gann and Peter Duignan, eds., *Colonialism in Africa, 1870-1960* (Cambridge, Cambridge University Press, 1970).

4. Dennis Austin, *Politics in Ghana 1946-1960* (London, Oxford University Press, 1964), p. 253.

5. Cf. David Apter, "Ghana," in James S. Coleman and Carl Rosberg, eds., *Political Parties and National Integration in Tropical Africa* (Berkeley, University of California Press, 1964).

in 1949-1954 occurred in fierce competition with the long-standing hegemony of the upper-level elites in nearly all spheres of modern Ghanaian society.[6] The bitterness of this political enterprise was not easily forgotten; nor was it forgotten among the younger members of the lower-level elites who had the dogged task of keeping the C.P.P. alive in the countryside and in the large network of Ghanaian hinterland towns.[7] Neither did the central leadership of the C.P.P. forget the party's difficult early days: but having assumed the governing roles they perforce had to surmount their bitterness toward the upper-level elites who, after all, monopolized many of the skills and the experience required to run a modern state in a backward area. Indeed, this pragmatic outlook had already determined the original decision of the dominant leaders in the C.P.P. to embrace men like Aaron Ofori Atta and E. O. Asafu-Adjaye in the early years of C.P.P. government. Another factor operative here — and one that complicated the effort of the C.P.P. leadership to harness politically the upper-level elites — was the tremendous sway the upper-level elites had over the social aspirations of the dominant leaders in the C.P.P. The latter saw the former as their reference group: apart from gaining political power, their ambition was to attain the status, prestige, and style of life long associated with the upper-level elites in the modern sector of Ghanaian society.

Regulating Intra-Elite Tension

Utmost political astuteness and acumen were required in order to regulate the interaction between the two sets of elites who ran the regime. To a surprisingly high extent, the astuteness necessary for such regulation was forthcoming, particularly from Kwame Nkrumah himself and from several advisers or confidants who never held seats in parliament but filled a variety of appointive positions in government. Among the latter were E. Aye-Kumi, an Nzima businessman who brought the Gold Coast Chamber of Commerce (comprising middle-sized merchants, contractors, and so on) behind the C.P.P. in its early days and later amassed a sizable fortune; and W. M. Q. Halm, a Ga businessman of marginal upper-level elite background who opted for the C.P.P. rather than for the party of the social group he was nearest, namely the United Gold Coast Convention led by Dr. J. B. Danquah, a lawyer and the most prominent political personality among the upper-level elites during the C.P.P. era.

6. David Apter captures this aspect of the early rise of the C.P.P. rather well in his *Gold Coast in Transition* (Princeton, Princeton University Press, 1955).

7. See Martin Kilson, *Chiefs, Peasants and Politicians: Grass Roots Politics in Ghana 1900-1970's* (forthcoming).

As already indicated, intra-elite tension under the single-party rule of the C.P.P. occurred at two basic levels of the system. One level of tension concerned the endeavor of the central leadership, largely of lower-elite background, to absorb upper status Ghanaians into the regime. The other level of tension occurred within the ranks of the dominant lower-level elites. This entailed, *inter alia,* the effort of the central leadership to pacify opposition to the policy of accommodating upper status Ghanaians. Party activists from the lower-level elites could hardly be ignored: they performed the linkman role for the central leadership in respect of key popular forces like workers and their unions, the ubiquitous traders and their marketing associations, and the hundreds of thousands of cocoa farmers and their cooperative societies. Moreover, it was precisely among the activists or functionaries in trade unions, youth associations, marketing associations, and farmers' cooperatives that the central party leadership expected the more serious bid for their own positions. These popular organizations harbored many men who possessed enough ambition, drive, and ability to attain such national political prominence as party leaders like Krobo Edusei, N. A. Welbeck, and Kwame Nkrumah.[8]

Thus the very social basis of the pecking order of elites within the C.P.P. single-party setup contained a built-in propensity toward political instability. But this situation was perhaps a mixed blessing: to checkmate it the party was forced to undertake a policy of political development that might not otherwise have occurred. More specifically, in order to minimize the threat to positions of the central leadership implicit in the aforementioned pattern of intra-elite tension, it was necessary to create, so to speak, tributaries to the mainstream of party power. Such an undertaking was no doubt hazardous: the tributaries might attempt to usurp the power of the mainstream. But it had its advantages as well: the tributaries would not only go far toward satisfying the political ambitions of thousands of party activists but would extend the central leadership's contact with and control over popular forces—the latter goal being always necessary in a single-party system.

Accordingly, from 1960 onwards the C.P.P. assumed a structure far more extensive and intricate, touching the lives of many more Ghanaians, than at any earlier period. The tributary structures to

8. The urge for national prominence on the part of functionaries in the lower echelons of the C.P.P.'s power structure was actively asserted during the period of free elections in 1951-1957. In the 1954 general election, for example the central committee of the party confronted some 1,005 claimants for the 104 seats in the legislature. See Austin, *Politics in Ghana 1946-1960*, pp. 210, 217-225.

mainstream party power were not, however, fashioned from scratch. The C.P.P. had always possessed many structural features of what Thomas Hodgkin calls a "congress-type" party; as a vote-getting instrument before independence, the C.P.P. relied heavily on the machinery of voluntary associations like trade unions, farmers' cooperatives, and marketing associations.[9] It was, then, this infrastructure which became what I have called tributaries of mainstream party power.

Insofar as none of the voluntary associations linked to the C.P.P. like the Trade Union Congress, the Ghana Farmers' Marketing Cooperatives (later the United Ghana Farmers' Cooperatives Council), and the National Council of Ghana Women (mainly women traders) possessed resources to undertake the transformation into veritable tributaries of mainstream party power, the central leadership had to utilize the administrative, financial and even coercive resources of the state to this end. The coercive and regulatory resources of government were especially important in this enterprise because even though cessation of free elections had seriously limited the political capacity of those voluntary associations not linked to the C.P.P., such associations were still functionally quite competitive with those that were C.P.P. satellites. For example, in 1961, the year the Ghana Farmers' Marketing Cooperatives was granted by authority of the government a monopoly over the marketing of cocoa, the non-C.P.P. linked cooperatives (especially the Ghana Cooperative Marketing Association and the Ashanti, Brong-Ahafo, and Sefwi Cooperative Organization) were responsible for marketing some 30 percent of the cocoa crop.[10] Thus the party-linked United Ghana Farmers' Cooperatives Council (U.G.F.C.C.) could overcome such stiff competition in cocoa marketing only with support of the coercive and regulatory powers of the state. The same applied to the other party-linked associations which were developed into a tributary of mainstream party power, gaining thereby a statutory monopoly in their special fields of action.

Armed with this monopoly and possessing the political, technical, and financial support of the C.P.P. government, the Trade Union Congress, the U.G.F.C.C., the National Council of Ghana Women, the Young Pioneers (embracing all youth associations) among others, were in position to become veritable subsystems of mainstream C.P.P. power — in a word, parastatal agencies. Their ultimate purpose was to

9. See Thomas Hodgkin, *African Political Parties* (London, Penguin Books, 1962). The best material on the role of voluntary associations in the C.P.P. between 1951 and 1960 is found in *Politics in Ghana 1946-1960,* passim.

10. *Report of the Committee of Enquiry on the Local Purchasing of Cocoa* (Accra, State Publishing Corporation, 1967), p. 6.

relieve the pressure on intra-elite tension at the center of the system. The politically ambitious heads and functionaries of these tributaries were expected to direct their energies not to posts at the center (for example, legislature, cabinet, party executive, government boards, and so on) but to the periphery of influence which the tributaries themselves constituted. This arrangement for regulating intra-elite tension in the C.P.P. single-party system was not, however, easy to legitimate. The heads of the tributaries of mainstream party power knew what was up and some held out for at least a toehold at the center of power. A few were satisfied, after a fashion, through simultaneous appointments as ministers plenipotentiary (for example, John K. Tettegah, head of the Trade Union Congress, and Martin Appiah Danquah, head of the U.G.F.C.C.) and, after 1964, as members of parliament.[11]

Moreover, this second-echelon party leadership was expected to become the political reference group for potential leaders down the line. The tributaries of the mainstream party were, in a word, expected to become a dead end for most rising leaders emanating from Ghana's expanding lower-level elites.[12] At the same time, however, the tributaries provided the central leadership with a testing ground for the kinds of men they might eventually recruit into upper-echelon posts.

To a surprising extent, the method of regulating intra-elite tension in the C.P.P. single-party system worked reasonably well. The heads and thousands of functionaries of the parastatal agencies were permitted wide sway over daily operations and, free of effective accountability, were not unhappy with their lot.[13] Tension stemming from political ambitions, among other things, was not absent, but it was now manageable. A well-ordered division of labor between different echelons of party leaders was now available — the respective spheres of influence were demarcated and transgression was known to carry dire penalties. As Henry Bretton has put it, "All machine functionaries, regardless of status, had been conditioned by frequent examples to avoid making false assumptions concerning their positions, power, and influence.

11. See Jon Kraus, "Ghana's New Corporate Parliament," *Africa Report* (August 1965), pp. 6-11. The 1965 parliament, members of which were selected largely by Nkrumah himself, was the first change in the legislature since 1957. Membership was expanded from 104 to 198.

12. On Ghana's growing lower-level elites, see Philip Foster, *Education and Social Change in Ghana* (London, Routledge and Kegan Paul, 1964).

13. Politically relevant functionaries of the U.G.F.C.C. like regional officers, district officers, marketing officers, depot officers, and secretary receivers totaled nearly 3,000. See *Report . . . on the Local Purchasing of Cocoa*, p. 137.

They were never allowed to forget the choke chain held by the President (Nkrumah)."[14]

Leader Cult as Cleavage Regulator

Thus far I have not mentioned the particular role of Kwame Nkrumah, life chairman of the C.P.P. and by 1964 virtual life president óf Ghana, in my description of the method of regulating intra-elite tension. Professor Bretton's suggestion that Nkrumah held the "choke chain" of the whole mechanism is apt, but it does not adequately portray Nkrumah's relationship to the daily operation of the mechanism. Nkrumah seemed not the least bothered with the operation of the parastatal agencies, so long as they reduced pressure on central leadership roles, including his own.[15] The manifold duties and tasks imposed on these agencies went far toward guaranteeing such reduction, or at least a major degree of it. There was as well the large realm of unaccountability permitted the parastatal agencies, enabling many functionaries to satisfy material if not political ambitions on a large scale. For example, Martin Appiah-Danquah, General Secretary of the U.G.F.C.C. told the commission of inquiry into the council's operation that his wealth included four houses, three cars, and seven farms.[16] The commission's report offers the following examples of ill-acquired wealth: "Farmers often referred to the opulence of the Secretary Receiver. It was alleged that these officers who earned £180 per annum owned cars, trucks, buildings, etc. and often supported as many as three wives. We saw some Secretary Receivers owning Mercedes Benz cars, Peugeot cars, and transport trucks . . . Farmers, particularly in the Ashanti Region complained about levies of from £G500 to £G100 demanded from them by some senior members of the Council including Opanyin Kwame Poku, National President . . . before agreeing to establish societies in their villages . . . Opanyin Kwame Poku . . . was alleged to have demanded £G40 and a sheep before officially opening any of the many new sheds of the Council."[17]

14. Henry Bretton, *Rise and Fall of Kwame Nkrumah* (London, Pall Mall Press, 1967), p. 111.

15. Cf. Jitendra Mohan, "Nkrumah and Nkrumahism," in Ralph Miliband and John Saville, eds., *The Socialist Register 1967* (London, The Merlin Press, 1967), p. 217. Mohan, a keen observer of the C.P.P. era who lectures at the University of Ghana, remarks that "Nkrumah had little time or taste for party activities and affairs. He was content to take the party's health for granted on the strength of sheafs of telegrams of felicitations and loyalty from party functionaries across the country on certain specified days in the year."

16. *Ghanaian Times*, November 15, 1966.

17. *Report on the Local Purchasing of Cocoa,* p. 20.

These means of redirecting tension away from central leadership were, moreover, reinforced by the contrived cult of personality that surrounded Kwame Nkrumah. This put all heads and functionaries of the parastatal agencies on notice that the premier position of Nkrumah was beyond the pale of legitimate striving. The cult of personality also helped protect other party leaders at the center: threats on their posts from second-echelon leadership were easily interpreted as potential thrusts at Nkrumah himself. In general, then, the function of the cult of Nkrumah, endowing him with special "powers," was to allow the political system to smoke out what Mary Douglas describes in her comparative study of witchcraft as "the existence of an angry person in an interstitial position which is dangerous."[18]

Nkrumah seems to have been actively concerned largely with the process of regulating the absorption of upper-level elites into the system. Under the 1960 Republic constitution it was provided that "the appointment, promotion, dismissal, and disciplinary control of members of the public services is vested in the President." The Judicial Service Act (1960) gave Nkrumah full authority to appoint, dismiss, and discipline all judges and magistrates. Armed with such wide authority over the bureaucracy, Nkrumah was most attentive to ensuring that upper-level elites brought into government did not distort or subvert its policies. As Bretton has put it, "The civil service was, if not incorporated into the political machine, certainly sensitized to its demands."[19] At the regional and district levels of administration (there were 8 regions and some 80 districts, administering a population of around 7,000,000), Nkrumah utilized the party machinery to oversee bureaucrats in the field. The bureaucrats worked under the watchful eyes of regional and district commissioners who were appointed by Nkrumah. The commissioners in turn functioned in lose consultation with officers of the Regional and District Executive Committees of the party, also appointed by Nkrumah. Party men also executed Nkrumah's personal will in the many state corporations like the Cocoa Marketing Board; some were made chairmen of these public bodies, and all party members of these public bodies were Nkrumah's watchdogs, protecting the single-party system against subversion by the bureaucrats.[20]

18. Mary Douglas, *Purity and Danger: An Analysis of Concepts of Pollution and Taboo* (New York, Frederick A. Praeger, 1966), p. 102.

19. Bretton, *The Rise and Fall of Kwame Nkrumah*, p. 51.

20. For membership of 48 state corporations, see *Ghana Gazette*, March 4, 1965, no. 11, pp. 131-140.

Dynamics of Single-Party Change

Contradictions in the structure and behavior of the Nkrumaist single-party system furnished the dynamics of change in the system. For example, ideology was officially meant to be a guide to policy choices, but in reality the most active use of ideology was as a cog in the machinery of the Nkrumaist cult. Moreover, in order to ensure the service of ideology to the Nkrumaist cult, Nkrumah turned to men of his own tribe, the Nzima, to control key communication networks like the Guinea Press, which operated the party's newspapers and other organs. By 1964 the Ministry of Information was also put in charge of one of Nkrumah's tribesmen. As the educational system was put to service of the Nkrumaist cult from 1964 onwards, it too was entrusted to a minister who was an Nzima. Then, too, there was always a chance that the "powers" the cult of personality bestowed upon Nkrumah would fail to convince possible detractors. If so, the personal security of Nkrumah becomes of paramount importance. To guarantee this, Nzima were given charge.

This admixture of what I described earlier as vertical and horizontal forces in the polity, emanating now from no less a figure than Nkrumah himself, tended to confuse and demoralize party ranks. Further demoralization ensued as party functionaries discovered for themselves that the official ideological framework for articulating demands or policy was often irrelevant to what demands gained a hearing and what policy was decided. But such demoralization was not in itself sufficient to spark upheaval in the party ranks and tributaries. It was, however, a precondition of any possible upheaval. Then, too, there was a question of the impact of demoralized functionaries on the system's relationship with popular forces. Much of what the general populace knew about the system was derived, after all, from contact with its functionaries.

In any political system demoralization among the functionaries is invariably translated into corruption and malfunction. And *demoralized corruption* is a different species from *instrumental corruption*: it lacks hope or perspective. What I call demoralized corruption differs in kind from that corruption that entails accumulating wealth for some long-range, transforming goal like entering a contracting business, opening a factory, and the like. The corruption that involves a long-range goal is what I call instrumental corruption. Demoralized corruption is on the other hand rather ad hoc or sporadic in scope and purpose, seeking immediate satisfaction of rather petty or frivolous needs and tastes, like an additional mistress, a second or third and bigger automobile, a third and more garish house, and the like.

In most African political systems these two modes of corruption currently vie for ascendancy and it is yet too early to know which will prevail. Since one or the other must prevail, insofar as corruption is fundamental to what Huntington calls the praetorian type of modernizing polities like those in Africa, one would rather see instrumental corruption win the race.[21] Such corruption would appear to be much less of a barrier to viable political institutionalization than demoralized corruption.[22] Suggestive of the political implications of demoralized corruption is evidence uncovered by an official audit of the erstwhile C.P.P.'s finances. A district commissioner in Brong-Ahafo Region pocketed $5,500 collected for building a regional office for the party; another district commissioner failed to account for $482 contributed for the same purpose—and another regional party officer was granted by regional headquarters some $10,119 from the building fund to liquidate personal indebtedness.[23] Similar evidence was turned up by a special audit of the finances of the erstwhile U.G.F.C.C.: "Investigations carried out by the Auditor-General's Department in 1965 into the distribution of gammalin to the Regions and Districts by one Mr. L. E. K. S. Gyambiby, former Senior Cutting-Out Supervisor in charge of gammalin supplies, disclosed some serious irregularities involving a shortage of 1,856 cartons of gammalin valued at £G7,424. The investigations established that 1,810 cartons of gammalin which were supposed to have been supplied to certain districts of the Council by the Senior Cutting-Out Supervisor never reached the consignees. It further revealed that a stock of 20 cartons returned by Jasikan District to the Senior Cutting-Out Supervisor in Accra, although received by him, were not brought to account. Again the Senior Cutting-Out Supervisor made some cash sales himself but failed to account for the proceeds. There were also instances of short supplies to some Districts involving a quantity of 13 cartons for which Mr. Gyambiby was held responsible."[24]

Such corrupt functionaries under conditions of backwardness unwittingly ensure that the masses really feel the weight of the system.

21. Samuel P. Huntington, *Political Order in Changing Societies* (New Haven, Yale University Press, 1968), pp. 192-198.

22. Cf. N. H. Leff, "Economic Development Through Bureaucratic Corruption," *The American Behavioral Scientist* (November 1964), pp. 8-14.

23. Auditor-General, *Convention People's Party: Report of Special Audit Investigation Ordered by the National Liberation Council* (Accra, State Publishing Corporation, 1967), passim.

24. Auditor-General, *Special Audit Investigation into the Accounts of the United Ghana Farmers Cooperative Council* (Accra, State Publishing Corporation, 1966), p. 28.

Malfunction merely compounds the matter.[25] For example, in local government, dominated by the C.P.P.'s district and regional apparatus from 1960 onwards, the malfunction was widespread.[26] Audit of accounts for 1964 of the Kumasi City Council, one of the wealthiest local councils,[27] revealed instances of malfunction common to many other local councils. The council executed 20 transactions for contracts worth £37,231 without requesting tenders, as required by law; it purchased 5,000 bags of cement from a private firm at cost per bag much greater than if it had purchased from the government's Ghana National Trading Corporation—instead advances to staff for personal consumption totaling £33,907 (figure was   82,245 in previous year); and expended £29,132 on beautifying the private home of the council's chairman, an act for which "no specific provision existed in the Council's Estimates."[28]

Demoralized corruption and malfunction generate more than demoralization among the masses: they spawn alienation, reinforced by cynicism. Popular alienation from government and politics does not, however, necessarily produce fundamental change: certain masses endure alienation for long periods, often seeking relief in some form of institutionalized other-worldly activity. Indeed, this tendency was apparent in Ghana during the C.P.P.'s authoritarian era. Anthropologist informants have reported an increase in witch-finding cults in rural Ghana in the 1960's.[29] The C.P.P. government kept a watchful eye on herbalists and healers, organizing some into an "integral wing" of the

25. My examples of malfunction concern local government. But they could have been selected from central government whose policies, born of confusion and bad fortune, registered few gains for the lower orders of Ghanaian society. Two gross instances of such malfunction may be noted. One was the government-sanctioned expenditure of £G12,339,127 by the U.G.F.C.C. for 3,780 tractors and tractor implements without any consideration of subsequent recurrent costs of maintenance, spare parts—especially since in 1962 onwards Ghana experienced a major foreign exchange crisis—or the availability of requisite skilled mechanics to service the tractors. As a result a major quantity of the tractors were left to rust in the harsh tropical climate. The other instance was the government's expenditure of some £G10,000,000 on a 14 story hotel to house delegates to a three-day conference of the Organization of African Unity in 1965. For other instances of such malfunction, see *The Budget 1965* (Accra, State Publishing Corporation, 1965), passim.

26. Local government consisted of local councils and urban councils, which collected much of their own revenue and performed local services.

27. Revenue in 1964 was £1,749,771.

28. *Annual Audit Report on the Accounts of the Kumasi City Council for the Year Ended 31st December, 1964* (Accra, State Publishing Corporation, 1965).

29. For witch-finding cults at earlier periods when popular estrangement from modern changes and institutions was rather pronounced, see Debrunner, *Witchcraft in Ghana* (Accra, SCM Printers, 1961), pp. 105-133, 163 ff.

party. The government was also apprehensive about the growth of prophet churches in Ghanaian towns; the subject was debated in parliament one year before the military seizure of power.[30]

Even when the potential for political upheaval inherent in popular alienation is contained or neutralized in the foregoing manner, the very existence of such alienation creates a context receptive of basic political change, as well as an atmosphere — however inchoate — of impending transformation. All that must be added is the appearance of a flaw in the national pecking order of elites and influentials. The military coup d'état of February 24, 1966, was, of course, evidence of such a flaw.

Conclusion: A Theory of Breakdown in African Single-Party Systems

It is doubtful that the experience of single-party government in Ghana or any other African state can be taken as representative of the single-party process in Africa as a whole. Yet the Ghanaian experience does put in relief a range of problems encountered in some fashion or other by most African single-party systems.

Regulating intra-elite competition and tension looms large in the concerns of African single-party systems. This is the first issue these systems confront; and the confrontation offers them a major opportunity for political development or growth. This is what the organization of tributaries to mainstream party power in the C.P.P. regime was about: they are additions to the structure of authority and influence available to the political system: they widen access to political influence.

But political development creates one special problem: legitimation. Legitimation in African single-party systems is difficult, at best. Political development in these systems is a function of intra-elite tension, and the stratum of elites affected by this development must find it satisfactory. In the C.P.P. experience the central leadership assumed that the political leverage at the periphery of power offered by the tributaries like the Trade Union Congress would serve to legitimate these structures among those who ran them. Absence of accountability was also thought to aid such legitimation, allowing functionaries room for material gain through corruption and extortion. To some extent this arrangement did prove satisfactory to these functionaries. But the issue of legitimacy is seldom left here. Ideology is involved too.

In African single-party systems the professed role of ideology as a guide to policy choices is distorted by the leadership's use of it to control

30. See *Parliamentary Debates, 22nd January 1965*, 38.8 (Accra, State Publishing Corporation, 1965). On prophet churches in general, see C. G. Baeta, *Prophetism in Ghana: A Study of Some "Spiritual" Churches* (London, SCM Printers, 1962).

or regulate the legitimation process. The cult of personality is particularly troublesome here — the leader and his cohorts contrive it to protect their own status and privileges. When middle and lower-level functionaries, whose appetites are whetted rather than satisfied by political leverage and material gain at the periphery of power, confront this confusion they are demoralized. This happened in the C.P.P. regime from 1962 onwards, and has occurred as well in Guinea, the Ivory Coast, Senegal, Malawi, and elsewhere.

Demoralized and corrupt functionaries are a liability in backward conditions because their behavior produces popular alienation from the polity. And popular alienation, especially in African politics, must be dealt with because of the forms it takes. For many Africans these forms include a growth in dysfunctional concerns like witch-finding cults and other traditional or neotraditional religious activities (all entailing major demands on peasants' and workers' incomes) and internecine tribalistic conflict. For the more articulate elements among the masses, like skilled workers, petty traders, and cash-crop farmers, alienation may spawn wildcat strikes, profiteering, and smuggling. In the last year of the C.P.P. regime, for example, it was necessary to combat the smuggling of cocoa into francophone African states. No figures are available for the amount of cocoa smuggled, but figures for the first year of the military regime (1966) are put conservatively at 20 percent of the marketed crop, valued around £12,000,000. In short, the consequences of popular alienation must be dealt with by African single-party regimes — they must be regulated or repressed. They signify, after all, that legitimation of the system is ineffective.

The regulation or rationalization — as opposed to repression — of popular alienation requires political development: the basis of access to authority and command in the system must be extended. But for most African single-party systems, the political development associated with tributaries of mainstream party power is about their limit. Neither the ideology of the central elites — particularly its use in the cult of personality — nor their definition of their status and role will permit more. Hence the system is stymied; malaise sets in — as it did in the last two years of the C.P.P. regime — and breakdown awaits a flaw in the pecking order of power at the center.

Although the military was the flaw in this respect under the C.P.P. regime and elsewhere as well (for example, Upper Volta, Togo, Sierra Leone) the flaw might well appear in another quarter. For example, civil servants might, when they obtain more nerve and skill at handling the coercive aspects of their role under single-party systems or military regimes, produce the flaw at the center of these systems, thereby shifting authority to a new set of men.

5. The Cameroon Federation: Laboratory for Pan-Africanism?

Willard R. Johnson

Cameroon has tested the practicality of pan-Africanist aspirations. Any vision of African unity including both English- and French-speaking countries must focus on the problems this federation faced during its early life. Created in 1961 through a reunion of a part of the British-administered Trust Territory of Cameroons with that formerly administered by France, it had the distinction of being the longest surviving political union in Africa between the widely shared British and French colonial legacies. The emergence, in 1973, of the Unitary Republic of Cameroon marked the success, rather than the failure, of this experiment.

Given its unique experience, Cameroon offered something of a laboratory test of some crucial, practical facets of closer political union in Africa. It is important to know, therefore, how this union came about, what, if any, factors predisposed and facilitated such a union and what ones may have hindered it. The problems which the leadership of this federation faced and their approach to their solution are of signal significance to the partisans of African unity.

Background to Federation

The fundamental basis of the Cameroon experiment was the fact that the might of German imperialism wrought a distinct entity out of its peoples — the colony of Kamerun. It was perhaps in a fit of Christian charity toward the Germans, that Reuben Um Nyobe, one of the principal champions of the idea of Cameroon reunification, justified it by saying, "Everyone knows that God created only one single Kamerun." The political union which was borne out of the United Nations supervised plebiscite of 1961 was thus considered really a restoration of a former, but lost, unity.

How much common ground did the period of German administration really create for the peoples of the two uniting territories? Enough to create a semblance of historic unity, and to inspire a vision of its restoration. Enough to make the subsequent division of the country between victorious military occupational forces seem cruel and arbitrary. Enough to make the justification of the reunification idea seem axiomatic to many. But not enough to provide the substance of a real sense

Note: For a comprehensive study of the economic and political life and character of the federation see my book *The Cameroon Federation: Political Integration in a Fragmentary Society* (Princeton, Princeton University Press, 1970).

of community, or the means for overcoming the disparities and discontinuities in their society.

The period during which Germany ruled a pacified Kamerun colony lasted scarcely more than a decade, though officially their suzerainty spread over more than thirty years. During this brief time they made some contributions which have endured the subsequent division of Kamerun between British and French trusteeship administrations. Most of the German plantations still are productive, though now they operate under the direction of the statutory body, the Cameroon Development Corporation. German roads and railways are still principal routes of commerce and communication. Much of the early German road and rail survey work was utilized by the successor administrations. Old German buildings, particularly castles and forts, still serve as important prestige symbols in each state; during the period of the federation — 1961 to 1974 — the prime minister of West Cameroon has his official residence in "das Schloss," built halfway up the side of Mount Cameroon for the first German governors. In the eastern state one of the ex-prime ministers had his home on the site of one of the German forts, on a hill commanding his home town of Ebolowa.

The impressively sturdy old forts and government buildings, some roads, and a dwindling collection of German-speaking ex-Beistande are about all of the German heritage that survived the British and French "civilizing missions." All, that is, save the name Kamerun itself. This was no mean legacy, for it served as a symbol of unity as artificially denied as it was artificial in character. This symbol became the principal inspiration of nationalists in both states.

The most eloquent testimony to the effectiveness with which the British and French administrations blotted out previous social, cultural, and political patterns is the vehement denunciations of these very "Kamerun" nationalists. They complained bitterly of the introduction of different languages, systems of law and administration, and different cultures on each side of the Mungo River frontier between the two states. Brothers became strangers to each other, they claimed.

The idea of "reunification" was a popular one. Over 70 percent of the eligible Southern Cameroons voters in the 1961 plebiscite favored union with the then independent Cameroon Republic. However, the leaders of the nationalist movements in each territory came to be rather wary of their success. This resulted from the fact that the goal of reunification was a secondary one, central to a stratagem to achieve other more immediate, though no more authentic objectives. Initially these movements, in each territory, were directed by the spokesmen of southern, coastal, modernized, and better educated and more socially privileged groups who sought home rule—the devolution of power onto autonomous local (territorial) structures. Each of these powers had administered their trust as an integral part of others under its dominion. Southern Cameroons formed an integral part of Nigeria, and Cameroon a part of the French Union. In both these states, reunificationists sought to pry their homeland loose from such larger systems. They hoped to so balance the ambitions of each administering authority as to prevent the permanent incorporation of the country into the British Commonwealth, Nigeria, or the French Union.

Success of the early efforts brought territorially based authoritative institutions. This fragmented the nationalist movements, however. New spokesmen then emerged who represented northern, more traditionalistic, and less educated or socially privileged groups. They took over the symbols of the reunification movement in an effort to gain advantage in a competition to determine who would rule at home once home rule itself was granted. These latter-day reunificationists appropriated slogans that had come to enjoy a widely based popularity but which had ceased to be of central importance to their creators.

In both territories the reunificationists sought to increase their political support by playing on this theme, but in different ways. In the Southern Cameroons the shift in the leadership of the campaign to the northern "Grassfields" groups represented heightened parochialism among peoples who harbored considerable resentment of the political preeminence of southern-based leadership. Since these peoples were numerically superior and had more direct and authentic ethnic affinities with the sister territory, the reunification slogan permitted them to question the sincerity of the southern leadership and reduce the latter's support.

The situation in French-speaking Cameroon was the reverse of that just described. Here, the northern groups had the less authentic and less direct interest in reunification (save for a union including Northern British Cameroons as well—a campaign which took shape too late to become effective.)[1] Moreover, the northern groups had already

---

1. Political parties in Southern Cameroons repeatedly asserted their desire for union of their sector of the Trust Territory with the north but they never received much support from northern leaders. Historically a part of the Islamic emirates of Northern Nigeria, the traditional Muslim leadership favored even closer association with that region. Not until a United Nations plebiscite was conducted in November 1959 was there a significant expression of opposition to the idea of amalgamation with the Northern Region. Voters in that plebiscite unexpectedly rejected immediate incorporation and decided instead to delay a determination of the territory's future status. Many observers attributed this

acquired predominant power. Theirs was a precarious predominance, however. In the interest of gaining support among the southerners, the northern Moslem leadership espoused the reunificationist cause.

In both territories the new leadership enjoyed remarkable success in consolidating their political position. Once having done so, they, like their predecessors, no longer found it necessary or convenient to push for the implementation of this program. By that time, however, the United Nations was tired of the issue and insisted it be resolved.[2] Thus, at the time of the plebiscite on reunification, none of the Cameroon political factions was fully satisfied with any of the alternatives presented them. The initial reunificationists in Southern Cameroons called for regional status within Nigeria, though they seemed to prefer full independence for their tiny state. The latter-day reunificationists campaigned for union with the independent Cameroon Republic but also evidenced a real preference for independence or a delay in the termination of trusteeship, possibly for as long as five years.[3]   The top leadership of the republic is thought to have preferred no union at all to that with only the Southern Cameroons, which they tended to identify politically with their own opposition.

result to desires, especially among pagan groups, for local government reforms and to the fact that suffrage was not extended to females. The northern Kamerun Democratic Party, inspired by the secessionist, pro-reunificanist party to the south (the KNDP) began to campaign for a merger with Southern Cameroons during the 1959 plebiscite and continued to work for a break with Nigeria but was unable to get this campaign off the ground, especially as the territory approached a second plebiscite in February 1961 when the full weight of the Northern Regional Administration was placed on the side of integration into the region. Intimidation of the NKDP opposition and of southern and French-speaking Cameroon visiting leaders and various "irregularities" in the conduct of the campaign were charged against the Northern Administration, in a case which went to the International Court of Justice. These charges were rejected or ignored by the court and the territory was fully integrated into Northern Nigeria, as Sardauna Province, in June 1961.

2. The Trusteeship Agreements governed the relations of each Administering Authority and the United Nations and could not be terminated or altered without the latter's approval. Thus the final legal authority for determining the procedures for terminating trusteeship rested with the United Nations, which was sensitive to but not bound to the aspirations of the political leadership and people of the territory itself.

3. *Cameroons Champion* (Buea, bi-weekly), November 21, 1960, reports that Foncha requested a grant of fourteen million pounds from the United Kingdom government and a period of independence following the plebiscite or at least continued trusteeship. The editorial of that issue indicates a belief that Foncha was thinking in terms of a five year delay in unification.

The Nature of the Federation

Perhaps the term federation is a misnomer for either the structural organization of reunified Cameroon, or the style of its operation. Despite the fact that Cameroonians called their constitution a federal one, and despite the existence of both central and state governments, power concentrated in the chief executive of the central government. The distribution of political power, even among East (French-speaking) Cameroonians, was more centralized under the "federal" arrangements than it was under the structures of the former unitary constitution.

Southern Cameroonian (West Cameroonian) partisans of reunification had not expected or desired such an outcome. The constitutional discussions which preceded federation revealed serious disparities between the political values of the leaders of each state. Rather than a synthesis of the views and proposals of each side, however, these discussions gave expression to those of only one side, in all save quite minor respects. In retrospect, it appears that this outcome advanced the prospect of success for the union.

The constitution makers drew up their proposals hastily. Neither side gave much thought during the early stages of the reunification movement to the form the union might take. Both sides tended to present the idea of a unitary system however. In the period of political turmoil and uncertainty following their rise to power John N. Foncha, the champion of reunification in Southern Cameroons, and Ahmadou Ahidjo, the latter-day spokesman for the issue in ex-French Cameroon, both switched to a federalist view of the union. Foncha was so preoccupied with the problems of the campaign itself, first for accession to power, which he waged around the theme of secession from Nigeria, and then for "the white box" (union with the Cameroon Republic) that he had little time to elaborate detailed constitutional proposals. Ahidjo could and did give considerably more penetrating and purposeful attention to these matters, though he refused to commit himself and his government to any very elaborate view of the constitution before the plebiscite. He argued that until it became clear which of the two sections of British Cameroon, if either, were to unite with the republic, it was useless to attempt to define too closely the constitutional arrangements for such a union.[4]

The demands of the plebiscite campaign itself and pressures from the United Nations Plebiscite Commission, and the British trusteeship administration all conspired to force Ahidjo and Foncha to declare

4. *The Two Alternatives,* publication of the Administering Authority on behalf of the U.N. Plebiscite Commission, January 1961, p. 4.

themselves on at least a minimal constitutional program.[5] The two leaders thus met several times in the fall and winter of 1960 and signed an agreement presenting in very vague outline the principal features of a federal constitution.[6] They alloted a minimum number and quite orthodox cluster of powers to the central government but left way for the later addition of more powers. President Ahidjo doubtless insisted on this. Agreement on having a bicameral federal legislature, a cabinet system wherein the prime minister would be bound to the advice of his council of ministers and a presidency with only ceremonial powers, all satisfied Foncha's plebiscite campaign promises. All along, however, President Ahidjo probably really preferred and he finally got a centralized presidential regime.

It is not clear whether Foncha was fully aware of the disparities between his own view of the impending federation and those of Ahidjo. Certainly by the time the proposals of the republic were formalized, these disparities were evident. It is thought that Ahidjo's proposals were secretly communicated to Foncha well before the official constitutional convention held at Foumban in August of 1961.[7] If this was so, perhaps the glaring differences in the points of view of the two leaders is what prompted Foncha to call a conference of all the political parties of Southern Cameroons, prior to the official convention, to discuss the proposals of his government. Rather than meeting the challenge of Ahidjo's position head on, Foncha failed to disclose the republic's proposals and attempted to marshall the support of all the minority parties behind his own. The Foncha government consistently appeared more suspicious and frightened of its own opposition than of the government of the republic or of the federation.

In any case, the proposals of Foncha's party, the Kamerun National Democratic Party (KNDP) failed to eliminate the fundamental disparity in the approaches to union of the two partners — the difference between linking the states in a tight and centrally controlled union, or only loosely associating them, leaving them nearly autonomous powers and political structures.[8]

5. *Presse du Cameroun* (Douala, daily), January 14, 1960 (reporting on a press conference Ahidjo gave in Garoua, January 3, 1960).

6. *The Two Alternatives,* pp. 13-15. Cf. also United Kamerun Federal Constitution, by KNDP, January 1961.

7. Members of opposition parties, as well as the members of the republic's government advanced such claims in interviews accorded to me in 1963.

8. *Report,* All Party Conference on the Constitutional Future of the Southern Cameroons, held at Community Hall, Bamenda, June 26-28, 1961. Cf. Constitutional Amendments proposals of Cameroon Republic for Constitutional Conference Foumban, July 17-21, 1961. For a full discussion of the

Curiously, some of the provisions of the KNDP's proposals were more appropriate to the centralized and strong union Ahidjo wanted: federal control over the planning and supervision of the economy, including development, fiscal policy, trade, and foreign technical and financial assistance. Direct election of the president, as proposed by the KNDP, also suited a presidency richly endowed with powers more than a ceremonial office. Perhaps Foncha placed too much faith in a provision for a list of "second stage" federal powers, those which the states would continue to exercise during an unspecified "transitional" period. Without a fixed time-table for, or clear definition of, this period, these powers were actually federalized rather rapidly.

At the all-party conference, the official opposition party, the Cameroon Peoples National Convention (CPNC) agreed, in the main, with the KNDP proposals. Their criticisms did not spring from any denial of the victory of the reunification idea, or any desire to sabotage the union at the last moment. In fact, their position reflected perhaps a more honest approach to the fact of this victory than did the position of the KNDP which had achieved it. For example, the CPNC rejected a KNDP proposal for dual East-West Cameroon nationality, arguing that this suggested there were two nations in the union instead of one. They alone suggested that a unitary constitution best suited a country the size of Cameroon. On the other hand, they also argued for inclusion of provision for legal secession, arguing that the plebiscite vote did not permanently bind their people.

Only the militant leftist party, the One Kamerun Movement (OK) came close to appreciating the contradictions embodied in the KNDP view of federation.[9] Unlike any of the other Southern Cameroons parties, their previous affiliation to the banned Union des Populations du Cameroun (UPC), which had waged the campaign for reunification on the French-speaking side and which bitterly opposed the Ahidjo government, had cause to fear and despise the president of the republic. Yet, perhaps purely from ideological commitments, the OK delegates consistently argued for a federal government with enough powers to

disparities and similarities between the constitutional positions of the two states see my "Cameroon Reunification: Political Union of Several Africas," Ph.D. dissertation, Harvard University, 1965.

9. The One Kamerun Movement (OK) was an offshoot of the Union des Populations du Cameroun (UPC) established in the Southern Cameroons when the UPC exiled leadership was expelled and the organization outlawed in that territory. Many persons considered the OK as the UPC under a different name. Structurally it was a separate organization, and although its leaders, especially Ndeh Ntumazah were closely associated with the UPC leadership, they seem to have enjoyed a certain autonomy from that group.

make the union real. They opposed CPNC and KNDP efforts to introduce schemes of dual nationality or legal secession. They did continually argue for a limitation of the powers of the president, who they thought would be Ahidjo.

The OK attacked outright the trepidations of the KNDP:

> We hear members of the Government Party threaten that if His Excellency President Ahmadou Ahidjo rejects their proposals they will reject unification. The statement implies that they shall declare the Southern Kamerun a sovereign state . . . this is both impossible and improbable. We can not declare sovereignty because we cannot assert it and defend it . . .
>
> When the Kamerunian people opted for Kamerun reunification . . . it was complete and entire. There can be no going back . . . we chose to achieve independence by joining the Kamerun Republic. There was never a condition attached thereto.

Perhaps Prime Minister Foncha considered that his signed agreement with President Ahidjo constituted conditions for the union. In reality the legal implications of that agreement are not clear. This much aside, however, Foncha did not enter the constitutional discussions on a footing of equality with Ahidjo. The OK delegates were right; Foncha had no alternative but to go through with reunification regardless of terms. Doing otherwise would have required considerable daring on his part and great appreciation of the nature and strength of Ahidjo's own opposition and of the features of Ahidjo's constitutional program which would arouse that opposition. He had none of these. Rejection of the obligations presumably imposed by the plebiscite results also would have required external support. The most likely source of this, the United Kingdom, had already indicated that it would not give it.[10]

Ahidjo also used the rhetoric of the long reunification campaign to fence off the constitutional debates from a free-ranging discussion and to guide it to his own ground. Reuben Um Nyobe had asserted the unity of the Cameroon, now Ahidjo echoed him: "[There is] one sole historic unity—the Cameroon Nation; one sole moral unity, the Cameroon

10. Representatives of the British government visited the Southern Cameroons in October 1960 and made it known that HMG would not support an independent Southern Cameroons. The British government also announced during the Bamenda Conference, as twice before in the House of Commons, that she was withdrawing British troops from the territory on October 1st, 1961. Britain did give the territory's government a terminal grant of $1.59 million, which some observers have interpreted to constitute an attempt to pursuade Prime Minister Foncha to accept the republic's constitutional proposals.

Fatherland."[11] But if this were so, there was no denying that the then independent republic, larger and more populous, endowed with a juridical personality internationally recognized—this surely was the chief expression of the Cameroon unity. A transformation to accommodate the distinctive features of its long separate fragment would permit expression of that unity once more. Thus, rather than creating a completely new political reality, theirs was a job only of creatively restoring an old one.

The effect of this stratagem was to place the entire constitutional discussion on ground which Ahidjo fully controlled. This meant that instead of elaborating a new constitution, they had only to amend the existing one of the republic. The procedures for doing so permitted the assembly of the republic to have the final say, and Ahidjo's party, the Union Camerounaise (UC) controlled this assembly by the required two-thirds majority. The Western Assembly did debate the final draft, but by that time little could be done to change it. The advantages of initiative and arbitrament which fell to Ahidjo were overriding.

The consequences of these advantages are clearly evident in the record of the constitutional convention at Foumban. Because the western proposals were not based on the model of the republic's constitution, and because the prior all-party conference had not prepared the Western delegates to give informed consideration to a program of amendments to that constitution, they had first to meet among themselves to study Ahidjo's amendments. All but one hour and thirty-five minutes of the five-day conference was spent in these separate meetings, only to end with a brief and unadorned speech by Ahidjo in which he picked out of the Western revisions those few recommendations that did not significantly challenge his own conception of the federation. All the rest was rejected by omission.[12] Though Foncha and Ahidjo held several subsequent meetings to discuss their differences, these resulted in only minor alterations of the results of the Foumban convention.

Perhaps equally as important, Ahidjo's approach to the constitutional discussions preempted a general public debate on the new constitution even among East Cameroonians. A completely new constitution would probably have required a public referendum. Ahidjo seemed unwilling to risk such a procedure, lest there be a repeat, with even worse results, of their 1960 experience with a constitutional refer-

11. *Record,* Conference on the Constitutional Future of Southern Cameroons Foumban, July 17-21, 1961.

12. Cf. *Constitution,* La République du Cameroun, February 21, 1960.

endum in which ten of the twenty-one districts rejected it.[13] In the absence of a national constitutional debate, such as had preceded the adoption of the first one, and lacking strong public protests from West Cameroon, the East Cameroon opposition was unwilling to campaign against the federal constitution, lest this make them appear opposed to the idea of reunification precisely at the moment of its realization.

The implications of the constitution-making process for the process of political integration in the Cameroon are serious. Some have conceptualized political integration as the emergence of a sense of community, leading to a high-fidelity system of social communication, a heightened sensitivity of people to each others' needs coupled with a willingness and capacity to accommodate those needs.[14] If this is so, then the experience of constitution making did not advance this process very much. West Cameroonians did not communicate their needs very clearly, and where they did, there was no response which could have left them gratified.

The Experience of Federation

A hiatus of considerable proportions and significance existed between the political values of the two merging communities in Cameroon. These were more than paper differences, for the general tenor of the constitutional document was very much reflected in its implementation and in the exercise of the federal prerogatives and institutions during the initial stages of the federation's life.

The implementation and embellishment of the federal structures continued to surprise West Cameroon officials and to increase the importance if not the magnitude of the disparities in the two political cultures by making them explicit and operational.

This was especially true with respect to the powers to legislate by decree and ordinance invested in the presidency. The nature and scope of these powers were poorly understood by the western officials, whose experience with such practices was limited and, in any case, had always involved close parliamentary scrutiny. The ordinance power for the president was a carryover from the first Cameroon Republic and took its inspiration from the Fifth French Republic. Formerly in Cameroon the president was given the power to enact rules and measures having the full effect of law. This was granted by specific parliamentary act,

13. Despite a common program of reunification, UPC elements exiled in West Cameroon ran candidates against Foncha and his KNDP leadership.

14. The 1960 constitution passed with a vote of 796,957 for, and 529,002 against. It failed to carry a majority of 10 of the 21 electoral districts. See *La Presse du Cameroun,* February 25, 1960.

however, and with respect to only designated subjects for a specified time. In the new federation, the only explicit reference to ordinance-making powers limited these to an initial six month period during which time the president could establish any of the federal institutions.

The full significance of this provision must have escaped the West Cameroon leadership for they proposed during the constitutional discussions that this period be extended to two full years, no doubt thinking that this would extend rather than limit the period of state autonomy. As it turned out the president made quick and extensive use of the ordinance powers. During the initial six month period the president proclaimed about thirty ordinances that established almost all the federal institutions. Many of the laws of the old republic were continued in effect in this manner, and other ordinances provided for the organization of the military, judicial, administrative, and commercial institutions of the state. The federal constitution specifically allocated many of these domains to the legislature. However, by the time even the transitional legislature had met, all the principal institutions and the procedures governing them were already established.

It made little difference to the eastern legislators that the president had played such a singular role in embellishing the federal regime. They were accustomed to tight presidential leadership. Not so for the western politicians. They had expected to play a more significant part in this process.

The scope of the presidential decree-making powers and the frequency of its utilization came as an even greater shock to the western officials. They expected that this power would be utilized only during the transitional period. However, long after the first six months during which the president was the sole rule maker, presidential decrees often covered subjects which had been within the sole competence of the assembly of the first Cameroon republic. The organization of the judicial system, military and civil, including the rules governing the magistracy, as well as the electoral system for the states and the rules governing the eligibility of candidates for the federal assembly, the elaboration of the federal administrative machinery, and the declaration of emergencies were all subjects of ordinances during the initial period or decrees thereafter. In addition some twenty or more subjects fell within the scope of the decree-making powers. Exclusive presidential competence in these fields surprised westerners, since this competence derived, in most cases, not from explicit constitutional allocations but rather from inferential allocations. Though all these subjects fell within the federal domain, the specifically legislative domain, defined by explicit enumeration of the assembly's powers, covered only some of these. Thus, all else went to the only other federal rule-making institution, the presidency.

One consequence of the broad range and frequent use of presidential power was a diminutive role for the federal legislature. Virtually none of the federal institutions was established by the assembly. Nor did many of the federal legislators, save occasionally the western deputies, have much influence in the designation of the personnel to staff these institutions. Initially the deputies preoccupied themselves mainly with fiscal and budgetary matters, including provision for the construction of a new assembly place and occasionally the ratification of certain international agreements. The eastern deputies generally were not used to lively substantive discussion in the plenary sessions of the assembly. Conditioned to accept party discipline and to limit substantive discussion to the working commissions, they seldom added much to government bills and almost never presented any of their own.

The state legislative assembly of East Cameroon reflected this same pattern, though to a markedly less degree. Despite the presence in the eastern assembly, until the spring elections of 1965, of a tiny but aggressive opposition, plenary debates were sterile because the procedures limited substantive discussion to the commissions from which the opposition, too small to qualify, were barred. Elder statesmen, particularly the few traditional notables in the assembly, did on occasion assert themselves, notably to thwart the government's attack on the bridewealth (dowry) system, and once to delay and modify important changes in the laws of land tenure.

Animated, even bellicose, debates set the West Cameroon assembly apart. Not only was the opposition usually relatively larger than in the East, it enjoyed the full panoply of parliamentary instruments traditional to British democracy. Government bills seldom suffered defeat or serious mutilation, but neither did they escape the sharp-witted and sometimes quite justified criticism of the opposition, themselves former occupants of government ministries.

The western government party had much more to fear from its opposition than did that of the eastern state. The leaders of the CPNC once threatened to partition the state rather than accept the plebiscite results. They were recognized as highly intelligent men with a significant popular following. Unable to suppress them, ignore them, or defeat them, the government party, after suffering a damaging internal split, finally invited the opposition leaders into a coalition government.[15]

15. On the process of political integration, and the role of communications within it, see Karl Deutsch, *Nationalism and Social Communication* (Cambridge, MIT Press, 1963).

The schism in the ruling party of West Cameroon, inspired by conflicting ambitions for succession to the prime minister's seat following
the constitutionally required separation of that post from the federal
vice-presidency, seems to have complicated and slowed the emergence
of a single party regime in West Cameroon but hastened it at the federal
level. East Cameroon tended toward such a regime steadily from
independence and realized this dubious status in the elections of June
1965. There, the process required imprisonment of the principal
opposition leaders and withdrawal of their right to participate in
politics. Despite the realization of such a regime the government was
slow to win the enthusiastic support of many of the following of the
emasculated opposition. At the federal level, the two dominant parties
from each state often speculated about creating a unified national
party, but the West Cameroon leadership, always conscious of the
strength of its own opposition and embittered by past relations with it,
always stopped short of serious negotiations on the subject. The
emergence in 1965 of a new opposition party, the Cameroon United
Congress, a splinter of the KNDP, helped convince the government
coalition to accept President Ahidjo's call, in June 1966, for the fusion
of all political parties into a single national movement in an effort to
squeeze out this new group. Thus, the Cameroon National Union party
was created to make the country a defacto one-party state.

From the start the federal system of territorial administration had
also enhanced close federal supervision over the political life of West
Cameroon, much to the surprise and consternation of West
Cameroonians. Federal inspectors of administration were appointed not
only to supervise but also to coordinate the functions of the various
federal departments operating in the various administrative territories.[16] One of these territories was all of West Cameroon, and thus
a direct representative of the president was placed in Buea, the capital of the western state. This person was initially authorized to establish rules and regulations within the framework of the executive powers
and to enforce these rules, with police and armed forces if necessary. As
more and more of the governmental responsibilities were federalized, the
scope of the inspectors' authority expanded apace. But what displeased
the Buea officials most was the fact that the federal system of administration incorporated many of the state's administrative officials, making

16. The Opposition Party (CPNC) has dwindled over the years. One of its
prominent members crossed to the government side in 1965 and was subsequently given a ministerial post. The top two leaders of the party, Dr. E.M.L.
Endeley, ex-prime minister became Speaker of the House of Assembly, and N.
N. Mbile was given the post Secretary of State (minister) of Public Works, a
ministry he held in the former Endeley government.

them the focal point of a dual chain of command. As federal responsibilities increased, these state officials were correspondingly federalized. The effect was to deny the state of West Cameroon any autonomous administrative structure at the district or local level.

As the supervisor and coordinator of federal operations and as liaison between the local federal administrators (most of whom were also state administrators) and the federal ministries and other governmental bureaus, the federal inspector for West Cameroon received copies of their correspondence. Copies of communications between the local bureaus and even the state ministries were sent to the inspector so that he might keep surveillance over federal interests. And as federal responsibilities extended to subjects like health services, judicial matters, postal and telegraph and information services, secondary and technical education, an increasing percentage of the time of these administrators was devoted to the coordination of federal rather than state services. Not familiar with either the personalities or the practices and regulations of the eastern (French) oriented federal government, the western officials faced difficulties in supervising these services which they had not faced when they operated according to British influenced custom. To protect themselves and avoid confusion, they sent more and more of their communications directly to the federal authorities, through the inspector, sometimes even on matters juridically within the domain of state authority.

These arrangements seriously threatened the power of the western state, and quite naturally, inspired consternation in its prime minister. Consequently all state officials, whether also federal or not, were ordered to refrain from any direct communication with higher federal officials.[17] Communications, even on truly federal matters were to pass through the prime minister, who as federal vice-president claimed higher rank than the inspector. After a period of cautious experimentation, the federal inspector in Buea found his level and was able to operate effectively in a limited area of strictly administrative responsibilities.

Surprise and resentment on the part of West Cameroonians also resulted from the provisions made for the preservation of law and order in the territory following reunification. Unlike most historic examples of

17. The Union Camerounaise provided the sole list of candidates in the state elections of June 6, 1965. In districts which formerly had been the strongholds of oppositional leaders, it is alleged that abstentions and blank ballots were significant. Official electoral returns reveal nothing lower than 88 percent turnout (casting valid ballots). Most of the districts returned 98 percent or above, however, and a few, especially those of politicians slipping from the president's favor, revealed a suspicious 100 percent response.

political union, fear of external military threats had not figured significantly in the motivations for Cameroon reunification, despite the
dearth of either police or armed forces in the tiny state of Southern
Cameroons. In fact, quite the reverse was true; the existence of an armed
rebellion in the republic replete with acts of unspeakable brutality on all
sides, generated widespread fears of a spillover of terrorism and violence
into "gentle, peaceful Southern Cameroons." This situation hurt the
prospects for reunification. Moreover, the pro-Nigerian leaders had
pledged never to accept reunification and had called for partition of the
territory. This prospect, combined with the outbreak, shortly before, of
violence and secession in the ex-Belgian Congo spread anxiety throughout the state, particularly among foreigners. At least one embassy drew
up plans to evacuate its nationals.

Nearly everyone recognized the need for West Cameroon to acquire a
much larger and better equipped and trained army and police force.
Ironically, however, the most obvious source of such forces, the partner
state, only complicated matters. The republic's armed forces,
particularly the gendarmes, were reputedly as brutal as the terrorists
against whom they fought. Some West Cameroonians warned of the
"dangers of armies of occupation" should the state be "flooded" with the
troops from the east. The brutal massacre of twelve unarmed West
Cameroon plantation workers near the border of East Cameroon, about
six weeks prior to reunification, seemed to confirm the dangers in the
minds of the westerners. Many of them attributed the massacre not to
the terrorists but to overzealous gendarmes. Without explanation, an
appointed commission of inquiry was never convened.

Such fears notwithstanding, about four hundred gendarmes were
stationed in West Cameroon following reunification.[18] Though one
could hardly call this "flooding the state," serious consequences did
occur. Rumors of manhandling and brutality on the part of these
gendarmes spread rapidly, inspiring many letters to the editors of local
newspapers.[19] Rapid expansion of the police force of West Cameroon
did little to help the situation because these forces often came into direct
conflict with the gendarmes, in large measure because of ill-defined
jurisdictions. On one occasion, gendarmes allegedly forced their way
into a West Cameroon jail to retrieve one of their suspects then under
custody of the police. Reportedly, the prisoner was then beaten and
hospitalized. On the other hand, even the West Cameroon police were
also often accused of misconduct, which led some officials to suggest
their centralization under federal control.

18. Decree 61-DF*15 of October 20, 1961.
19. See *Cameroon Times,* May 7, 1962.

Political pressures on the federal officials more effectively to control the gendarmes, as well as growing familiarity and sensitivity of these forces to the cultural mores of the westerners gradually reduced complaints about gendarme behavior. The police forces were not amalgamated. Some tension remained between them and the federal armed forces until late in the 1960s, but this issue had ceased to be the great source of anxiety and disappointment it was to the West Cameroonians during the initial period of federation.

The union produced serious hardships in commerce. Loss of Commonwealth preferences, coupled with steadily declining world prices on many agricultural exports drove many West Cameroon African farmers out of production. Hardest hit were the independent banana producers. The total 1964 banana crop was the smallest in a decade, down a third from the peak production at the time of reunification.[20] The crop of the small producers fell to less than half its prefederation figure, though sharp reductions in the plantation efforts devoted to this crop permitted small producers to increase their relative share of export tonnage. Prices fell even more precipitously, by nearly two thirds. Moreover, the burden of these setbacks fell particularly on West Cameroon. Total production of East Cameroon, while substantially below peak production rates achieved in 1957, showed a net increase of more than 20 percent over the immediately prefederation figures. What threatened to be a critical situation for West Cameroon in early 1964 was checked, literally by a windfall; a hurricane in the Caribbean, which destroyed the total crop of a major competitor, suddenly reopened closed British markets and at peak prices. Producers in both states of Cameroon enjoyed a boon year. Thenceforward, the principal problem in this sector was to gain entry into new markets. Ultimately the eastern-dominated federal government came to look after the interests of the western producers as vigorously as it did those of the east.

Replacement of Nigerian currency with the republic's CFA franc heralded the first impingement of the union on the economic life of the western state. As illiterate market women struggled to master conversion rates, and as cautious Nigerian traders, hurt by artificially high costs for Nigerian pounds, consistently resolved uncertainties in their own favor, prices rose apace. Many people doubted the value and stability of the new currency and consequently refused to convert it. Their confidence was unnecessarily jeopardized by the refusal of French

---

20. Two years after unification two companies (thirteen platoons) of gendarmes were still stationed in West Cameroon and the special branch (security) of the police had been federalized.

commercial firms to honor any specie under five francs, the standard practice in the more affluent markets of East Cameroon. These practices quickly depleted the kerchiefs of the poor western shoppers, however. Many of their purchases were calculated in franc equivalents of their old sterling prices—which seldom provided the convenience of summing to multiples of five. "Dis money too light," one shopper stated in pidgin English, "i no fit buy proper t'ing self."

The establishment of a common federal tariff regime and complicated import license procedures in mid-year 1962, augmented the inflationary pressures on West Cameroon markets. Price advantages on Nigerian goods, or items imported through Nigeria, were generally eliminated. Because the bulk of petty trade traditionally lay in the hands of Ibo tradesmen from Eastern Nigeria, these goods became scarce and replaceable primarily by higher priced goods from the French areas. The cost of living allegedly rose between 70 and 100 percent during the first year and a half of federation. Import regulations were then relaxed for Nigerian tradesmen.

Until the withdrawal of Commonwealth preferences on West Cameroon exports, at the beginning of 1964, British goods were exempted from the stiff and discriminatory (against non-EEC goods) federal tariffs. British importing firms in West Cameroon suffered difficulties nonetheless. The new license requirements obliged them to place their orders for foreign exchange a year in advance. The market was seldom that predictable. Many firms found it easier to switch to French products, which did not require foreign exchange or special licenses. Thus Britain's share of the West Cameroon market declined sharply and was replaced by a westward flow of products from overstocked French firms in Douala. Some of the French firms laid out grand plans for development in the new markets. In the first two years of federation East Cameroon exports to western markets multiplied forty-fold, twice the rate of increase in the opposite trade flow, and twenty-eight times its absolute value. Most of these firms found the venture unprofitable however. Whatever else thirty-five years of British rule had failed to achieve, it succeeded in implanting a taste for British goods. West Cameroonians were unwilling to switch overnight to French items, especially the staple items like rice, sugar, and canned foods. The high trade figures were misleading; many of the French firms came to have overstocked shelves and warehouses in both states.

By switching back to British and other Commonwealth products, many of the French firms operating in the western market created new headaches for themselves, in the form of foreign exchange problems akin to those faced by the firms they had replaced. Since Cameroon was a net creditor to the franc zone, its merchants did not normally have to worry about limited exchange. Members of the zone seldom had any difficulty in drawing on Paris foreign exchange holdings. In the Cameroon case, however, it was the government that restricted exchange quotas to the large expatriate firms, apparently in the favor of a growing number of African importers. The government did not grant the small and still largely inefficient African firms quotas anywhere near those of the expatriate giants, but their inclusion limited the total supply of exchange. Several large firms claimed their quotas were far below their capacity to effectively employ foreign exchange and arbitrarily restricted their operations and thus the size of the African work force they could employ and their contribution, through taxes, to government revenues.

African importing firms were beginning to impinge on large expatriate firms not only by favor of bounteous exchange quotas but also through price advantages. These resulted from the opportunities for smuggling resulting from continuation of the prereunification customs barrier between the two states. Denounced during the period of trusteeship as a symbol of the cruel and arbitrary separation of brother from brother, the barrier remained as a protection both to the higher priced sellers of East Cameroon and to the less affluent buyers of West Cameroon. Enterprising businessmen of both states and bargain-hunting shoppers of the east also benefited from it. Goods from non-EEC countries, entering the country via the western port at Victoria, enjoyed certain tariff exemptions. The internal customs barrier was supposed to ensure against transshipment of these goods into the east where they might undersell imports entering the country through Douala, where they suffered higher tariffs and fiscal charges. Many small African firms, profiting from the inefficiency of their bookkeeping procedures, their knowledge of the many jungle paths across the boundary, and from well-placed friends, became reasonably big firms. Even automobiles were allegedly included in this contraband trade. In the mid 1960s, for the first time in the history of the country, a group (they did not yet constitute a class) of African businessmen were finding it possible to gain a real foothold in the expatriate-controlled markets. Despite the cries and threats of the big firms, one might regard this turn of events as having been favorable to the long-run interests of the country.

The dual market situation which prevailed in the country could not endure. As the expatriate-firm share of the general retail trade shrunk, these firms had been forced to reduce their network. Many branch stores of firms like R. W. King, the only firm which traditionally operated in both British and French Africa, closed. Unilever's Kingsway sold out to its French affiliate Printania. One large French firm withdrew entirely from the general retail trade and others threatened to follow suit. More important, this situation could not last because the federation became part of an even larger common market and customs union, that of the Equatorial African States.[21] Common external tariffs came into effect for the five-state region in mid-1962 and certain common fiscal and other regulations took effect the beginning of 1966. It was difficult for Cameroon to persist in granting special procedures to importers in West Cameroon. At least this is an argument the expatriate firms often made. However, the obvious need for some special measures for West Cameroonians, whose general level of income remained far below that of their compatriots, supported continued customs and fiscal privileges for a while.[22]

The burden of adjustment and change arising from federation fell disproportionately heavily on West Cameroon in several other fields as well, the educational, legal, and communications fields, especially.

The allocation of federal and state prerogative in the field of education reflected the disparities in the values and approach of the two political elites. Perhaps President Ahidjo realized that the educational system could serve to strengthen regional loyalties and cultural distinctiveness. Thus, he insisted that all education above the primary school level should fall under federal control. As a spokesman for regional interests, Prime Minister Foncha pressed during the constitutional discussions for state control over all local educational institutions, save perhaps a federally run and supported university. The president's view prevailed.

Federal officials supervised the secondary and technical schools in West Cameroon. Because of personnel shortages, for a time these federal officials, reassigned from the state ministry of education, also continued to supervise the primary schools and teacher training operations as well. A natural consequence of this approach was to slow down the impact of federalization on the West Cameroon educational system. Eventually the disparities between the two systems, most striking in terms of calendar, but more important, in terms of curriculum and conception, demanded tighter coordination and adjustment. In general, the pattern of adjustment remodeled the western system along the lines of its eastern counterpart. One of the first changes harmonized

21. See especially *Cameroon Times* and *Cameroons Champion,* 1962 and 1963 (the latter ceased publication in February of 1963).

22. For a general survey of agricultural production see "Agriculture: The Economic Potential of West Cameroon — Priorities for Development," Stanford Research Institute, May 1965.

the calendars on the basis of, first, a seven-year primary program for West Cameroon, and later, a six-year program in each state. Proposed reforms called for up to seven years of secondary training, in two cycles of unequal length in each state.[23]

Examinations and certificates continued to follow their colonial models, but the syllabi faced important reforms in each state, and though this effort derived primarily from the achievement of independence, reunification of the country gave it an impetus in the west which it might otherwise have lacked. History and geography, especially, acquired an African and Cameroonian framework. Vocational and more general and limited terminal secondary programs were added, facilitated by a dual-cycle secondary program. Thereby, they eliminated the French mid-secondary exams (*brevet*). The diversification which was sought through these reforms began, in East Cameroon at least, at the primary level. Here too a dual cycle was introduced, which permitted vocational training for terminal students, some with a rural orientation.

These reforms, based primarily on East Cameroon patterns, required a significantly higher degree of harmonization of the two educational systems. The first step in this direction was a plan for standardizing throughout the whole federation the entrance examination to the first cycle of secondary school. This exam, alike in the substance of the basic subjects, but given in either French or English, was to replace the West African School Certificate used throughout ex-British Africa. Common qualifying examinations added pressure for closer coordination if not full standardization of primary school programs as well as the secondary programs.

One of the chief differences between the two states in the pattern of primary school education was the role played by private, especially missionary, institutions. About 85 percent of the students attended such schools in the west. French-speaking educational officials are used to a system which historically, even during the colonial period, placed the greatest responsibility for education on the government. They sometimes described the system which existed in ex-British Cameroon as one with "a free enterprise spirit," leading to a situation of "semi-anarchy." The place for private schools, especially secular ones, steadily shrank; the government closely inspected and monitored their activities. General secular, private, secondary schools, often called general

---

23. *Cameroon Times* of June 18, 1962 asserted that exchange rates CFA-Nigerian Pound prior to reunification had been £800 CFA. The new official rate was £692 CFA. Most traders could obtain sterling only on the black market which continued at the old rates or higher.

colleges, were on their way out in the east. Only in the church-supported in the east was religious instruction permitted. Here it was left to the unfettered control of the sponsor. The secular curriculum of all schools, government or missionary, was carefully prescribed and rigidly supervised. In the west it was different. Religious instruction was almost universal, because historically so many of the schools were missionary in sponsorship, and the secular program is less rigidly supervised. Missionary officials were fearful that the general intensification of governmental supervision would endanger religious instruction in the west. Indeed, at one point overzealous officials in the federal ministry called for its elimination throughout the system. Any threat to the deeply rooted tradition of religious instruction in the schools considerably endangered popular and especially official enthusiasm for the federation among westerners.

In the field of education more than in any other, hopes ran higher, and perhaps disappointments were more profound for a true give-and-take between the two Cameroon systems to take place. Rather than because the differences between them were any less fundamental here, this situation resulted from the fact that education was seen as the keystone of almost all the rest of the cultural superstructures of each state, or at least of the peculiar attachments to, and ways of perceiving these cultures. What West Cameroonians looked for in the federal program of educational reform was a sincere commitment to cultural synthesis. Because the true meaning of the Cameroon experiment, at least to the few intellectuals, was the opportunity provided to bridge the colonial legacies in Africa, a blending of the best of all the African worlds was considered more important than merely bridging the regional, tribal, and linguistic differences by assimilating one culture to the other. Given such a spirit, West Cameroonians might have adapted more happily to the ways of the east, at least temporarily. Lacking such a spirit, the pursuit of national integration could be expected to breed only resentment.

Educational policy symbolized this situation in two other fundamental areas. The more technical and perhaps less crucial was that of harmonization and instruction of the law. Second was that of the creation and propagation of a common communications system.

Almost every new African state faced an acute problem of creating a harmonized legal system.[24] In both the British and French dependencies, two or more rather distinct legal systems operated. Everywhere the colonial power introduced its own metropolitan law, but African

24. See the speech of the minister of education, *Cameroon Pedagogical Review,* no. 3 (1965).

customary law was generally permitted to continue alongside the metropolitan system. This was true even in those areas the French administered by "direct rule." The colonial power often supported the highly organized and positive Islamic legal codes and judicial systems as well. Also these regimes usually made a distinction between "assimilated" or "civilized" on the one hand and "natives" or *indigènes* on the other. Whatever may have been the justification for these last distinctions was eliminated by independence, but the other problems remained. Secularism even threatened the Koranic codes. Re-examination and adaptation of these various legal traditions was therefore, and everywhere, an item of high priority. Cameroon was the first African state to tackle not only the problem of synthesizing the various customary systems with the European ones but of synthesizing them with each other. Here especially was an opportunity for creative and balanced cultural melange.

Cameroon officials, both state and federal, repeatedly professed a commitment to rational and balanced syntheses of their legal systems, but this came about very slowly. It is still too early to evaluate adequately their success. There are indications, however, that in this domain as in so many others many consider size the determinant of what is wise.

The law faculty of the Federal University exemplifies this. Their approach to the training of Cameroonians in the British legal system caused no small amount of concern among westerners. West Cameroonian recipients of federal scholarships to the "bilingual" faculty thought they were off to Yaoundé to pursue studies principally in the legal traditions of their own state and in English. Not only did they discover that almost nothing was taught about the British common law tradition, but that all the classes were conducted in French. After some months of stumbling along these students were sent to Paris to learn French. Some did surprisingly well both in the language studies and in the legal studies. A few students, with extraordinary energy and enterprise, took correspondence courses in British law while finishing their studies in the code system at Cameroon University. Ultimately a truly bilingual, comparative legal studies program emerged, the first in Africa, if not the world.

There was greater give-and-take between legal specialists of the two states in the discussions relating to the fusion of the more technical aspects of legal systems, respecting procedures for the supreme court, the rules governing the qualifications and recruitment procedures of judicial and other legal personnel, the procedures for civil and criminal cases, and the tenets of the civil and criminal codes. All these incorporate some elements of each system. The framework of the new system seems to have remained French, however, with a few innovations here and there.[25]

The task of rationally constructing a new, essentially Cameroonian legal system out of the materials of the previous ones was somewhat complicated by the fact that the rapid pace of political change in West Cameroon made it difficult to determine what its laws really were. Nigerian legislation was carried over into the federal period, along with certain parts of British common law. New state and federal legislation superceded some of this heritage but no one knew for sure which part. In order to establish a sound basis for discussion of a unified federal system a codification of West Cameroon was necessary. Overworked officials and legal advisers undertook this work, but its significance diminished with each indication that the eastern officials intended to push their own system largely intact.

The balance of federal-state authority affected this issue as well. Pressures for true legal synthesis at the federal level would have been greatest had there been some autonomy for the states if not the preservation within them of their traditional legal precepts and procedures. The fact was, however, that very little of "the law" was left within the states' domain. It was suggested, for example, that state legislation could not carry its own provision for penalty, because "criminal law" was included among the federal powers. Thus the states were potentially left with no power of their own to enforce any of their rules.

If we turn to an examination of the communications system in the federation we see that greater success was achieved in mutual accommodation. The problem of overcoming discontinuities in the communications patterns among Cameroonians was severe but distinctive only in the need to bridge the gap between two world languages as well as myriad vernaculars.

Cameroon fared better than one might have expected in terms of having a capacity to provide translation of discussions between top officials. Centuries of contact with British commercial and missionary establishments along the coast left a residue of an English-speaking community even in the East Cameroon port city of Douala and surrounding areas. Most of its members speak only pidgin English, however. This language is one of the real continuities between the two states. The hold on standard English is tenuous, even in West Cameroon, among the masses. Many of the federal and eastern officials converse with their anglophone compatriots in pidgin. One highly

25. For a wide-ranging examination of the problems of legal synthesis in Africa see the various papers and report of the Interdisciplinary Colloquium on "The Development and Adaptation of Legal Systems in Africa," UCLA, Spring 1963.

placed West Cameroonian even suggested that pidgin be utilized as something akin to an official language.

The initial, extraordinary translation needs of the federation were met through French and UNESCO aid. Such aid may have provided the means to Ahidjo to present his constitutional proposals in English. The official gazette appeared as a bilingual edition from the start.

Low literacy rates throughout the country, even in the more advanced east, continue to limit the impact of written communications. even where translations are provided. Oral media also find it difficult to bridge the many communications gaps. No real lingua franca exists. French is perhaps the most widespread language and the sole link between the north and south of Cameroon. Hausa and Fulbe (Fulani) are both widespread in the north. Pidgin English serves as the trading language along the coast and frontier regions between the two states. But in West Cameroon standard English is not an adequate link between the ruling elite and the masses. Either the vernaculars or pidgin must be used for this purpose. The radio services hardly ever used pidgin, which would have been necessary were Cameroonians to come to know each other. Only major news items are diffused in both official languages. Otherwise, the English broadcasts referred to West Cameroon only, or perhaps to the English-speaking world in general. Those who listened in French heard items only about East Cameroon or the French-speaking world.

The long-run solution to this language problem rests, of course, with the schools. Both official languages theoretically were compulsory at the secondary level. The western officials feared, however, that initiating studies in French too early might jeopardize some students' knowledge of English, resulting in their learning neither of the official languages well. Initially they asserted that for a while bilingualism would mean the two language communities would operate side-by-side.

Language later became an important symbol of the whole of the distinctive culture of each of the two states. The sudden association of these two communities, vastly unequal in numbers and resources, in a single political system made each of them self-conscious about their cultural heritage, including the colonial legacies. This was especially true of the minority region. For the first time in the long debate among Africans concerning the need for "national languages," the official languages inherited from European rule competed with the vernaculars as a legitimate vehicle for the expression not only of official business but also of the authentic culture and personality of their speakers. West Cameroonians, especially, considered the place accorded English in the life of the federation as a symbol of their contributions to the cultural development of the country. Their goal, of course, was cultural equality with the east. This goal confronted the dominance of French culture in the east and the dominance of the east in the life of the federation. Mere juxtaposition of the two language traditions, therefore, seemed an insufficient guarantee of cultural equality and true cultural synthesis. Indeed, expectations of anything more than preserving cultural distinctiveness in the west quickly waned. The difficulty here was that this issue involved the political stability of a regime, the prestige of its leaders, and their relative claim to national resources and power. To bolster their position some West Cameroonians even pointed to the dominance of English in Africa as a whole. They found more than idealistic reasons to become pan-Africanists.

The scale of costs versus benefits to West Cameroonians from reunification was not as unbalanced as the problems imply. Most westerners asserted confidence in Cameroon unity. The advantages it brought to them were of two sorts, principally. First, there was the undisputed economic advance of the country and financial gains of the government. Second, and somewhat ironically, there was what many felt to be enhancement of their political security and freedom.

Reunification brought considerable benefits to the feeble budgets of West Cameroon. An area of limited resources, laggard in social and economic development, its plight was consistently one of financial crisis during the period it was administered as part of Nigeria. Not only did it lag behind the other regions in locally generated income, but there is good reason to believe that it seldom received its just due from the redistributed Nigerian federal revenues.[26] Reunification reversed this financial situation. The total revenues of the government increased considerably.

Various formulae of revenue allocation applied by Nigeria to the territory failed one after another to stabilize an adequate revenue for its recurrent and capital investment budgets. The Nigerian central government first pledged to return "every penny" it received from the territory above the costs of its own services to it, then it attempted to guarantee a fixed income, and finally applied the system in use for the other regions of Nigeria. These schemes all proved either too costly to the central government or discriminatory and inadequate to Southern Cameroons. The territory's share of federal revenues amounted to about $1.7 million during the first year it participated in Nigeria's revenue allocation

---

26. Harmonizing the criminal code entailed relatively few difficulties, since both systems contained roughly similar or compatible definitions of crimes. Greater difficulty arose in criminal procedures and substantive aspects of the civil code, particularly the rules governing the admission of evidence, protection of the accused, and preliminary hearings.

system on a par with the other regions. But this figure did not eliminate a small deficit on recurrent account.

Cameroon federal subsidies to West Cameroon rose steadily over the first five years of the life of the federation, until, in 1965-66 it is estimated to have reached $5.4 million, accounting for 48.5 percent of the total revenues of the state and about 60 percent of the revenues for the recurrent budget. The subsidy was about 5 percent above the federal subsidy for East Cameroon and sufficient to permit West Cameroon to balance its budget. The capital budget also rose to about 80 percent above prefederation levels. Available figures on costs of the various federal departments which operated in the state and the revenue they collected do not permit a precise comparison between federal revenues which were derived within, and subsidies returned to, the state. It is thought, however, that the amount of the subsidies was greater, thus representing a net redistribution of national resources in favor of the west.[27]

Tangible evidence of basic development was evident to all who traversed the state's highways and byways. The most noticeable improvements were in the roads, formerly a source of great embarrassment and inconvenience to Southern Cameroonians. In 1965 President Ahidjo inaugurated work on "Reunification Road," thirty-five miles of highway to link Douala with Victoria, the principal commercial districts of each state. Formerly travel between these centers required five hours of driving, or travel by canoe through marsh and bog. United States AID equipment transformed long sections of almost all the principal routes throughout the country into well graded and tarred highways. Over one and a half million dollars of U.S. aid went to West Cameroon during fiscal year 1962-63 alone, most of this for road development. A large contingent of Peace Corpsmen was teaching in West Cameroon schools or assisting community development projects. During the same year European Development Fund assistance agreements amounted to over four million dollars, and the Fond d'Aide et de la Coopération (FAC) brought in another two and three quarters million. These figures are blind to the significant contributions of aid received which were not itemized and given a monetary measure by the Cameroon government. In the years following 1962-63 the amount of aid received by or pledged to West Cameroon increased.

Comparisons between the experience of West Cameroon after reunification with what might have been had it remained with Nigeria

27. A report on the financial situation in the Cameroon prior to reunification can be found in the report by Sir Sydney Philippson, "Financial Implications of Separation of Southern Cameroons from Nigeria," September 1958.

can only be speculative. It seems safe to say, however, that the state fared better in terms of foreign aid than it would have as part of Nigeria. During the year 1962-63, for example, only about 27 million dollars of Nigeria's capital investments came from foreign sources, and the great bulk of this went into federal projects. There is no reason to believe that very much of this would have gone into federal projects in tiny, out-of-the-way Cameroon. Moreover, even for the eastern region, for which the foreign aid component of the capital budget was highest of the regions, this figure amounted to only one and a half million dollars. This is far smaller than the sum actually received by West Cameroon for that year.

It is true that the total capital expenditures of any of the Nigerian regional governments which existed in 1962-63 surpassed that of Cameroon, even considering the combined expenditure of all its governments. The 1962 figure nearly equaled the 1966 Cameroon figure. Even the poorest Nigerian region, the north, spent nearly $12.5 million on capital projects. However, if one takes relative size, economic importance, or political weight of West Cameroon into consideration, its likely percentage of the total Nigerian figure ($190 million) would be about 1 percent, perhaps amounting to two million dollars, much less than it steadily received in the Cameroon federation during the first half decade of the federation. It is hard to imagine that it would have enjoyed claims as strong within Nigeria as it did in Cameroon, where it is seen as a special ward of the English-speaking world, and reaped the major share of U.S. aid to the country. Even East Cameroon acknowledged a special obligation to its sister state. Of course, West Cameroon missed out on the huge oil revenues which Nigeria ultimately acquired.

With respect to their political and personal security and freedom, unexpected benefits accrued from federation to a number of West Cameroon groups and individuals. This resulted in part from the advantages of federalism, offering dissidents and offended officials a course of higher appeal. More important, this result derived from the presence in the highest seats of authority of judicious men, considerate and not inclined to precipitous action.

Exemplary of such benefits is the case of several West Cameroon civil servants who, at various times, found themselves in conflict with the top politicians or accused by them of participating in politics on behalf of the opposition. In a few cases, such persons were actually dismissed from their posts. In other cases they may have been subjected to administrative harassment. Some of these difficulties seem to have arisen from tribal or regional prejudices, the weight of which fell on many official acts and judgments of the West Cameroon regime during the first three years of federation. For some of the victims, the federal services proved an alternative. The growing federal departments continually needed competent personnel and could sometimes attract the better educated or more experienced people. West Cameroon officials at the federal level seem to have been freer of tribalist pressures and freer also of local political pressures in their hiring and general administrative policies. In several cases administrative officials who lost favor or were otherwise in conflict with the state regime acquired a federal post through sympathetic and sometimes dissident colleagues well placed in the federal government.

An even more important example of the role of the federal government sometimes as guarantor of the independence from state level pressures of some western politicians is provided by the case of the dismissal in July 1965 of two West Cameroonian federal ministers from the Kamerun National Democratic Party. Despite the fact that their positions had initially been acquired as a result of their political strength in the state party, constitutionally these appointments were made by the president. Thus, despite their fall from favor with the state level political leadership, these ministers could continue to fill their posts at the will of the president. The president may have desired, in part, to demonstrate his own independence from purely local or personal political pressures.

Federalism became an issue in the conflict between the expelled ministers and their party. The dispute arose from conflicting ambitions for the post of prime minister following the constitutionally required separation of that post from the vice-presidency in April 1965. In an attempt to limit to the state parliament where he was thought to have the greatest support the authority to choose the successor, one of the federal ministers wrongly asserted that a decision on this matter by the party's national congress would violate the president's constitutional prerogative to nominate the state prime ministers. The president, aware of the pitfalls of hasty action, carefully and systematically canvased the members of parliament before formally proposing a different name to that body. His unwillingness to act without full knowledge of local attitudes won him the respect of both camps, and strengthened the role of the federal government. Several years later President Ahidjo did nominate, and the state Assembly confirmed this person, Solomon Muna, as Prime Minister of West Cameroon.

The attempt of West Cameroon politicians and other political and social groups to wed the federal machinery to their own causes serves as an important indication of the reality of federal authority and power in the country. Effectiveness at many levels of life and administration in West Cameroon required a shift from state to federal levels of activity and organization. District officers found it increasingly necessary to meet with their counterparts from the French-speaking zone, labor union federations likewise found it necessary to communicate with each other more frequently, and finally to fully amalgamate. The business community in each state also established mutual contacts. Even religious organizations, especially those of West Cameroon, felt it important to acquire a knowledge of federal procedures and officials. Common organizations, outlooks, or patterns of behavior emerged in many of these spheres of interest. Cameroonians in all walks learned more about each other, and found it increasingly necessary to collaborate. This process embellished the social and political super-structures necessary for the achievement of a true sense of national community.

Conclusion

The Cameroon experience of political integration inspires at least two questions: was it successful and was it instructive for any future attempts at political union between English- and French-speaking Africa?

Success requires more than durability, at least if one takes the Cameroon experience as a model. Partisans of African unity or lesser conceptions of closer political union in Africa can hardly consider the mere achievement of union as success if the aspirations which motivate this desire go unfulfilled. Despite the many disappointments of reunifi-cation, especially to West Cameroonians but also sometimes to their eastern compatriots, most people throughout the country seemed to consider the benefits as greater than the costs. The hiatus in living standards, political values, and social patterns between the peoples of the two states has not yet disappeared. But it has significantly diminished. Given the meagerness of the initial continuities between the two territories of Cameroon, the slowness to achieve truly common political and social behavioral patterns is hardly justification for calling the whole experiment a failure. What it does justify, perhaps, is the emphasis which the federal authorities, particularly the president, placed on establishing and embellishing the legal, organizational, and even coercive capacities of the federal government. It is already evident that many of the processes of realignment and refocus which worked at the federal level stemmed from the reality of federal power. The federation in time, became a unitary republic. This change was a con-tinuity of previous trends, not a break in them.

The Cameroon does offer some lessons to the partisans of African unity. For one thing, it adds new strength to the counsel: "Seek ye first the political kingdom and all things else shall be added unto you." Cameroon certainly does not demonstrate the futility of a gradualist and functional approach to political union, but it does indicate the possibility of achieving it and making it work despite the lack of extensive homogeneity or bonds of social intercourse between the merging units.

Additionally, this case highlights what may be the more troublesome aspects of any union between British and French legacies. Undoubtedly the most intractable problems for Cameroon came in the economic and commercial spheres. Any other similar union would probably face a similar plight. Association of these legacies might also deepen the sense of cultural and political competition and difference between them, rather than the reverse. Unless offset by cross-cutting affiliations and identifications, this might increase the disintegrative pressures on the union; the pressures are initially likely to be high anyway. On the other hand, some parochial loyalties within each state may be overcome or reduced in the process.

That some of the measures which were undertaken in Cameroon to secure union may have angered some of its leaders is no proof that they were not the more helpful in securing the long run interests of all concerned. Initially the easterners tended to regard the process of integration as primarily one of assimilating the westerners to the ways of the east. Later, however, they recognized the need for moderation in implementing the powers won for the central authorities and accepted the obligations incumbent on bigger, wealthier, and more advanced East Cameroon with respect to the advancement of the western state. Goodwill and a sincere desire for success were perhaps the most crucial elements in this experiment, and on both sides these were in plentiful supply.

Part Two
The International Order and Emergent States

6. Domestic Jurisdiction and Colonialism

Inis L. Claude, Jr.

A familiar feature of political argument is the tendency of antagonists to begin with a skirmish over jurisdiction, before locking polemical horns on substantive issues. The "who may do what" issue frequently takes precedence over the "what should be done" issue, and the latter question may be concealed beneath the former throughout the controversy. While the total relationship between law and politics is not exhaustively analyzed by this observation, it is often true that debate over legal competence provides a convenient forensic form for battles over matters of policy. Americans are accustomed to the discussion of such political issues as the rights of Negro citizens in the terminological guise of learned debate concerning the constitutional residue of states' rights in the federal system. On the international plane, the world is rapidly becoming accustomed to the similar utilization of the concept of domestic jurisdiction as the key to the sublimation of political controversy within the form of legal debate.

While the problem of jurisdictional controversy is inherent in the multiplicity of sovereignties which is the basic characteristic of the modern state system, the international stage was not set for the playing scenes closely analogous to the stylized comedies of American states' rights debates until the framers of the Covenant of the League of Nations devised the conceptual prop of domestic jurisdiction. Even then, the dramatic potentialities thus opened up were not fully exploited for a generation: it remained for the United Nations, equipped with a modified version of that prop, to assemble the *dramatis personae*, and for the postwar anticolonial movement to inspire the drafting of the appropriate script, for truly gripping performances of the jurisdictional drama on the global stage. The charter's prohibition of intervention by the United Nations "in matters which are essentially within the domestic jurisdiction of any state," contained in Article 2 (7), has figured in debates on a variety of subjects,[1] but its greatest impact upon international dramaturgy has occurred in connection with the rebellion against colonialism.

The definition of domestic jurisdiction—the determination of the extent and limits of the domain reserved to states against international intrusion—is a legal matter, a problem which a host of international lawyers have made their own. Such questions as what is encompassed by the jurisdictional fence, how the fence is shifted, and what sort of United Nations action constitutes improper penetration of the fence have been

1. See M. S. Rajan, *United Nations and Domestic Jurisdiction* (Bombay, Orient Longmans, 1958), for a comprehensive survey.

subjected to intensive legal analysis. To acknowledge and approve this, however, is not to assert or admit that domestic jurisdiction is exclusively a legal problem. It is, in fact, a political matter par excellence, in the sense that the politicians sometimes ignore the lawyers and even more in the sense that they frequently undertake to use the lawyers; the handling of the domestic jurisdiction issue is never more political than when it is being argued in legal terms.

This may sound cynical — but one should reflect that, in the domestic setting, the use of lawyers is regarded as entirely legitimate. They are, after all, advocates of the parties who employ them. It is judges who are not to be used. Strangely and unfortunately, most discussion of the ideal of assigning a major role to law in international affairs focuses upon the image of the legal arbiter, while tending to forget that of the legal advocate. It conjures up a never-never land where there are judges but no lawyers, objective judicial opinions but no partisan legal briefs — where law is simply an instrument of even-handed justice, never a set of weapons for heavy-handed dueling. A moment's reflection will suggest that this is not an accurate picture of the functioning of the legal system in, say, the United States, and ought equally to suggest that it does not portray a situation which can reasonably be expected to develop in international affairs. In the functioning of real legal systems, as opposed to fanciful ones, lawyers' arguments on behalf of their clients are as significant as judges' rulings in the interest of justice. One can hope that judges may acquire a larger role in the relations of states, but no vision of a working system of international law is complete without a view of politicians in conflict, using lawyers to advance and defend their competing interests by presenting rival versions of the legal situation.

The denial of the legal authority of an institution to interfere in a given situation is essentially a conservative tactic, a device for heading off possible disruption of the status quo. Moreover, this kind of restrictive device is typically employed by conservative forces that feel themselves outclassed, or likely to be outclassed, politically. They undertake to prevent by legal means what they despair of preventing by political means. In the United States, the assertion of states' rights can be translated as an effort to debar the federal government from acting to alter existing arrangements in certain fields. In the United Nations, the claim of domestic jurisdiction has a similar function with respect to the world organization. In both cases, the restrictive effort is a defensive maneuver, reflecting the assumption that whatever action the broader institution might take would be determined by the "wrong" political forces, in the long run if not in the immediate future.

Given this analysis, one can see that the logic of the political situation has virtually predetermined the manner in which the domestic jurisdiction clause has figured in the battle over colonialism: it has been invoked by the colonial powers, and its invocation has been resisted by the anticolonial forces. Article 2 (7) of the charter has served as the documentary shield of the custodians of the colonial system, while Article 73 has been used as the major documentary sword of the liquidators of that system. The latter provision, which along with Article 74 constitutes chapter 11 of the charter with the title, "Declaration Regarding Non-Self-Governing Territories," provides the broad if not absolutely firm foundation for the contention that the United Nations is constitutionally authorized to supervise and control — and terminate — the operation of the colonial system. In the hands of anticolonial enthusiasts, Article 73 is a sharp instrument for penetrating the colonial domain; its cutting edge has been persistently and lovingly honed by the proponents of rapid and complete decolonization. On the other side, Article 2 (7) has been raised to blunt the thrust of Article 73, and much of the sound and the fury of the battle has resulted from the clanging together of these two provisions of the charter.

In legal terms, the crucial question pertains to the relationship between the charter's espousal of the principle that colonial policy is a matter of international concern (stated not only in chapter 11, but also in the two following chapters, which deal with the trusteeship system, and implied in still other provisions), and its declaration of respect for the reserved domain of states. Which limits and qualifies the other? Is international intervention into the colonial situation restricted by the proposition that a state's colonial policy is its own national business, as the possessors of colonies are wont to insist? Or do the charter's provisions concerning the colonial problem remove that entire matter from the protected zone of domestic jurisdiction, uprooting the "Private Property — No Trespassing" signs planted there in earlier times?

The framers of the charter appeared to believe that such a clear-cut choice could be avoided. They sought to promote international regulation of colonial property, modifying the old laissez-faire colonial system without going to the extreme of international confiscation. In setting up the trusteeship system, they enabled colonial powers to exercise the option of subjecting particular dependencies to international arrangements that implied the relinquishment, or the willingness to move toward relinquishment, of sovereign title over them. Beyond this, they were satisfied to establish the public international regulation of colonies without formally challenging the theory of private national ownership. In essence, they left colonies in the domestic domain of their possessors but removed their management from the realm of unfettered domestic jurisdiction. If the evidence suggests that they did not purport to revoke national sovereignty over colonies, it also indicates that they did not propose to respect national privacy in dealing with colonies. In ratifying the charter, with its extensive provisions relating to the colonial problem, the possessors of colonies gave up any reasonable claim to such privacy.

It would be inaccurate to suggest that the treatment of colonial matters in the United Nations has been characterized by a continual debate over the fundamental question of whether the world organization or the colonial possessor is properly in ultimate charge of a given territory. Colonial powers have accepted numerous applications of the principle that the United Nations can legitimately concern itself with developments in their possessions, and anticolonial states have accepted the proposition that those who administer colonies have a certain authority as well as a distinct responsibility in those territories. Within the framework of the United Nations, an elaborate mechanism has been developed to deal with many aspects of the affairs of dependent territories, including the process of advancing many of those territories to independent status, and much of the detailed work undertaken through this mechanism has been accomplished without significant controversy and with notable cooperation on both sides.

However, the disagreement on basic principle has never lain far beneath the surface of cooperation on detail. When controversies have arisen regarding the wisdom or propriety of particular manifestations of United Nations concern with colonialism, the clash over jurisdiction has tended to come into the open. Thus, the establishment of the Committee on Information from Non-Self-Governing Territories to deal with reports submitted by administering powers under Article 73(e) was grudgingly accepted by the colonial states, despite reservations concerning its constitutionality, but recurrent efforts to enhance its status by formalizing its permanence evoked opposition, which was expressed in terms of the denial that chapter 11 constituted an abridgment of their sovereignty over colonies.

Even more, the accumulation of disagreements over detail has led to the formulation of opposed doctrinal positions. It may be possible to discern a kind of typical life history of such ideological developments: one side attributes to the other an extreme position in principle: the allegation is repaid in kind; the first side strings together detailed evidence in support of the charge that the other is conspiring to give effect to the doctrine attributed to it; reciprocity operates again, and thus, by a process that might be called the interaction of self-fulfilling prophecies, doctrinally based opposition emerges. Something of this sort seems to have occurred in the relationships of the colonial and anticolonial forces in the United Nations. The colonial powers interpreted the policy of the anticolonial group as a gradually unfolding scheme to destroy their authority in dependent territories and to achieve the rapid and total abolition of the colonial system. The anticolonials developed the conviction that the other camp was dedicated to the complete frustration of the United Nations enterprise in colonial supervision and the perpetuation of unmitigated colonialism. Pressure mounted, resistance stiffened, and incidental disagreement concerning the implementation of chapter 11 and related sections of the charter came to be construed, not altogether inaccurately, as evidence of sharp doctrinal conflict.

The invocation of the domestic jurisdiction clause as a check upon the elaboration and intensification of international involvement in colonial affairs has led to the development of a number of subordinate doctrines, related to each other across the battle line as theses and antitheses and, in some instances, contradicting each other on the same side of the line.

The Belgian Thesis

The earliest and one of the most prominent of these is the position known as the Belgian thesis in recognition of the primary role of Belgian representatives in its development and espousal.[2] In essence, this is the proposition that chapter 11 of the charter logically and properly applies not only to the peoples of territories commonly designated as colonies, but with equal justice and on equal terms to all other population groups, no matter where situated, which fall below the level of first-class citizenship of the states under whose authority they live. Reference is made to non-self-governing groups, relatively primitive and ill-equipped to participate in the political, economic, and cultural life of the larger societies to which they are joined, in several Latin American countries, India, Burma, Afghanistan, the Philippines, Iraq, Syria, Saudi Arabia, Liberia, the Soviet Union, and so on. The point that peoples such as these, typically residing within the metropolitan territories of their states, should be regarded and treated as beneficiaries of the Declaration Regarding Non-Self-Governing Territories is argued on several grounds. The broad language and general purpose of that declaration offer no justification in law or in logic for the exclusion of such peoples from its application. In moral terms, it is inexcusable to provide less adequately for the protection and advancement of these groups than for those living in acknowledged colonies, often under far

2. For one of several expositions of the thesis by its leading proponent, see F. Van Langenhove, *The Question of the Aborigines before the United Nations: The Belgian Thesis* (Brussels, Royal Colonial Institute of Belgium, Section of Social and Political Sciences, 1954). My analysis of the case for the Belgian thesis is based largely upon this work.

better circumstances. Many of the states harboring such groups recognize their non-self-governing status by making special legal and administrative arrangements for dealing with them, closely analogous to those prevailing in colonies. Some international organizations, including ILO, UNESCO, and the Organization of American States, consider these peoples within the same category as colonial inhabitants. Historically, the principle of international concern for the welfare of such groups was well established before 1945. Article 23(b) of the covenant provided the basis for action on their behalf by the League of Nations, and served as the starting point for the elaboration of chapter 11 of the charter; it cannot be presumed that the framers of the charter intended to effect a retrogression in this area of international law. Thus runs the argument.

The Belgian thesis contrasts sharply with the familiar "salt water" theory of imperialism, according to which the conquest of territory is classed as an instance of imperialist behavior only if the territory involved lies across an expanse of salt water—that is, overseas. While this theory originally served the convenience of states which specialized in continental expansion rather than island hopping, notably Russia and the United States, the pressure of the Belgian thesis has forced the anticolonial states to make it their own. Reacting against the effort to expand the coverage of chapter 11, they have insisted that its provisions were intended to apply only to territories commonly regarded as colonies—in effect, to overseas possessions of European powers. The anticolonial rejection of the Belgian thesis ultimately triumphed in the General Assembly. This victory was implicit in the adoption, on December 14, 1960, of General Assembly Resolution 1514 (XV), the highly significant "Declaration on the granting of independence to colonial countries and peoples." As the title suggested and the text emphasized, this resolution interpreted the concern of the United Nations with non-self-governing territories as a concern with colonies: *colonialism*, a term not used in the charter, was repeatedly designated in Resolution 1514 as an evil which the United Nations was determined to abolish. The assembly's repudiation of the Belgian thesis in favor of a position modeled after the salt water theory was made explicit on the following day in Resolution 1541 (XV); the first item in an annexed list of "Principles which should guide Members in determining whether or not an obligation exists to transmit the information called for in Article 73(e) of the Charter" contained the flat assertion that "The authors of the Charter of the United Nations had in mind that Chapter XI should be applicable to *territories which were then known to be of the colonial type*."[3]   In short, "non-self-governing territories" means colonies, and

3. Italics mine.

the Belgians and their cohorts should not be allowed to confuse the issue!

This proves only that the critics of the Belgian thesis had the votes, not that they had logic or truth on their side. It might well be argued that the position was not rejected on its merits and would not have been rejected if its merits had been given dispassionate consideration, since a thoroughly plausible if not absolutely convincing case can be made for the Belgian thesis. However, it must also be said that the thesis was not advanced or supported on its merits; its proponents were as little concerned as its opponents with its objective validity. Its espousal was a political maneuver, and its rejection a political response.

Since a political phenomenon deserves a political analysis, it is not amiss to point out that the state which gave its name to the Belgian thesis and the states which joined it in espousing that doctrine were not the most ardent admirers of chapter 11. They were colonial powers, states which had become increasingly worried about what they regarded as an anticolonial campaign to expand unreasonably their obligations and vulnerabilities under chapter 11. They had reacted by arguing that the Declaration Regarding Non-Self-Governing Territories was a unilateral statement of their enlightened colonial policies rather than a legal basis for international surveillance of their colonial administration, by demanding a strict construction of their reporting responsibilities under Article 73(e), by insisting that the General Assembly was incompetent to challenge national decisions to place dependencies upon or remove them from the roster of non-self-governing territories, and, in general, by invoking the domestic jurisdiction claim as a defense against the expansive development of the implications of chapter 11. Belgium, in particular, had displayed sensitivity to the use of chapter 11 as a vehicle of anticolonialism and had restricted its cooperation in the implementation of that section of the charter.

Under these circumstances, a Belgian doctrine which purported to extol chapter 11 as a beneficent instrument whose blessings should be extended beyond the colonies to all other population groups having a status analogous to that of colonial peoples could hardly be accepted at face value. It represented, in fact, an effort to turn the tables on the anticolonials, to demonstrate they did not approach the task of supervising colonial policy with clean hands, to discourage the exploitation of chapter 11 by insisting that its most avid champions were themselves vulnerable to its impact. Belgium was attempting to combat the intensification of the application of chapter 11 by demanding the extension of its range of applicability. What Belgium and its cohorts really wanted was not to get all non-self-governing peoples under the protective umbrella of chapter 11, but to get their colonies out from under that umbrella—or, at any rate, to reduce the interference with their domestic jurisdiction resulting from the continued coverage of their colonies. In essence, the tactic of the colonial powers was to relieve United Nations pressure upon their domestic jurisdiction by threatening to use the organization to bring equal pressure upon the domestic jurisdiction of their antagonists.

The anticolonial states interpreted the move in this way and succeeded in gaining United Nations support for their resistance to it. From their point of view, Belgium was, indeed, trying to confuse the issue, to slow down the campaign against colonialism.

Moreover, the articulators of the Belgian thesis took no great pains to conceal their basic political motivation. In the exposition referred to above, Dr. Van Langenhove accepted the characterization of the thesis as a "counteroffensive" against those who had undertaken to stretch chapter 11, making it the basis for a "system of quasi-trusteeship."[4] He noted that the tactic had succeeded to some degree:

> Certain [delegates at the United Nations] have apparently recognized the difficulty of contesting its merits in the case of their aboriginal peoples. For this reason, it has prompted them to maintain an attitude of prudent reserve, for it has given them to understand that an offensive aimed at the colonial powers might have repercussions in their countries by raising questions with respect to their own indigenous peoples.
>
> They consider it unwise, in these circumstances, to weaken the provision of the Charter which, in paragraph 7 of Article 2, forbids the United Nations to intervene in matters which are essentially within the domestic jurisdiction of any State.[5]

Significantly, the success upon which he commented consisted not in the persuasion of certain states to place their aborigines under chapter 11, but in the dampening of their enthusiasm for vigorous application of chapter 11 to colonies, and the increase of their respect for the reservation of domestic jurisdiction. Observing that other states had not reacted in this way but had resisted the Belgian thesis while treating it as a threat to their sovereignty, he maintained that they had brought this challenge upon themselves by their stubborn effort to use the United Nations for improper interference in colonial matters.[6]

The implication was clear: the Belgian thesis was designed to exert pressure upon the anticolonials to moderate their use of chapter 11 for making inroads upon an area regarded by the colonial powers as falling within their domestic jurisdiction. It could best serve this purpose if its

4. Van Langenhove, *The Question of the Aborigines,* pp. 79-83.
5. Ibid., pp. 83-84.
6. Ibid., p. 84.

political motivation were not completely concealed by the legal verbiage in which it was stated. While it did not succeed in the larger sense, it did have the effect of putting the anticolonials at least temporarily on the defensive and may thereby have affected the pace of their advance.

The Integration Thesis

Another response of the colonial powers to the pressure of anti-colonialism has been the assertion of what I shall call the *integration thesis*: the claim that certain overseas possessions of European states, having been formally incorporated into those states on the same footing as the metropolitan territories, are not to be regarded as colonies, put within the scope of chapter 11, or otherwise treated as falling outside the protective fence of domestic jurisdiction. This doctrine is intimately associated with the assimilationist brand of colonial policy, which emphasizes the goal of transforming natives of overseas territories into full participants in the civilization of the metropole; the integration thesis goes a step farther, by envisaging the assimilation of the *land* as well as the people in the metropolitan state. Given this background, it is not surprising that France and Portugal have been the most prominent advocates of the integration thesis.

This thesis was put to the test in the Algerian case, in the mid-fifties, when France opposed repeated moves to have the General Assembly consider the situation resulting from nationalist revolt in Algeria.[7] France had begun the legal establishment of the position that Algeria was an integral part of the state, rather than a colony, in 1834, shortly after the beginning of its occupation of Algeria. This work of legal construction had been continued by the French Constituent Assembly in 1946, and it culminated in 1958 with the entry into effect of a *loi cadre* reaffirming Algeria's status as part of France. On this ground, France insisted that the Algerian war was wholly a matter of domestic juris-diction, outside the range of United Nations concern.

The French position achieved fleeting victories but encountered ultimate defeat. In political terms, the issue was whether France should be allowed to succeed in fending off United Nations intrusion into a colonial conflict, and the initial choosing up of sides followed a predictable pattern: the colonial powers supported France against the anticolonials. Although the General Assembly passed two innocuous resolutions in 1957, expressing hope for a peaceful solution,[8] it was not

7. I am indebted to Mohamed Alwan, *Algeria Before the United Nations* (New York, Robert Speller and Sons, 1959), for many of the details in the following account.

8. General Assembly Resolutions 1012 (XI) and 1184 (XII).

until December 19, 1960, that the anticolonial group succeeded in having the Assembly adopt a resolution clearly asserting that Algeria had a right to self-determination and independence and that the United Nations had a responsibility to promote the realization of that right — in short, repudiating the French claim of domestic jurisdiction and treating the case as a colonial matter within the legitimate purview of the world organization.[9] By this time, the French had virtually surrendered the claim; President De Gaulle had declared in a speech in Algeria, on December 10, that:"It is vain to pretend that it [Algeria] constitutes a province like our Lorraine . . . It is so vain that it is not worth saying because it is not true. It is something else. It is an Algerian Algeria."[10] It is doubtful that the United Nations contributed substantially to the final triumph of the Algerian independence movement, but it did ultimately rebuff the French contention that the Algerian problem lay beyond its jurisdictional reach.

Upon its admission to United Nations membership in 1955, Portugal was immediately confronted with the question of joining the ranks of states submitting reports on colonies in accordance with Article 73(e). The Salazar regime had prepared itself to give a negative answer; although it had proudly referred to its overseas dependencies as colonies in the 1930s and 1940s, it had transformed its colonies into "provinces" by a constitutional revision in 1951.[11] Thus, Portugal relied upon the integration thesis when it submitted to the United Nations that it was not a colonial power and had no non-self-governing territories to declare.

Portugal was even less successful than France in gaining respect for the doctrine that its dependencies were integral parts of the national territory, safeguarded against United Nations intrusion by the barrier of domestic jurisdiction. Flatly refusing to accept this line, the anticolonials worked systematically to refute it and achieved the overwhelming passage, on December 15, 1960, of General Assembly Resolution 1542 (XV), which listed the Portuguese colonies and declared that Portugal was obligated, under chapter 11, to transmit information concerning them to the United Nations.[12] Moreover, the Assembly adopted, on the same date, a statement of principle to the

9. General Assembly Resolution 1573 (XV).

10. Unofficial translation in the *New York Times,* December 11, 1960.

11. James Duffy, *Portugal's African Territories: Present Realities,* Occasional Paper No. 1 (New York, Carnegie Endowment for International Peace, 1962), pp. 9, 25.

12. For an excellent analysis of Portugal's battles over the colonial issue in the United Nations, see Patricia Wohlgemuth, "The Portuguese Territories and the United Nations," *International Conciliation,* no. 545 (November 1963).

effect that "Prima facie there is an obligation to transmit information in respect of a territory which is geographically separate and is distinct ethnically and/or culturally from the country administering it," and that other elements indicative of a subordinate relationship of such a territory to the metropole strengthen the presumption that the territory should be regarded as falling within the scope of chapter 11.[13] This amounted to a repudiation, in general terms, of the integration thesis, whether advanced by France or by Portugal.

The two major doctrinal devices developed by colonial powers in their effort to use the shield of domestic jurisdiction against the thrust of anti-colonialism, the Belgian thesis and the integration thesis, require joint as well as separate analysis. In rejecting the Belgian thesis, the anticolonials insisted that only colonies, in the commonly accepted sense of the term, fall within the scope of chapter 11 and related provisions of the charter and that dependent or primitive peoples living within metropolitan territories are safely ensconced behind the wall of domestic jurisdiction. This position may well have inspired the resort of France and Portugal to the integration thesis. The integrationists attempted to exploit the argument that dependent noncolonies should escape the attentions lavished upon colonies by the United Nations; by taking more or less elaborate measures to establish a formal status different from that of colonies for their dependencies, they sought to conform to the formula proclaimed by the anticolonials. In a superficial sense, the latter appeared to be inconsistent when they rejected claims based upon the integration thesis. After all, they relied upon some version of that thesis to justify their denial of the Belgian contention that they were obligated under Article 73(e) to submit reports concerning their indigenous dependent peoples. However, their rejection of the French and Portuguese claims was based upon factual rather than doctrinal considerations. The anticolonials simply refused to be taken in by the pretense of integration, to believe that colonies were any the less colonies for being called something else. They did not reject the doctrine of integration but its abuse as a device for evading the jurisdiction of the United Nations. Their basic attitude toward naked colonies applied also to colonies thinly disguised in provincial garb.

The incompatibilities of the Belgian and the integration thesis posed greater problems of consistency for the colonial powers, which tended to support both whenever they seemed to offer any promise of effectiveness in the struggle against the anticolonial offensive. The essential point of the Belgian thesis was that *all* population groups of inferior cultural,

13. General Assembly Resolution 1541 (XV), Annex, Principles IV and V.

economic, and political status were encompassed by the provisions of chapter 11, regardless of whether they lived in colonies or in metropolitan territories; in contrast, the integration thesis held that such groups were excluded from United Nations jurisdiction if it could be maintained that they had metropolitan status, even if such status were conferred by the artificial device of assimilating overseas territory to the national domain. From the standpoint of the Belgian thesis, integration, however genuine, made no difference; from the standpoint of the integration thesis, it spelled the difference between domestic jurisdiction and vulnerability to intrusion by the United Nations.

It does not appear that the colonial powers were greatly troubled by the problem of logical consistency. Most of them could turn without discomfort from supporting the Belgian line that India or Bolivia should recognize the authority of the United Nations with respect to aborigines within their metropolitan territories, to endorsing French or Portuguese claims that the conferment of metropolitan status upon overseas possessions exempted the latter from United Nations jurisdiction. Indeed, Belgium itself was not deterred by its thesis from defending the French and Portuguese claims; Belgian logic declared those claims invalid, but Belgian votes supported them. It would be hard to find a more striking demonstration of the supremacy of policy over principle in state behavior than the spectacle of Belgium's denying the Belgian thesis in voting against General Assembly Resolution 1542 (XV), which declared that Portugal's possessions were covered by chapter 11.

The point is, of course, that the colonial powers opted for a higher consistency—a consistent effort to find some shelter behind the wall of domestic jurisdiction from the winds of anticolonialism which have been funneled through the United Nations. This is not to say that they have consistently opposed or obstructed decolonization. Clearly, they have not done so. They have distinguished between decolonization and anticolonialism; while tending generally to accept and even to promote the former, they have maintained their resentment of and opposition to the latter.

The Indian Thesis

On the other side of the colonial division, the doctrinal development of fundamental importance has been the emergence of the thesis that colonial powers have no valid claim to sovereignty over non-self-governing territories beyond their metropolitan bounds, regardless of whether they call them colonies or provinces. Quite simply, "their" colonies are not theirs. In positive terms, this is the doctrine of national self-determination, uncompromisingly applied to the European colonial system on behalf of non-European peoples. Colonial possession can no longer be deemed to give good title. If sovereignty over colonies was sanctified by traditional international law, that was because the law was formulated by and for the advantage of Europeans. Such law cannot be accepted by the non-European peoples which have now advanced, or are striving to advance, to independent statehood; indeed, their rejection of the legality of colonial rule has been confirmed by the United Nations. In a long series of General Assembly resolutions, the key item of which is Resolution 1514 (XV), the organization has proclaimed the replacement of the old legal rule by a new one which asserts the sovereign rights of all peoples and denies the legitimacy of colonialism. For reasons which will become evident below, I call this the Indian thesis.

This no-sovereignty-over-colonies doctrine, frequently asserted in abstract terms, was given its most concrete — and controversial — application in the Goa case, considered by the Security Council on December 18, 1961.[14] Portugal appealed for United Nations action against India's invasion of Goa; relying upon the integration thesis, it held that the attack clearly infringed upon Portugal's sovereign domain and thus constituted aggression. India denounced the claim of Portuguese integration of Goa as a transparent myth, maintained that Goa was a colony, and then applied the Indian thesis: Portugal had no valid sovereign title to Goa; hence, an attack on Goa could not constitute aggression against Portugal.[15] On the contrary, Goa was a part of India, and the Indian invasion was a mission of liberation designed to end the long-continuing occupation, *l'agression de tous les jours*, by Portugal. Perhaps India's action violated the old international law — but that law had been repealed. By refusing to terminate its colonialism, Portugal violated the new international law. Thus ran the Indian case.[16]

14. Security Council, Official Records: 16th Year, 987th and 988th Meetings.

15. It could be argued that, by basing its case upon the integration thesis, Portugal implicitly accepted the Indian thesis. Its zeal to prove that Goa was not a colony suggests that Portugal believed its claim to sovereignty would be weakened if Goa were regarded as remaining in colonial rather than integrated status. In any case, the Portuguese claimed that their colony was not a colony, and the Indians retorted that it was not theirs.

16. For contrasting views of the issues in this case, see J. S. Bains, *India's International Disputes* (New York, Asia Publishing House, 1962), pp. 195-208, 210, and Quincy Wright, "The Goa Incident," *American Journal of International Law 56.3* (July 1962), pp. 617-632.

The upshot of the debate was that the council divided, seven votes to four, on two resolutions. Ceylon, Liberia, the USSR, and the UAR supported a pro-Indian draft, and opposed a pro-Portuguese draft; the first failed of adoption because of inadequate support, and the second because of the Soviet veto. The issue was not put to the Assembly, and the United Nations never declared itself on the case. In a very real sense, this was a victory for the Indian thesis, since India used it in justification of a resort to force and escaped condemnation by the United Nations.

The American Thesis

The major retort to the Indian position in the Goa case can properly be labeled the American thesis, since Ambassador Adlai Stevenson of the United States made himself its chief proponent. Its basic point was that the charter's prohibition of unauthorized violence overrides everything else, including the Assembly's call for the termination of colonialism; even if the Indian thesis were accepted as entirely valid, it could not justify unilateral coercive action by India—and India could cite no mandate to take military action on behalf of the United Nations. India responded by denying the absolutist interpretation of the charter's restriction upon violence—an interpretation which few if any states are prepared to maintain when their own policy is in question—and by asserting that it acted in self-defense, to counter continuing Portuguese aggression against the Goan fragment of Indian territory and the Indian nation. The failure of the council to adopt a resolution meant that this part of the debate, like the rest, ended in a draw.

The American thesis represented a possible line of final defense against the anticolonial onslaught: if Portugal's position in Goa could not be protected against United Nations intervention by the domestic jurisdiction claim, or against Indian invasion by the assertion of sovereign title to the area, it might yet be protected against the latter by the "thou shalt not start a fight" rule of the charter. Even this, however, did not work. Although the debate ended in a draw, the case did not. In the end, nothing served to prevent an Indian victory in Goa which was applauded on one side as a triumph for anticolonialism and deplored on the other as a defeat for international law and order.

Conclusion

The use of the claim of domestic jurisdiction as a barrier to the advance of anticolonialism has been a losing battle all along, and it must now be declared that the war has been lost. The colonial problem has become firmly established as the central issue on the agenda of the

United Nations and will be removed only when decolonization has proceeded so far that no issue is left. That day may never come. European colonialism in the old style may well disappear entirely and even the fear and the reality of European neocolonialism, but human history promises no ultimate respite from conflicts arising out of the urge and power of some groups to dominate and subjugate others. So long as such problems plague international relations, international institutions will be pressed to deal with them — and to leave them alone. Insofar as the United Nations continues to develop as a vital and relevant organization, it will assert the competence and assume the responsibility to deal with them as best it can, for such problems must always be focal points of international concern.

7. The Right of Self-Determination in International Law

Leo Gross

This chapter is exclusively concerned with the status of the concept or right of self-determination in the sense of the right of an entity — a people or nation or another group — to establish itself as an independent state. Consequently the right of a people already organized into a state to choose its form of government — democracy, autocracy, and so on — or to give itself a political or economic system or to adopt a certain ideology is left out of account. This right is well established in international law although its scope and range have not been precisely defined. The Draft Declaration on Rights and Duties of States prepared by the International Law Commission in 1949 states in Article I: "Every State has the right to independence and hence to exercise freely, without dictation by any other State, all its legal powers, including the choice of its own form of government."[1]

More recently the General Assembly adopted Resolution 2131 (XX) on December 21, 1965 in which this right is recognized. Thus paragraph 1 declares: "No State has the right to intervene, directly or indirectly, for any reason whatever, in the internal or external affairs of any other State. Consequently armed intervention and all other forms of interference or attempted threats against the personality of the State or against its political, economic and cultural elements, are condemned."[2]

In view of the general though somewhat imprecise acceptance of this right of self-determination in international law, it seems unnecessary to deal with it any further. It may be enough to recall that this right may be limited by the charter of the United Nations, by bilateral treaties, or by policies and principles adopted by intergovernmental regional organizations such as the Organization of American States.

Insofar as self-determination in the first sense is concerned, the questions have frequently been raised by whom the right may be claimed and who has the duty to grant or recognize it. It has been

1. Annex to GA Res. 375 (IV), 6 Dec. 1949. UN Doc. A/1251, p. 67. See also GA Res. 2625 (XXV) "Declaration on Principles of International Law Concerning Friendly Relations and Co-operation among States in accordance with the Charter of the United Nations," adopted on Oct. 24, 1970. GAOR: Sess., Supp. no. 28 (A/8028), pp. 121, 123.

2. "Declaration on the inadmissibility of Intervention in the Domestic Affairs of States and the Protection of their Independence and Sovereignty," GA Res. 2131 (XX), Dec. 21, 1965, GAOR: 20th Sess., Supp. no. 14 (A/6014), p. 12. See also Declaration, cited above.

argued that unless a satisfactory answer can be given to these two questions it is not possible to speak of a right, properly so-called, of self-determination. This argument has merit, since usually when a right in the legal sense is created by a proper authority, the bearers of the right and the corresponding duty are ascertained or ascertainable as individuals generally or individuals or corporations belonging to a certain class or category.

The United Nations resolutions and declarations on the subject of self-determination are sometimes general and sometimes addressed to particular states. Thus colonial territories or peoples are referred to or particular governments such as Portugal are singled out. It is submitted that for the purposes of this chapter the questions of the identity of the bearer of the right and of the corresponding obligation are of no importance. The reason for this is that in any event the existence of the alleged right of self-determination in the legal sense will depend upon the authority or competence of the organs of the United Nations, particularly of the General Assembly, to create such a right or obligation. Thus if the General Assembly has no law-making competence it will be lacking this competence regardless of whether the resolution in question proclaims a right of self-determination for peoples or nations generally or for peoples or nations under colonial domination or for particular peoples like the peoples of Portugal or under Portuguese colonial rule.

Attempts are sometimes made to circumvent the question of the law-making competence of the General Assembly by arguing that the right of self-determination is included in the charter and that the relevant resolutions merely interpret the charter in an authoritative or authentic manner, that is, with a binding effect for members of the United Nations.

It is unnecessary to discuss this approach in any detail. There is an abundant literature on the subject. It may be enough to recall that there is not and never has been any consensus on the question whether the seven references to human rights in the charter are binding, singly or together, on the members. The fact that the General Assembly devoted more than 20 years to the elaboration of two Human Rights Covenants which depend for their binding force upon ratification by the members militates against the attribution of binding force to the human rights provision in the charter.

As to the right of authentic interpretation of the General Assembly there is still an unresolved controversy. No such right is conferred upon the Assembly in the charter and no such right can be derived from any relevant document such as the San Francisco Statement on the interpretation of the charter.[3]   The Advisory Opinion of the International Court of Justice in the *Expenses* case may be read as a confirmation by the court of the right of an assembly to interpret authentically and with binding force the expenditures of the organization which fall within the meaning of Article 17 (2) of the charter. Two points, however, need to be made: in the first place this right would be derived, as indeed it was derived by the court, from Article 17 (1), which confers upon the Assembly the power to "approve the budget of the Organization" and from Article 17 (2), which established the obligation of the members to bear "the expenses of the Organization . . . as apportioned by the General Assembly." In the matter of human rights there is no comparable, clear statement of legal obligation. In the second place, the Advisory Opinion of the Court has failed to resolve the conflict with respect to this matter. Members continue to resist what appears to some of them an unwarranted enlargement of the Assembly's power to interpret the charter obligations. If this is so with respect to an undoubted legal obligation, it will be all the more so when there is no solid legal anchor to which an interpretation of human rights could be attached.

The conclusion then emerges, at least provisionally, that the alleged right of self-determination cannot be derived from a simple interpretation of the charter. This aspect of the problem albeit in a somewhat different approach will be discussed in the following section.

Generally it may be said that a right which is claimed to be grounded in international law must be the product of a law-making process. The classic law-creating agencies—the formal sources of international law—are treaties and custom. Article 38 of the Statute of the International Court of Justice adds "general principles of law recognized by civilized nations." It is controversial whether these principles are those of municipal or of international law. Be that as it may, they will be left out of account here for two reasons. First, there is no space to undertake a systematic comparative study of the different systems of municipal law, and second I have a strong suspicion that the results of such an effort are not likely to be productive.

Finally, the question will be raised whether the General Assembly has a law-making competence, in particular whether its resolutions and declarations are legally binding upon the members. It may be said at once that certain resolutions of the Assembly, namely those relating to the internal functioning of the organization such as appointments, admission to membership, and others of this variety are undoubtedly legally binding providing they are in conformity with the charter itself.

3. See Leo Gross, "The United Nations and the Role of Law," *International Organization,* 19 (1965), 538f.

Political discretion does not mean that the rules of the charter can be disregarded. As Judge Bustamante said in the *Expenses* case, "The real reason for the obedience of States Members to the authorities of the Organization is the conformity of the mandates of its competent organs with the text of the Charter." He went on to say: "It cannot be maintained that the resolutions of any organ of the United Nations are not subject to review: that would amount to declaring the pointlessness of the Charter or its absolute subordination to the judgment—always fallible—of the organs."[4]

In order to avoid confusion between the two meanings of self-determination, I shall use "right to self-determination" in referring to the right of a people or nation to establish itself as a state,[5] and "right of self-determination" in referring to the right of the people of a state to choose its form of government, economic system, and so on.

The charter being a multilateral treaty may be and is the source of legal obligation for its members. "Self-determination of peoples" is referred to in Article 1 (a) of the charter of the United Nations as a "principle." It is mentioned in Article 55 which restates the purposes in more specific language. Paragraph *c* of this article refers generally to "human rights and fundamental freedoms" among the purposes which the United Nations shall promote. Self-determination is not specifically included in the list of objectives in Article 73 relating to non-self-governing territories. Development of self-government is, however, included in Article 73 (b). "Self-government or independence" is one of the basic objectives of the Trusteeship system but its implementation is made dependent, in Article 76 (b), on the terms of the trusteeship agreements.

The members which were responsible for the administration of non-self-governing territories and trust territories have largely divested themselves of their responsibilities.

From the recital of the relevant charter provisions it is *clear that nowhere has a right to self-determination* in the legal sense been established. I have no intention to disparage the potency of self-determination as a principle and a purpose of the United Nations. But no matter how potent it may be in the actual operations of the United Nations, still it is not a right in terms of the charter.

However, treaties may be interpreted and what is known as subsequent conduct of the parties is relevant in this context. Subsequent

4. International Court of Justice *Reports* 1962, pp. 151, 304.
5. This is in conformity with General Assembly Resolution 1514 (XV) and the Declaration cited above, p. 124.

conduct of the parties may also be considered as a method of amending the treaty apart from any formal procedure for amendment which may be laid down in the treaty. The formal procedure for amending the charter is the subject of chapter 18 (Articles 108 and 109), but this procedure has not been applied in connection with self-determination. To put it in another way, the principle of self-determination has not been converted into a right to self-determination by an amendment of the charter. It remains to be examined whether such a transformation has occurred as a result of subsequent conduct.

The International Law Commission included in Article 27 (3) of its Draft Articles on the Law of Treaties devoted to the "General Rule of Interpretation," the following clause: "There shall be taken into account, together with the context: (b) any subsequent practice in the application of the treaty which establishes the understanding of the parties regarding its interpretation."[6]

In its commentary the commission pointed out that recourse to subsequent practice as an element of interpretation is well established in the jurisprudence of international tribunals. The question obviously arises how widespread subsequent conduct must be in order to qualify as a tool of interpretation. On this point the commission was quite specific by stipulating in its 1964 draft that the practice must be one which "establishes the understanding of *all* the parties." In the 1966 final draft the word "all" was omitted but the commission stated that:

> By omitting the word "all" the Commission did not intend to change the rule. It considered that the phrase "the understanding of the parties" necessarily means "the parties as a whole." It omitted the word "all" merely to avoid any possible misconception that every party must individually have engaged in the practice where it suffices that it should have accepted the practice.[7]

The clause quoted above was considered by the Vienna Conference on the Law of Treaties in 1968 and the Committee of the Whole recommended its adoption.[8] In the committee the United States proposed an amendment the object of which appears to have been to

6. Reports of the International Law Commission on the Second Part of its seventeenth session . . . and on its eighteenth session . . . GAOR: 21st Sess., Supp. no. 9 (A/6309/Rev. 1), p. 49. The text is identical with Art. 31(3b) of the 1969 Vienna Convention on the Law of Treaties except for the replacement of "understanding" by "agreement."

7. Ibid., p. 53. Italics supplied.

8. Draft Report of the Committee of the Whole on its work at the first session of the Conference, Doc. A/CON. 39/G.1/L.370, p. 141.

incorporate in the text the essence of the commission's commentary. This proposal, however, was rejected.[9]

It is relevant to note that the Committee of the Whole modified the text of Article 4 submitted by the ILC to make it clear that the draft articles on the law of treaties do apply to treaties which are constituent instruments of an international organization "without prejudice to any relevant rules of the organization."[10]

As I am not aware of the existence of "any relevant rules" of the United Nations in this matter, Article 5 of the Vienna Convention may be applied to the charter of the United Nations. If this is so it would be necessary to examine whether the "principle of self-determination" has been generally understood or has been understood by all the parties to the charter as constituting a "right to self-determination." The same examination would then have to be made with respect to the human rights provisions. More specifically, it would have to be determined whether the practice established the understanding of all the parties that these provisions on human rights constitute rights and obligations in the legal sense and whether these rights and obligations have come to encompass the "right to self-determination."

It seems very doubtful, to put it no higher, whether the subsequent practice is sufficiently consistent to permit a positive conclusion along the lines indicated. There is no question that the oratory in the General Assembly and the resolutions of the Assembly are replete with affirmations of the "right to self-determination." But in testing the application of Article 31 (3b), the subsequent practice of the members, that is, the parties as distinguished from the practice of the organs of the United Nations, it is necessary to evaluate the behavior of the so-called colonial countries, along with the behavior of the parties which have advocated unconditional and speedy decolonization. The negative attitude and behavior of some of the parties would defeat any attempt to attribute to the subsequent practice the degree of universality indicated in the commentary of the International Law Commission. In the present submission subsequent practice as an element of interpretation does not support the proposition that the *principle* of self-determination is to be interpreted as a *right* to self-determination or that the human rights

9. Ibid., p. 136. The text of the proposed amendment was as follows: "Any subsequent practice in the application of the treaty which establishes the *common* understanding *of the meaning of the terms as between the parties generally.*"

10. Ibid., p. 32. The commission's draft made the applicability of the articles to constituent instruments "subject to any relevant rules of the organization." Ibid., p. 26. Same text in Art. 5 of the Vienna Convention.

provisions have come to be interpreted as rights with corresponding obligations either generally or specifically with respect to the right to self-determination.

As indicated above, subsequent practice is also relevant as a process for modifying treaties. As formulated in Article 38 of the ILC's draft, it reads as follows: "A treaty may be modified by subsequent practice in the application of the treaty establishing the agreement of the parties to modify its provisions."[11]

This article was deleted by the Committee of the Whole of the Vienna Conference.[12]

However, the clause proposed by the ILC has the support of at least one arbitral tribunal to which the commission refers in its commentary, namely a tribunal between France and the United States which was concerned with the interpretation of a bilateral air transport agreement. In the context of the award of 1963 the tribunal's statement was probably no more than a *dictum*. The commission refers to no other authority. For the purpose of this discussion and subject to Article 5 of the Vienna Convention, let us assume that Article 38 was declaratory of customary international law and not merely an attempt at progressive development of the law. The commission, in its commentary, pointed out that: "In formulating the rule in this way the Commission intended to indicate that the subsequent practice, even if every party might not itself have actively participated in the practice, must be such as to establish the agreement of the parties *as a whole* to the modification in question."[13] Applying the rule as interpreted by the commission to the question of self-determination the conclusion appears inescapable that the practice of the parties as distinguished from the practice of the organs of the United Nations has not been sufficiently consistent and not as widespread as would be necessary to support the conclusion that the principle of self-determination has been modified and is now to be regarded as a right to self-determination with a corresponding obligation on the part of the colonial or other states involved.

The relevance of the practice of the organs, that is, of the resolutions and declarations adopted by the organs of the United Nations, will be taken up below.

To sum up, the charter does not establish a right to self-determination; the principle of self-determination and the articles of human rights in the charter cannot be interpreted as having been trans-

11. *International Law Commission Report,* p. 65.
12. *Draft Report of the Committee of the Whole,* p. 165.
13. *International Law Commission Report,* p. 66.

formed into legal rights with corresponding legal obligation as a result of subsequent practice, and they cannot be construed as having been modified by subsequent practice.

The next formal source of international law to be considered is custom, or in the words of the Statute of International Court of Justice, "international custom, as evidence of a general practice accepted as law" (Article 38 [1b]). It is generally agreed that in order to constitute a rule of customary international law two elements must be shown to be present. General practice in the first place, and acceptance of this practice as law in the second place. The first element is generally characterized as objective and the second as subjective or psychological. Obviously the first is more easily ascertainable from the behavior of states than the second but in proceedings at law proof of both elements has been required.

The pronouncements on the subject by the Permanent Court of International Justice and the International Court of Justice are infrequent but remarkably consistent. The Permanent Court in the *Lotus* case (1927) had the opportunity to elaborate the distinction between mere usage and usage which is required as a matter of legal obligation. The court held first that the rules of law emanate from the will of states as expressed in treaties or "by usages generally accepted as expressing principles of law," and second that custom must have "the force of law establishing it," and third that the party invoking a rule of law must prove that the states have not merely performed certain acts or abstained from performing them, but that they did so out of a sense of legal obligation. In the *Lotus* case the question related to the exercise of criminal jurisdiction and the agent for the French government referred to a number of judgments to the effect that states have refrained from exercising jurisdiction in certain circumstances. On this point, which is relevant to the present analysis, the court said that the judgments relied upon by the French agent: "would merely show that States had often, in practice, abstained from instituting criminal proceedings, and not that they recognized themselves as being obliged to do so; for only if such abstention were based on their being conscious of having a duty to abstain would it be possible to speak of an international custom."[14] The judgment went against the French government, France having failed to prove the existence of the sense of duty, or what is commonly called, *opinio juris*.

In a more recent case, the International Court of Justice had occasion

---

14. *Permanent Court of International Justice,* Series A, no. 10, p. 28.

to set forth its view on customary international law. In the *Asylum* case the court stated:

> Finally, the Colombian Government has referred to a large number of particular cases in which diplomatic asylum was in fact granted and respected. But it has not shown that the alleged rule of unilateral and definitive qualification was invoked or . . . that it was, apart from conventional stipulations, exercised by the States granting asylum as *a right appertaining to them and respected by the territorial States as a duty incumbent on them and not merely for reasons of political expediency*. The facts brought to the knowledge of the Court disclose so much uncertainty and contradiction . . . and the practice has been so much influenced by *considerations of political expediency* in the various cases, that it is not possible to discern in all this any constant and uniform usage, accepted as law.[15]

In another context, the court made its position abundantly clear:

> The Party which relies on a custom of this kind must prove that this custom is established in such a manner that it has become binding on the other Party. The Colombian Government must prove that the rule invoked by it is *in accordance with a constant and uniform usage* practiced by the States in question, and that this *usage is the expression of a right appertaining to the State granting asylum and a duty incumbent* on the territorial State. This follows from Article 38 of the Statute of the Court.[16]

The court adhered to this position in the *Fisheries*, *Rights of Nationals* and the *Continental Shelf* cases, in which the *Lotus* case was expressly confirmed.[17]

If these criteria of customary international law are applied to the right to self-determination the conclusion is inescapable that this right is not or not yet one that can be characterized as based on customary international law. True, self-determination has been granted or conceded to an impressively large number of peoples or nations but it would not be possible to supply the missing element, namely that practice was based on a sense of legal obligation. On the contrary, the practice of decolonization is a perfect illustration of a usage dictated by political expediency or necessity or sheer convenience. And moreover, it is neither constant nor uniform.

It was to be expected that the stand taken by the court on the concept of customary international law and the exacting standards of proof were subjected to a good deal of penetrating criticism. But while it is easy to

15. Reports 1950, p. 277. The court referred again to political expediency, pp. 285, 286. Italics supplied.

16. Ibid., p. 276. Italics supplied.

17. ICJ *Reports* 1969, pp. 3, 44.

criticize the court for supporting an excessively rigid position, it is extremely difficult to suggest a concept which, operationally, would be more satisfactory by opening the way to greater flexibility. Only one approach will be discussed here which merits serious consideration by virtue of the great authority supporting it.

The late Judge Lauterpacht while fully aware of the difficulties of proving the *opinio juris* was opposed to dispensing with it altogether on the ground that to do so would be contrary to practice. But he offered an alternative in the following:

> Unless judicial activity is to result in reducing the legal significance of the most potent source of rules of international law, namely the conduct of States, it would appear that the accurate principle on the subject consists in regarding *all uniform conduct* of Governments (or, in appropriate cases, abstention therefrom) as evidencing the *opinio necessitatis juris except when it is shown that the conduct in question was not accompanied by any such intention.* The Judgment in the *Asylum* case is not inconsistent with some such approach. The solution may not be altogether satisfactory, but it is probably more acceptable than the alternative method of exacting rigid proof of the existence of international customary law in a manner which may reduce to a bare minimum its part as a source of law. Of this, the decision in the *Lotus* case . . . provides an interesting example. While it is impracticable to demand positive proof of the existence of legal conviction in relation to a particular line of conduct, it is *feasible and desirable to permit proof that in fact the opinio necessitatis juris* was absent.[18]

It is of secondary importance whether Lauterpacht's alternative approach is compatible with the jurisprudence of the court. What is important is to ask whether it really offers an alternative and secondly, whether this alternative would lead to a result different from that based on the jurisprudence of the court. A state which claims the existence of a rule on the ground of "uniform conduct" or "uniform abstention" of governments would be hard put to it to furnish the required evidence. In the second place, it would still have to prove that this conduct has become binding on the other state or, following Lauterpacht's alternative, that the other state was not unaware of the *opinio juris* implied in its conduct. On the other hand, that state would probably be able to show that its conduct was not accompanied by any sense of legal obligation.

It is consequently submitted that in so far as self-determination is concerned the acceptance of Lauterpacht's alternative would not lead

---

18. Sir Hersch Lauterpacht, *The Development of International Law by the International Court* (New York, Praeger, 1958), p. 380. Italics supplied.

to the finding that it has become a rule of customary international law in the sense of creating a right on the one side and a duty on the other. Practice there is but it falls short of "uniform conduct of Governments" and even if it did meausre up to it—and there is room here for differences of opinion—it would be easy to argue the absence of the *opinio juris*.

Faced with the difficulty of accelerating the growth of customary international law in an international system subject to accelerating change and the difficulty of invoking or proving rules of that law, governments and writers have taken to argue that certain resolutions and declarations of the General Assembly have law-creating effect. In particular such effect has been claimed for the General Assembly Resolution 1514 (XV) adopted on December 14, 1960.[19]

Whether salvation, or escape from the confinement of the classic law-creating procedures, can be found by attributing law-making competence to the General Assembly generally or in some particular circumstances has become a matter of lively controversy. There is no room to examine this controversy in any detail nor is there any need for it, since the arguments on either side of the fence are well-known. Nonetheless it may be useful to indicate some salient points in the controversy.

At the outset it may be well to recall that the new dispensation has not yet received judicial imprimatur. The relevance of General Assembly resolutions and similar acts of other international organizations was argued extensively in the *South West Africa* cases. The International Court of Justice in its judgment in the Second Phase in 1966 limited itself to its traditional function, that is to apply the law as it finds it and not to indulge in judicial law making. In the dissenting opinions a variety of points of view was expressed ranging from a denial by Judge Jessup that the General Assembly has law-making competence to the affirmation of such competence by Judge Tanaka. The applicants argued: "that the practice of States and the views of the competent international organs are so clear, so explicit, and so unanimous in respect of the policies against discrimination, that such standards have achieved the status of an international rule of law, as a legal conclusion based upon the application of Article 38."[20]

Judge Jessup, while accepting the alternative proposition of the applicants, based on the same grounds, that there is "an international standard as an aid to interpretation," rejected the contention that "the

19. G.A.O.R.: 15th Sess. Supp. no. 16 (A/4684), p. 66.
20. ICJ *Reports* 1966, p. 431.

so-called norm of nondiscrimination had become a rule of international law through reiterated statements in resolutions of the General Assembly, of the International Labour Organization, and of other international bodies." Such a contention, he said, would be open to attack on the ground: "that since international bodies lack a true legislative character, their resolutions alone cannot create law."[21]

Elsewhere in his dissenting opinion Judge Jessup repeated that he did "not accept Applicants' alternative plea which would test the apartheid policy against an assumed rule of international law ('norm')," and that it was "therefore not necessary to discuss here whether unanimity is essential to the existence of *communis opinio juris.*" But, said Judge Jessup:

"the accumulation of expressions of condemnation of apartheid..., especially as recorded in the resolutions of the General Assembly of the United Nations, are proof of the pertinent contemporary international community standard . . . This Court is bound to take account of such a consensus as providing the standard to be used in the interpretation of Article 2 of the Mandate."[22]

Judge Tanaka, displaying a remarkable degree of judicial boldness, expressed his views as follows:

Of course, we cannot admit that individual resolutions, declarations, judgments, decisions, etc., having binding force upon the members of the organization. What is required for customary international law is the repetition of the same practice; accordingly, in this case resolutions, declarations, etc., on the same matter in the same, or diverse, organizations must take place repeatedly.

Parallel with such repetition, each resolution, declaration, etc., being considered as the manifestation of the collective will of individual participatant States, the will of the international community can certainly be formulated more quickly and more accurately as compared with the traditional method of the normative process. *This collective, cumulative and organic process of custom-generation* can be characterized as the middle way between legislation by convention and the traditional process of custom making, and can be seen to have an important role from the viewpoint of the development of international law.

In short, the accumulation of authoritative pronouncements such as resolutions, declarations, decisions, etc., concerning the interpretation of the Charter by the competent organs of the international

21. Ibid., p. 432. In a note, Judge Jessup added: "The literature on this point is abundant."

22. Ibid., p. 441.

community can be characterized as evidence of the international custom referred to in Article 38, par. 1 (b).[23]

In his dissenting opinion Judge Tanaka also said: "the method of the generation of customary international law is in the stage of transformation from being an individualistic process to being a collectivistic process.[24]

Judge Jessup, at the beginning of his Dissenting Opinion, quotes with approval a statement by Charles Evans Hughes, who was a member of the Permanent Court of International Justice and later Chief Justice of the United States. It was also quoted with approval by the late Judge Lauterpacht to whom he pays tribute:

> A dissent in a court of last resort is an appeal to the brooding spirit of the law, to the intelligence of a future day, when a later decision may possibly correct the error into which the dissenting judge believes the court to have been betrayed.[25]

Judge Tanaka's forward-looking reasoning may well belong "to the brooding spirit of the law" but the judicial caution of Judge Jessup is more in tune with current notions about the law-generating process. Indeed if we have already reached the stage where a community-centered process has taken the place of the classic state-centered process, that is, the process of consent, then it would be difficult to understand why the General Assembly itself is still using the method of treaty law as a vehicle for creating and making binding upon the states the political, civil, economic and other human rights, the duty of non-discrimination on racial grounds, and similar matters. If Judge Tanaka's view is accepted as a correct statement of the law then there is no doubt that self-determination has become a right based on customary international law through the repeated resolutions of the General Assembly over a number of years.

However, if Judge Jessup's view is the correct one, and in the present submission it is, then the resolutions and declarations on self-determination would at best be productive of a standard of interpretation. This standard could be used in the interpretation of an appropriate treaty clause which established an obligation in the matter of self-determination, just as Judge Jessup proposed to use it in order to test the execution by South Africa of its obligation under Article 2 of the mandate. But as has been shown above, there is no such clause in the charter establishing an obligation and none could be found in customary international law.

23. Ibid., p. 292. Italics supplied.
24. Ibid., p. 294.
25. Ibid., p. 32/15.

The International Court of Justice in the *Expenses* case attached some significance to the practice of the General Assembly in interpreting the range of Article 17 (2) of the charter and the resulting scope of the financial obligations of the members.[26] Judge Spender in his Separate Opinion took categorical exception to the view that subsequent practice of organs of the United Nations as evidenced in resolutions and declarations can be used in the same manner as subsequent practice of states for the purpose of interpretation. Judge Fitzmaurice shared this view in his Separate Opinion. The gist of Judge Spender's opinion is that "unless it is of a peaceful, uniform and undisputed character accepted by all current Members" practice of organs has no probative value.[27] The question of the proper role of the practice of organs of international organization while not new is of substantial complexity.[28]

In any event, subsequent practice of organs like subsequent practice of states parties to a treaty could only serve as a tool of interpretation and on condition that it is accepted by all member states. As indicated earlier, subsequent practice, whether of organs or of states, does not lead to the conclusion that the charter established a right to self-determination and a corresponding duty on the part of the member states in question.

It is now necessary to consider the question whether a single resolution such as General Assembly Resolution 1514 (XV) can be said to be legally binding on members of the United Nations, that is, the question of the law-making competence of the General Assembly. That members of the United Nations hold an affirmative view with respect to this question needs no proof. Some statements may be quoted for the purpose of illustration. Thus in the aftermath of the 1966 judgment in the *South West Africa* cases, the Soviet delegate expressed the view that the court "should have rendered a decision consistent with General Assembly resolution 1514 (XV), condemning racism and colonialism." The delegate of Iran stated that "the issue in the present case was that legislation enacted by the United Nations had not been put into effect," whereas the delegate of Pakistan, echoing Judge Tanaka, declared:

> The insensitivity of these Judges to current international standards or legal norms, their disregard of the mode of generation of

26. See on this Leo Gross, "Expenses of the United Nations for Peace-Keeping Operations: The Advisory Opinion of the International Court of Justice," *International Organization,* 17 (1963), 1-35.

27. ICJ *Reports* 1962, p. 195.

28. For a detailed analysis see Salo Engel, " 'Living' International Constitutions and the World Court (Subsequent Practice of International Organs under their Constituent Instruments)," *International and Comparative Law Quarterly,* 16 (1967), 865-910.

customary international law, their refusal to apply, in the performance of their functions in accordance with Article 38 of the Statute of
the International Court of Justice, directives manifested in the resolutions of the General Assembly, are things which are bound to perturb
enlightened public opinion throughout the world.[29]

The issue has thus been squarely raised whether the General
Assembly has indeed the competence which some members believe it
has.

In this connection, reference may be made to a memorandum by the
office of Legal Affairs in the U.N. Secretariat on the "Use of the Terms
'Declaration' and 'recommendation' " of April 2, 1962 appended to this
chapter.

Paragraph 4 of the memorandum states what I believe to be the
correct view on the subject. First, a declaration or recommendation of a
UN organ "cannot be made binding upon Member States," and second
insofar as the "strong expectation that Members of the international
community will abide by it . . . is gradually justified by State practice, a
declaration may by *custom* become recognized as laying down rules
binding upon States."

In a similar vein, the late Secretary-General, Dag Hammarskjöld,
stated that "all international organizations have under their charters or
constitutions only very limited powers of imposing legal obligations on
Member States without their consent. Thus there can be no question of
legislating international law in such organizations."[30]

There is a fairly widespread tendency to accord to resolutions of
international organs some relevance in the process of creating new
international law without going so far as regarding them as a means of
"instant" law. My own view has been that, depending upon the subject
of the resolution, the degree of preparation that was devoted to its
formulation, the extent to which it is supported and accepted by the
relevant members, resolutions represent a stage in the evolution of a
new rule of customary international law unless the General Assembly
decides to treat such resolutions merely as a step toward an international convention. The latter procedure was followed in connection
with human rights, the legal principles governing the activities of states

29. G.A.O.R.: 21st Sess., Fifth Committee, 1124th mtg., October 10, 1966,
pp. 23-25 (Iran). Ibid., 1414th Plenary mtg., Doc, A/PV. 1409-1431, p. 10.
30. Andrew W. Cordier and Wilder Foote, eds., *Public Papers of the Secre-
taries-General of the United Nations,* II, *Dag Hammarskjöld* (New York,
Columbia University Press, 1972), 602. See also Tammes, *Decisions of International Organs as a Source of International Law,* 94 Hague Recueil des Cours,
265-363 (1958, II).

in the exploration and use of outer space, racial discrimination, and other matters. Law creation then follows the traditional pattern of seeking and receiving formal consent through ratification.

In other instances, a resolution or declaration has so far at any rate been the first and last step. This has been so in connection with General Assembly Resolution 1803 (XVIII) on Permanent Sovereignty over Natural Resources of December 14, 1962, and the Resolution 1514 (XV) which is here relevant, the "Declaration on the granting of Independence to colonial countries and peoples," of December 14, 1960. Resolution 1803 (XVII) may have a very potent impact indeed on the *quantum* of compensation to be paid in case of nationalization of alien property. The old formula "prompt, adequate and effective" has been under attack at least since 1930 and the new formula "appropriate compensation" may well be on the road to becoming part of the customary international law. But it is well to bear in mind that *opinio juris* without practice can no more produce a rule of law than practice without *opinio juris*.[31]

In terms of Article 38 (1d) of the statute of the International Court of Justice such resolutions may serve "as a subsidiary means for the determination of rules of law." I suggested that they may rank with, or even ahead of, "the teachings of the most highly qualified publicists" but below judicial decisions.[32]

A somewhat similar intermediate position has been expressed as follows:

> Without having the character of a treaty, with all its constitutional implications, resolutions of this kind unquestionably are an important link in the continuing process of development and formulation of new principles of international law. In some cases they will be preparatory to formal international covenants; in other cases they will serve as highly authoritative statements of international law in certain fields.[33]

I cannot fully subscribe to the last part of the statement though it would be possible to apply it in fields such as cooperation in outer space, where there is little or no settled law at all.

31. On this see Leo Gross, "The United Nations and the Role of Law," pp. 555-558.

32. Ibid., p. 557.

33. Wolfgang Friedmann, *The Changing Structure of International Law* (New York, Columbia University Press, 1964), p. 139. See also S. K. Bailey, "Making International Law in the United Nations," *Proceedings,* American Society of International Law, 61st Annual Meeting (1967), p. 239.

Relevant in this context is the international cooperative effort to produce an impartial and objective textbook on international law, edited by Max Sørensen. According to this, resolutions and declarations of the General Assembly are not in themselves acts creative of new rules of international law because the General Assembly has no legislative power. On the other hand, a unanimous or nearly unanimous resolution may contribute to the formation of customary international law or be evidence of such a rule.[34] In this textbook it is also suggested that some resolutions may manifest a recognition of certain legal principles by members voting for them, a possibility which certainly cannot be excluded in some areas such as outer space but it would be a matter of proving that the vote was indeed intended to express acceptance of legal principles by the members concerned.

Finally, this textbook suggests that resolutions may be interpretations of rules or principles in the charter and which are themselves binding. This view has already been discussed. The General Assembly has no power of authentic, that is, binding interpretation. In the area of self-determination there are no binding rules or principles in the charter.

It may be worthwhile to include in this survey the views on self-determination of a distinguished Polish jurist, Manfred Lachs, who has been elected a member of the International Court of Justice. He agrees with the position I have taken that "the relevant provisions of the Charter were not creative of a new rule of international law. All they did was to confirm and lay down a principle which had long been growing and maturing in International Society."[35] But the issue of self-determination has become a permanent item on the Agenda of the United Nations. Resolution 1514 (XV) should "be viewed as interpreting the principles of 'self-determination' enunciated in Chapter I" of the charter. Lachs concludes that "under the circumstances, there seems no doubt that the interpretation given by the General Assembly is authoritative and binding."[36]

34. M. Virally, "The Sources of International Law" in Max Sørensen, ed., *Manual of Public International Law* (New York, St. Martin's Press, 1968), p. 162.

35. "The Law In and Of the United Nations," *Indian Journal of International Law*, 1 (1961), 432. Along similar lines the following statement is relevant! "Thus it might seem that it is only within the last generation that it has come to be admitted that there is a principle of self-determination of peoples which must underline all international law. Yet, as the foregoing analysis of the process of changes in territorial sovereignty and of state succession must sufficiently demonstrate, that principle has always underlain the system of international law." Clive Parry, "The Function of Law in the International Community," in Max Sørensen, ed., *Manual of Public International Law*, p. 19.

36. Ibid., pp. 438, 439.

Writing three years later, Lachs seems to have modified his views or perhaps given them a somewhat more precise formulation. The 1960 Declaration on the ending of colonialism like the 1948 Declaration on Human Rights are from the formal point of view only resolutions but they set in motion a process the political and legal effects of which go far. One cannot but agree with this proposition. Lachs goes on to say that these and other resolutions "lay solid foundations for obligatory norms, which, in general, constitute the work of those organizations. For this reason they have undoubtedly a part in the formulation of international law."[37]

I shall make no attempt to weigh the opinions on one side or the other of the argument. The weight of the reasoned argument as distinguished from sheer oratory may well be on the side of those who accord to resolutions of the General Assembly a role in the formation of law. From a legal standpoint all I can say is that I regard this view as a better one and as being more in accord with the prevailing system of international law and the character of the statal environment in which it functions. Both the environment and the system are far from satisfactory but we have to live in and with it.

Before leaving this part of my analysis, two or three factors relating to self-determination may be mentioned briefly. The first factor is that the General Assembly has recently characterized and condemned as "crimes against humanity" certain activities in the context of a denial of the right to self-determination. Thus in Resolution 2184 (XXI) of December 12, 1966, the Assembly "*condemns* as a crime against humanity, the policy of the Government of Portugal, which violates the economic and political rights of the indigenous population by the Settlement of foreign immigrants in the Territories and by the exporting of African workers to South Africa."[38]

The General Assembly has also condemned "the policies of apartheid practiced by the Government of South Africa as a crime against humanity."[39] Could denial of the right to self-determination be characterized as a crime against humanity at some future time?[40]

---

37. "Le Role des organizations internationales dans la formation du droit international," in *Mélanges offerts à Henri Rolin* (1964), p. 166. My translation.

38. G.A.O.R. 21st Sess., Supp. no. 16 (A/6316), p. 70.

39. G.A. Resolution 2202 (XXI) of October 16, 1966, ibid., p. 20. Both resolutions were recalled in Res. 2144 (XXI) of October 26, 1966, ibid., p. 47.

40. This has indeed been done indirectly by Resolution 2621 (XXV) of October 12, 1970, in which the Assembly declared, "The further continuation of colonialism in all its forms and manifestations a crime which constitutes a violation of the Charter of the United Nations, the Declaration on the Granting of

The second factor is the increasingly strident appeal to assist in the struggle for independence. Thus in the Resolution 2184 (XXI) referred to above, the Assembly "*appeals* to all States to give the peoples of the Territories under Portuguese domination the moral and material support necessary for the restoration of their inalienable rights." If this is not a call to what in other contexts is called "wars of national liberation" it comes close enough to it. It will be noted that the appeal is addressed to "all States" which, conveniently, includes The People's Republic of China.[41]

It is interesting that in the objective and impartial *Manual* Professor K. Skubiszewski considers that Article 2 (4) of the charter does not apply in the relations between a state and its people, that the right of the people to fight the government is deduced "from the principle of self-determination and the political right of revolution," and that the conflict while "formally domestic" in nature is nonetheless a "conflict between armed forces which represent different authorities and different peoples. Fighting by the local people for the independence of their country that is part of the colonial empire of an extraneous power, sometimes referred to as a war of liberation, is lawful."[42] If such fighting is lawful on one side, can it be lawful on the other side as well? Is military or other assistance to the "local people" also lawful?[43]

Independence to Colonial Countries and Peoples and the principles of international law." G.A.O.R.: 25th Sess., Supp. no. 28 (A/8028), p. 2.

41. See par. 2 of the above resolution, and Resolution 2627 (XXV) of October 24, 1970, ibid., p. 4, Resolution 2708 (XXV) of December 14, 1970, ibid., p. 7, and Resolution 2625 (XXV) of October 24, 1970, ibid., p. 124.

42. "Use of Force by States, Collective Security, Law of War and Neutrality," in Max Sørensen, ed., *Manual of Public International Law,* p. 771. The "inalienable right of all colonial peoples to self-determination" and the "legitimacy" of their struggle for freedom "by all appropriate means" or "by all the necessary means" at their disposal has been reaffirmed or recognized in Resolutions 2627 (XXV) of October 24, 1970, and 2708 (XXV) of December 14, 1970, ibid. See also Res. 2734 (XXV) of December 16, 1970, ibid., p. 23, par. 18, and Res. 2649 (XXV) of November 30, 1970, ibid., p. 74, par. 2.

43. In this connection Resolution 3103 (XXVIII) of December 12, 1973 entitled "Basic principles of the legal status of the combatants struggling against colonial and alien domination and racist régimes" is relevant. The resolution confirms that colonialism is a crime (see Res. 2621 [XXV], n. 38a above) and that struggle for self-determination is legitimate, and declares that any attempt to suppress this struggle is contrary to the Charter and various resolutions and "constitutes a threat to international peace and security," that armed conflicts involving such a struggle are to be regarded as "international armed conflicts," and that the Geneva Conventions of 1949 should apply to the combatants carrying on this struggle. In Resolution 3163 (XXVIII) of December 14, 1973, the Assembly urges in par. 7 "all States and the specialized agencies . . . to provide

The third factor is the increasing tendency to enlist the plenary powers of the Security Council for the purpose of achieving the policy objectives formulated in the resolutions of the General Assembly. Suppose that the Council would resort to enforcement action in order to assist a people to achieve self-determination, would such action transform the principle into a right to self-determination? If such an action were to be construed as a sanction in the legal sense then—to use Kelsen's terminology—the denial of self-determination would be a delict, that is, an infringement of a people's legal right to self-determination.

The standpoint from which the position of the right of self-determination has been considered so far may be identified as positivistic. It might be of interest to study the problem of self-determination from the point of view of the policy-oriented methodology. Characterized by the employment "of certain processes of thought—a frame of reference, a method of inquiry, a disciplined and contextual mode of analysis,"[44] it prefers to regard international law as part of the world power process,[45] as a result of which the law is drained of its normative character and content. The role of law in the process of power is broken down into seven functional phases of decision making, namely prescription, recommendation, intelligence, invocation, application, appraisal, and termination.[46] Each of these is broken down into a number of tasks. The reader may wish to consider the desirability of applying this multiphased approach to the problem of self-determination. The overriding goal of this policy-oriented approach is an international law of human dignity which is bound to reflect subjective value preferences and judgments.

Self-determination has a place in this mode of thinking as a goal but it is one of several goals:

> While according great deference to the principle of self-determination, such international law might, further, balance self-determination with capacity for, and acceptance of, responsibility and seek an organization of government in territorial units large enough to discharge responsibility. Contemporary techniques in community plan-

moral and material assistance to all peoples struggling for their freedom and independence in the colonial territories . . . in particular to the national liberation movements of the territories in Africa—in consultation, as appropriate, with the Organization of African Unity."

44. Myres S. McDougal and Associates, *Studies in World Public Order* (New Haven, Yale University Press, 1960), p. 990.

45. Ibid., p. 12.

46. Ibid., p. 14.

ning might be employed to encourage the establishment of appropriately balanced, economic regional communities. The goal of a law of freedom is not the extreme of anarchy but an ordered, productive, shared liberty and responsibility.[47]

From an impressionistic point of view it would seem that the deference thus accorded to self-determination falls short of the principles embodied in Resolution 1514 (XV). That resolution calls for transfer of "all powers to the peoples . . . without any conditions or reservations" and declares specifically that there must be no "balancing"—"Inadequacy of political, economic, social or educational preparedness should never serve as a pretext for delaying independence." Regional communities might be incompatible with respect for "the integrity of their national territory," that is, the territory of the dependent peoples. To the extent that this approach is policy-oriented the outcome of analysis may depend upon which country's policy is chosen implicitly or explicitly as the overarching goal.

The foregoing analysis suggests the conclusion that the "principle" of self-determination in Article 1(2) of the charter has not been transformed into a right to self-determination and that, independently of the charter, no such right has become part of customary international law, for the following reasons:

1. The General Assembly has no competence to interpret charter principles with binding force for all or some members;

2. The "principle" of self-determination has not been transformed into a "right" to self-determination by the subsequent practice of the parties as a means of interpretation of treaties or as a means of modifying treaty provisions;

3. The General Assembly has no law-making competence, neither generally nor with specific reference to self-determination;

4. The practice of organs of the United Nations has not become a new method or source of generating rules of customary international law;

5. Resolutions or declarations of the General Assembly may be a step in the formation of customary international law through practice accepted as law.

In my view, the potency of the principle of self-determination depends less upon its characterization as right to self-determination, that is, as a norm of contemporary international law—regardless of the persuasiveness of any particular line of legal reasoning which would permit such a characterization—than upon the effectiveness of the political pressure that can be mobilized in and out of the United Nations in order to make it prevail. For even norms of international law if not complied voluntarily must as a last resort be enforced.

47. Ibid., p. 1010.

Appendix

Commission On Human Rights
Eighteenth session

Use Of The Terms "Declaration" And "Recommendation"

Memorandum by the Office of Legal Affairs

1. At the request of the Commission on Human Rights, the following comments on the use of the terms "declaration" and "recommendation" are submitted by the Office of Legal Affairs.

2. The Shorter Oxford English Dictionary defines a "declaration" *inter alia* as: "The action of setting forth or announcing openly, explicitly or formally: a proclamation as embodied in a document, instrument or public act." It defines a "recommendation" *inter alia* as: "The action of recommending a person or thing worthy and desirable; Exhortation, advice." These definitions may provide the departure point for indicating the differences between a "declaration" and "recommendation."

3. In United Nations practice, a "declaration" is a formal and solemn instrument, suitable for rare occasions when principles of great and lasting importance are being enunciated, such as the Declaration on Human Rights. A recommendation is less formal.

4. Apart from the distinction just indicated, there is probably no difference between a "recommendation" or a "declaration" in United Nations practice as far as strict legal principle is concerned. A "declaration" or a "recommendation" is adopted by resolution of a United Nations organ. As such it cannot be made binding upon Member States, in the sense that a treaty or convention is binding upon the parties to it, purely by the device of terming it a "declaration" rather than a "recommendation." However, in view of the greater solemnity and significance of a "declaration," it may be considered to impart, on behalf of the organ adopting it, a strong expectation that Members of the international community will abide by it. Consequently, in so far as the expectation is gradually justified by State practice, a declaration may by custom become recognized as laying down rules binding upon States.

5. In conclusion, it may be said that in United Nations practice, a "declaration" is a solemn instrument resorted to only in very rare cases relating to matters of major and lasting importance where maximum compliance is expected.

8. Nationalism, Statesmen, and the Size of African States

Joseph S. Nye

> To determine the size of the polis — to settle how large it can properly be, and whether it ought to consist of the members of one people or several — is a duty incumbent on the statesman.
>   Aristotle

Nineteen hundred and sixty was the year of triumph of African nationalism. Yet as the coups of 1966 soon underlined, the independent states were not yet nations. A conclusion drawn from this, and one that is reinforced by the prevalent academic theories of political development, is that African leaders should forego their concern with their neighbors and focus their attention solely on the internal tasks of nation building.

But such a conclusion is too simple. It is one thing to turn inward to internal development in Nigeria or Congo-Kinshasa, but it is open to question whether any degree of concentration on internal problems would bring about significant economic or political development in Togo, Upper Volta, or Chad. Two thirds of the independent African states have only a few million inhabitants and per capita incomes of under a hundred dollars a year — a small market for industrialization and a thin base over which to spread the overhead of services that go along with sovereign status.[1] Several states, for instance Malawi, Gambia, and Dahomey, are dependent on the former colonial power for support of their recurrent budgets as well as for capital expenditure. It is doubtful whether African microstates can achieve a level of economic development on the basis of their present size which will allow them to develop governmental institutions capable of providing sufficient and effective rewards and punishments necessary for rapid nation building. In other words, some sort of external arrangements with other African states may be a necessary condition for internal nation building. Otherwise, military interventions which periodically focus attention on internal order will merely be part of a dreary cycle.

Why then has there been so little progress on improving the external conditions of development in Africa? Why have African leaders accepted the boundaries arbitrarily determined on the drawing boards of nineteenth century European chancellories? In the eyes of some

---

1. There is no absolute line for distinguishing "small" states. S. Kuznets sets the dividing line in the modern world at roughly 10 million population in "Economic Growth of Small Nations," in Austin Robinson, ed., *The Economic Consequences of the Size of Nations* (London, Macmillan, 1960), p. 14.

younger African elites, the explanation lies in the selfishness of the current generation of African leaders. In the eyes of some outside observers, the explanation lies in the intensity of African nationalism. The purpose of this chapter is not to provide solutions but to demonstrate the inadequacy of the above explanations and to interpret the dilemma of African nationalist leaders who are concerned about the development of their small states.

One thing to make clear at the outset is that I am not arguing that large size is good for states and small size always bad. Nor does small size necessarily mean, as is frequently said, that African states are "unviable." Viability is in the living, and in an age when a combination of nuclear bipolarity and international organization tend to dampen violent conflict and put a safety net below small states, many so-called "unviable" states will go right on vying for external support. But life can be lived at a variety of levels, and viability says nothing about the level at which equilibrium is finally achieved. After all, some Caribbean countries have limped along for more than a century.

One must also beware of too simple assumptions about the relation of size to development. Highly developed countries like Switzerland, Norway, and New Zealand have populations little larger than those of the small African states. But it is argued that the small developed nations began their economic growth in a period of more liberal international trade and thus were better able to specialize in manufactures for the world market rather than have to rely on small internal markets.[2] While this argument tends to underrate the possibility of developing countries producing manufactures for the world market today, one can still feel uneasy about alleged lessons from small developed countries.[3]

On the political side as well, one must avoid overly simple statements about the relation of size to development. The two Latin American states consistently judged by scholars as having the most highly developed stable democratic institutions are Uruguay and Costa Rica — two of the smaller republics, with populations of 2.8 and 1.2 million respectively. Other small states, however, tend to be ranked at the bottom of the list by Latin Americanists.[4] In short, the key variable

2. Sidney Dell, *Trade Blocs and Common Markets* (London, Oxford University Press, 1963).

3. On neglected possibilities, see Raymond Vernon, "Prospects and Problems in the Export of Manufactured Products from Less-Developed Countries," *Contributed Paper No. 2* (Geneva, UNCTAD, 1964).

4. Russell Fitzgibbon and Kenneth Johnson, "Measurement of Latin American Political Change," in John Martz, ed., *The Dynamics of Change in Latin American Politics* (Englewood Cliffs, Prentice-Hall, 1965), pp. 113-129.

seems to be the homogeneity of the populations—neither Uruguay nor
Costa Rica had large unassimilated Indian populations. Recognizing
this variable, an economist suggests that small states may have better
prospects for growth because they may tend to be more homogeneous.[5]
But whatever the merits of the propositions in general, they seem inaccurate in Africa. Gambia, one of the smallest sovereign states has the
same ethnic divisions as its larger neighbor Senegal. The politics of
Dahomey, to take another of the smallest states, has been plagued by
ethnic heterogeneity.

In summary, although we cannot come to simple conclusions about
the relation of the size of states to their economic and political development, we *can* say that most African states are severely restricted in terms
of their internal markets and in the services of sovereignty that they can
afford to provide—and further that under African conditions there is
no reason to believe that small size indicates a homogeneity that might
be a mitigating factor.

A frequently suggested solution to the problem is to consolidate
African states into larger units—whether federations or various more
limited forms of functional arrangements such as common markets or
common service organizations. Given the general verbal commitment to
overcoming "balkanization" on the part of African leaders, one might
expect that the prospects for such a solution are good. Some observers
have concluded that "Africans really have an advantage over every
other attempt . . . to bring about regional cooperation," and that
pan-Africanism has shown a trend away from "amorphous protest to
the fashioning of organized cooperation." Many younger Africans
believe that they will some day break out of the small state "cages"
inherited from colonialism.[6]

Thus far the evidence suggests the contrary. If anything, African
leaders have strengthened the bars of the inherited cages. One case
where ideology led to amalgamation—the Mali Federation—was a case
of "premature" union in which the coercive, utilitarian, and ideological
powers of the union were not sufficient to maintain it for more than a
few months of independence. Other putative amalgamations, such as
the Ghana-Guinea-Mali Union, remained at the purely verbal level —
even though all three states had constitutions providing for sacrifice of
sovereignty on the altar of African unity; two (Guinea and Mali) were
contiguous and shared a similar colonial background and ideological

5. Kuznets, "Economic Growth," pp. 28-31.
6. Herbert Spiro, "Political Stability in the New African States," *The
Annals,* 354 (July 1964), 106-107; Norman Padelford, "The Organization of
African Unity," *International Organization,* 18 (Summer 1964), 546.

outlook, and the third (Ghana) invested some $22.4 million in the project.[7] Efforts on the part of East African leaders to consolidate the high degree of economic and functional cooperation inherited from colonial rule by forming a federation in 1963 proved abortive. Indeed, with one exception, the few successful amalgamations of territories in Africa occurred before independence and more often than not involved United Nations action. The one exception, the union between Tanganyika and Zanzibar in 1964 involved the absorption of two little islands with the same linguistic background as the country 360 times their size and off whose coast they lay—an exception, but one from which it is difficult to generalize for more than the smallest enclaves.

More limited functional arrangements such as customs unions and shared services appear to be an attractive solution in Africa because they allow simultaneous pursuit of the three values of independence, development and unity without forcing a choice among them.[8] But functional arrangements and "technocratic federations" depend on a certain degree of at least short-run separability of economic or technical problems from political ones. Such separability is rare in Africa. The location of industry in a customs union, for instance, is not a simple problem of welfare benefits to be calculated, compromised, and redistributed. Industry is a key symbol of modernity and sovereignty is a game in which the ultimate stakes are racial dignity. Thus pan-Africanist Guinea was unable to accept a United Nations plan for the establishment of a West African steel industry. Pan-Africanist Tanzania was unable to tolerate an East African common market in which a disproportionate amount of industry tended to locate in neighboring Kenya,[9] and Chad, unhappy with the distribution of benefits, withdrew from the hopeful new Union Douanière et Economique de l'Afrique Centrale, which commenced in Equatorial Africa in 1966.

Even the most limited technical arrangements are frequently plagued by politics. When Senegal failed to break relations with Britain over the Rhodesia issue in 1965, Guinea related the question to cooperation in the Senegal River Committee. Despite its subsequent return, the scheme remained highly politicized. Common services shared by Niger and Dahomey broke down over a minor dispute in 1963. When Somali irredentism led to armed clashes with Ethiopia in 1963, the latter bombed the base of the joint Desert Locust Survey for fear that the light

7. See I. William Zartman, *International Relations in the New Africa*, (Englewood Cliffs, Prentice-Hall, 1966), p. 127.

8. Ibid., p. 150.

9. J. S. Nye, *Pan-Africanism and East African Integration* (Cambridge, Harvard University Press, 1965), chap. 5.

aircraft of the organization might be used by the Somalis for military purposes.[10] At the continental level, the technical commissions of the Organization of African Unity, such as the Health, Sanitation and Nutrition Commission and the Commission of Jurists, have failed even to attain quorums, while the former colonial Commission for Technical Cooperation in Africa (CCTA) has atrophied since incorporation by the OAU. Indeed, in general the OAU found personnel and budgetary assessments difficult to obtain from member states. The Secretary-General reported a $2.5 million debt and serious understaffing to the October 1965 meeting and in 1966 the member states decided to reduce the budget by two thirds.[11]

The obstacles to African unity whether in the form of amalgamation or functional arrangements are sometimes attributed to evil men or to outside interference. Yet if Africa were governed by angels in a vacuum, the problems would remain because of the postcolonial situation in which such leaders would find themselves. Similarly, it is inadequate to attribute the problems of common markets in Africa to "profound feelings of nationalism."[12] The problem in Africa is quite the contrary — the lack of profundity of the feeling of nationalism. To see the present problem in perspective, it is necessary to go back to the colonial period.

With the establishment of colonial rule, Africans gained a new racial identity. Even illiterate Africans were aware of the racial difference of their colonial rulers and of their disruptive influence on traditional communities. The result was a wide variety of diffuse reactions ranging from reformism to millennial escapism which Hodgkin called African nationalism and Lord Hailey labeled "Africanism."[13] Educated elites tended to reject the traditional community as the basis for political action at least in part because it could not provide the power necessary to achieve racial dignity on the world scene. Thus the elites expressed the sense of racial identity in continental terms and labeled politics based on traditional communities as "tribalism."[14] In Julius Nyerere's words, "Once the tribal unit had been rejected as not being sensible in

10. *West Africa,* January 1, 1966; Zartman, *International Relations in the New Africa,* p. 158.

11. *New York Times,* October 25, 1965; *West Africa,* October 16, 1965.

12. Dell cites this as an obstacle to common markets in developing areas, *Trade Blocs and Common Markets,* p. 172.

13. *Nationalism in Colonial Africa* (New York, New York University Press, 1957); *An African Survey: Revised 1956* (London, Oxford University Press, 1957).

14. French elites were more explicit about race in their concern with negritude. The role of Western Hemisphere Negroes in shaping this identity was considerable. For an introduction to pan-Africanism, see Colin Legum, *Pan-Africanism: A Short Political Guide* (New York, Praeger, 1962).

Africa, then there can be no stopping short of Africa itself as the political grouping. For what else is there? 'Nations' in any real sense of the word do not at present exist in Africa."[15]

Nyerere's formulation was a statement of preference as much as fact. Nations might not exist, but states did. The newness of the *inter*state system obscures a longer period of impact of state structure on African identities. African states did not spring full grown from the head of the United Nations; rather they developed in the womb of colonial rule. Political development does not begin with independence.

By constant use of the terms "nation" and "nationalism" we do ourselves a disservice. The "rising tide of African nationalism" suggests analogies with nineteenth-century Europe when a new formula of political community and legitimacy was used to destroy institutions and restructure the international order. Indeed, this may have been what educated African elites and sympathetic Western observers, perhaps unconsciously, wished the terms to suggest, since by using Western slogans of national self-determination, particularly in the period after the Atlantic Charter, they were able to shake the colonial sense of moral legitimacy. But seeing the change in Africa as "African nationalism" or "pan-African nationalism" as the elites sometimes phrase it, leaves us unable to explain the weakness of Africa-wide institutions.

The inadequacy of the analogy implied in the slogan was illustrated by the isolated position of the Somali, a linguistic, ethnic, and religious group trying to reshape state boundaries to their sense of community. "Somali nationalism began as an exclusive movement aimed at the amalgamation of the Somali territories in the Horn of Africa . . . There was no need in this situation . . . to appeal to a wider identity as 'Africans.' "[16] The uniqueness of the Somali case was dramatized by the July 1964 resolution of the O.A.U. recognizing that the colonial borders so often described as meaningless, "constitute a tangible reality," and pledging "to respect the borders existing on their achievement of national independence."[17] This caused a heated debate in Somalia's National Assembly and a resolution denying that the O.A.U. resolution

15. *An Address to the Norwegian Students Association in Oslo* (Dar es Salaam, Government Printing Office, 1963), p. 4. This simplification avoids the problem of defining "tribe." In reality many traditional African systems involved several levels of community. See Paul Bohanan, *Africa and Africans* (New York, Natural History Press, 1964), chap. 8 and 12.

16. I. M. Lewis, "Pan-Africanism and Pan-Somalism," *Journal of Modern African Studies,* 1.2 (1963), 159, 148.

17. "General Record of the First Assembly of Heads of State and Government: Resolution 16" (mimeo, July 1964).

was binding on the Somali Republic.[18] The Somalis continued to speak of "self-determination" in the postcolonial period. Kenya, which is more typical of the rest of Africa and within whose borders a large number of Somalis reside, insisted that "seeking to create new African nations on the basis of tribal or religious identities is a sin against Pan-Africa and a most dangerous weapon for destroying African solidarity."[19] Indeed, one of the remarkable features of the new African state system has been the comparative rarity of irrendentism. Paradoxically, the arbitrariness of African borders has enhanced rather than decreased their significance.

We can gain a somewhat different perspective if we switch temporarily from words which bear an implicit analogy to the nineteenth century, to words which imply an analogy with Europe of the sixteenth and seventeenth centuries. Unlike the slogans of nationalism which assumed the existence of a community, the slogan of "sovereignty" was used to subordinate both internal and external feudal loyalties to the monarchy.[20] That this centralization frequently proceeded under monarchs who denied any intention of reducing external loyalties and swore fealty to the Pope, suggests interesting comparisons with African leaders who wish to subordinate tribal loyalties to the state while simultaneously swearing fealty to pan-Africa.

We cannot understand the dilemma of the pan-Africanist leaders unless we see that the origins of the "sovereign revolution" lie in the colonial period. Not only was colonial rule a source of modernization, but it created the political *infrastructure*—budgets, bureaucracies, armies, police, propaganda devices—around which mobilized groups tended to cluster.[21] Loyalties tend to shift to the source of rewards. Thus even though the colonial state never became fully legitimate because it was colonial, the identities and attention of the educated and other mobilized groups became focused on it in order to influence rewards and to cope with the problems of the new way of life that it fostered.

18. Jeane Contini, "The Somali Republic: Politics with a Difference," *Africa Report* (November 1964), p. 8.

19. "Pan-African Unity and the N.F.D. Question in Kenya," unpub. ms., Addis Adaba, 1963. For the wider context, see Rupert Emerson, *Self-Determination Revisited in the Era of Decolonization* (Cambridge, Harvard University Press, 1964).

20. Even the analogy of the monarch may not be too farfetched in some cases. See David Apter, "Ghana," in James Coleman and Carl Rosberg, eds., *Political Parties and National Integration in Tropical Africa* (Berkeley, University of California Press, 1964), p. 311; and Immanuel Wallerstein, *Africa: The Politics of Independence* (New York, Random House, 1961).

21. See Martin Kilson, "African Political Change and the Modernization Process," *Journal of Modern African Studies,* 1 (December 1963), 427.

Clan and "tribal" associations were formed in such a way that they often enlarged identities to include peripheral groups to better compete or fulfill their new functions much as caste and associations have in India.[22] What was crudely called "tribalism" often concealed important social changes.

Because African "nationalism" was an ideology held by an elite wishing to call a nation into being rather than a widespread sentiment of community, organization was crucial in its propagation.[23] Before independence the critical organization for this purpose was the nationalist party which in nearly all cases was constructed at the territorial level.[24] It was there that the mobilized groups clustered and the important institutions existed. Both had to be captured to make the "self-determination" which had been expressed in broad terms a narrower but more tangible reality.

Ironically the approach of independence heightened general awareness of identity at several levels, including ethnic "micro-nationalism" or "tribalism" in the pejorative language of the pan-Africanist. At the same time, independence increased the importance of national loyalties as citizens become better placed to affect government rewards. For instance, in the Ivory Coast, where nearly a quarter of the population were alien Africans, increased governmental autonomy was marked by riots and expulsions of non-indigenous Africans.[25] Similar though less violent experiences occurred in Niger, Congo, and Uganda.

In short, the internal consolidation of "sovereignty" began with the foundation of the colonial state; and was reinforced by the formation of territorial "nationalist" organizations. When independence and Africanization removed the colonial stigma which hindered legitimization of the state, it would have been remarkable if internal consolidation had not increased regardless of the "good" or "bad" intentions of the leaders, or the differences in the nature of the new regimes.

Observers have been prone to dichotomize the new political systems

22. Compare Immanuel Wallerstein, "Ethnicity and National Integration in West Africa," *Cahiers d'Études Africaines,* no. 3 (1960), 129-139; and Lloyd and Susanne Rudolph, "The Political Role of India's Case Associations," *Pacific Affairs,* 33 (March 1960), 5-22.

23. Ernst Haas makes this distinction. *Beyond the Nation-State* (Stanford, Stanford University Press, 1964), p. 465.

24. Aristide Zolberg shows that even in the case of the major exception, the Rassemblement Démocratique Africain in the former French African federations, the important unit in the late colonial period was the territorial party. *One-Party Government in the Ivory Coast* (Princeton, Princeton University Press, 1964), p. 95.

25. Ibid., p. 245.

first by the numbers of parties; later, when the single party became the dominant institution, by the elite versus mass-mobilization nature or pragmatic versus revolutionary style of the major party and now, perhaps, as military versus civilian.[26] After independence, with a few exceptions and for a variety of reasons including personalist leadership in some cases (Ghana, Malawi) and governmental competition for the scarce resource of middle-level bureaucrats (Tanzania, Zambia), the more impressive party bureaucracies were weakened leaving the inherited colonial state the key institution.[27] Close identification of party and state tended to legitimize the state rather than strengthen the party.

Whether one distinguished African regimes by the nature of their dominant institutions or differentiates them according to the degree of their tolerance of traditional pluralism, they are all faced with a similar set of problems which tend to enhance the importance of the state—though not necessarily increasing its capacity. Rapid economic development is desired to assert racial dignity as well as for welfare, thus diminishing the time available to wait for payoffs from supranational schemes which might better enhance long-run effectiveness. Ethnic malintegration has been another common problem, and the state machinery—used both for punishment and reward—has been a vital instrument in strengthening the elite's ability to cope with it.[28] Insecurity has been another problem. The persistence of independence legitimacy which one might have expected to limit the violence and social effects of most revolts and mutinies was suprisingly brief. Even before the spectacular coups of 1965-66, the previous two years had seen seven heads of state or government forcibly deposed and plots discovered in a dozen other states, including all types of regimes.[29] Even where it does

26. Ruth Schachter, "Single-Party Systems in West Africa," *American Political Science Review*, 55 (June 1961); Thomas Hodgkin, *African Political Parties;* Martin Kilson, "Authoritarian and Single Party Tendencies in African Politics," *World Politics*, 15 (January 1964); Coleman and Rosberg, *Political Parties.*

27. Conversely, weak parties often gained strength from association with government. Also, the decline of party bureaucracies is only relative, and their role in legitimacy should not be ignored. See J. S. Nye, "The Impact of Independence on Two African Nationalist Parties," in A. Castagno and J. Butler, eds., *Boston University Papers on Africa* (Boston, Boston University Press, 1967).

28. Zolberg, *One-Party Government in the Ivory Coast,* p. 194; Nye, "The Impact of Independence."

29. Robert Good, "Changing Patterns of African International Relations," *American Political Science Review,* 58 (September 1964), 637; *The Economist,* London, April 27, 1963.

not lead to increasing centralization, build-up of security forces and military coups, the threat of instability diverts leaders' attention to internal affairs. In terms of Karl Deutsch's communications analogy, statesmen are less likely to hear and respond to each others' messages if their ears are continually full of the noise of internal problems.

Levels of social mobilization are low in African countries compared with economically more developed areas, but in terms of African institutional capacity, they are high. In general, the colonial education pyramid had a very narrow top and a comparatively broad base. The result was mobilization of considerable number of school leavers who are attracted to urban areas, creating urban unemployment rates of 20 percent or higher in some places. At the same time, the colonial education systems produced only a handful of university and secondary school graduates to staff governmental bureaucracies which were denuded of experienced personnel because of pressures for Africanization.[30] In addition, and in contrast to European history, most African states had universal suffrage and an egalitarian ideology before they proceeded far in capital formation. The single-party tendency can be seen as a partial retraction of the substance of universal suffrage — an interesting example of the notion that political development can be advanced by reducing the burdens of mobilization on institutions.[31] But in general Deutsch is probably correct in stating that in the race between rates of mobilization and institutional capability, the "only variable with which policy makers usually can work is capability."[32]

Cooperative arrangements can increase capability for economic development, but the payoffs are often long run, and such arrangements cannot solve the other problems of insecurity and party reintegration. Moreover, such arrangements run counter to the growing use of state loyalties to affect governmental rewards, and to the statist political culture within which most African elites have developed their ideas. Whatever else "African socialism" may mean, it generally implies a

30. For instance, Zambia came to independence in 1964 with approximately 100 (African) university graduates and 1,500 secondary school graduates but 50,000 youths seeking jobs in addition to 74,000 adult unemployed. *East Africa and Rhodesia* (October 22, 1964), p. 109. The extreme case of the colonial education pyramid was, of course, the Belgian Congo.

31. Samuel Huntington, "Political Development and Political Decay," *World Politics,* 17 (April 1965), 419. In waggish form this becomes "African democracy: one man, one vote — once." Tanzania which held meaningful elections in 1965, is an exception.

32. "Communication Theory and Political Integration," in Philip Jacob and James Toscano, eds., *The Integration of Political Communities* (Philadelphia, Lippincott, 1964), p. 71.

distrust of the private sector and reliance on state planning.[33] A pre-condition of planning is some degree of certainty about the boundaries within which resources are to be allocated. It is understandable in origin but rather ironic in practice that the strongest pan-Africanists are also the strongest African socialists.

A recent work on political integration suggests that international integration differs from other kinds because it means "integrating the integrated." The units involved are "sovereign." In a legal sense this means they have "the ultimate right to make decisions." In a realistic political sense, it means they have a "general competence to make decisions."[34] African states are not highly integrated and have little sovereignty in the latter sense. Thus international integration in Africa is "integrating the integrating." It seems less difficult to integrate the integrated or the unintegrated than the integrating—those with a high degree of realistic sovereignty than those with less, but an intense concern with getting more.[35]

In summary, the majority of African states are hindered in their prospects for economic and political development by their small size and internal heterogeneity. The roots of the problem lie deep in the colonial experience and the postcolonial situation rather than depending simply on (removable) bad leaders. Similarly, the problem lies not in the intensity of African nationalism (in the sense of a widespread national consciousness) but in the weakness of African nationalism. It is one of the tragic ironies of African development, that in spite of intensive pre-independence talk of rejecting artificial colonial boundaries on the part of African statesmen, it has been the despised colonial statesmen who so completely determined the size of the polis.

33. See W. H. Friedland and Carl Rosberg, eds., *African Socialism* (Stanford, Stanford University Press, 1964); Elliot Berg, "Socialism and Economic Development in Tropical Africa," *Quarterly Journal of Economics,* 78 (November 1964), 549-573.

34. Jacob and Toscano, *Integration of Political Communities,* pp. 9, 72.

35. For instance, the Indian half of the Guatemala population is largely unintegrated and this has not prevented Guatemala from playing a major role in the Central American Common Market. See J. S. Nye, "Central American Regional Integration," *International Conciliation,* 562 (March 1967).

Part Three
Problems of the New International Order

9. Regulating the New International System

Stanley Hoffmann

The rise of the new nations, largely with the help of the United Nations, the importance of the issues discussed by its political organs, the growing relevance to world politics of the subjects within the jurisdiction of the specialized agencies would all seem to vindicate the study of the UN system as a field of political science. And yet, specialists in the field of international organization have noted with some alarm a decline of interest among students and foundations. This decline is due in part to the new emphasis on transnational (as opposed to interstate) relations, an emphasis that reflects the importance of all those economic forces which the states do not control, as well as an external dimension of the current interest in relations between bits and pieces of the national bureaucracies. But even within the realm of interstate affairs, there has been a shift from international organization toward the study of regionalism and the theory of integration. The former shift reflects one reality of postwar world politics—the division of a huge and heterogeneous international system into subsystems in which patterns of cooperation and ways of controlling conflicts are either more intense or less elusive than in the global system. The interest in integration reflects both the persistence and the transformation of the kind of idealism that originally pervaded, guided, and at times distorted the study of international organization. We have come to understand that integration, in the sense of a process that devalues sovereignty, gradually brings about the demise of the nation-state and leads to the emergence of new foci of loyalty and authority, is only one, and by no means the most important, of the many functions performed by global international organizations. This has led only in part to a more sober and searching assessment of these functions. It has resulted primarily in a displacement of interest toward those geographically more restricted institutions (like the European communities) whose main task seems to be to promote integration.[1]

Those who have remained concerned with the UN system have also gradually shifted their efforts. The heavy emphasis, advocated some years ago, on a comparative study of the institutions still expressed a willingness to detach or abstract international organization from the international system. But in recent years there has appeared a new approach—both more sweeping and more modest though not incompatible with comparative research.

1. For an assessment of West European integration, see Leon N. Lindberg and Stuart A. Scheingold, *Europe's Would-be Polity* (Englewood Cliffs, Prentice-Hall, 1970).

It has become clear that international institutions, in their political processes and in their functions, reflect and to some extent magnify or modify the dominant features of the international system. Therefore, instead of concentrating on these institutions as if they were a closed universe, one ought to study them as patterns of cooperation and of muted conflict whose nature, evolution, effectiveness, and outcomes cannot be studied apart from the global system or from the relevant subsystem. In this respect the discussion of international organization by political scientists follows the same curve as the study of international law or of war.

Since international organizations provide procedures for cooperation or for the temperate pursuit of conflict, it is obvious that their effectiveness depends on the degree of moderation of the international system. A revolutionary system wracked by inexpiable power rivalries and ideological conflicts is one in which international organization is reduced to impotence as a force of its own and to the condition of a helpless stake in the competition of states. This was the fate of the League of Nations in its second decade. On the other hand, not every moderate international system need be one in which global international organization plays a major role. This is not because of any built-in conflict between the balance of power, the traditional moderating mechanism in international politics, and international organization: such a conflict exists only with respect to one function of international organization, collective security. Rather it is because of two other factors. A moderate international system will be one in which global international organization plays a major role in the muting of conflict and the spread of cooperation only if, in the first place, there exists a broad procedural consensus among states which makes of multinational institutions the legitimate channels for the management of conflict and cooperation and if, in the second place, there exists a preference for universal channels over regional ones. In other words, a moderate international system, or one in which there exist compelling reasons why even deep and lasting ideological and power conflicts must be kept under control, creates opportunities for international organization, but these opportunities may be meager and difficult to exploit (as in the nineteenth-century international system).

It is impossible here to provide a thorough analysis of the international system or of the United Nations. I have tried to be more analytic elsewhere. I would like only to sketch briefly first the relations between the United Nations and the international system in recent years and second some of the possible relations in the future.

A Sketch of the Past

The image of the United Nations which guided the founding fathers of Dumbarton Oaks and San Francisco suffered from the huge discrepancy between the international system it postulated and the international system that emerged from World War II. The charter assumed and required a pluralistic yet controlled world that never came into being. First, it was supposed to be managed and regulated by the concert of the Great Powers, a modern version of the European Concert. Second, it was supposed to be a moderate international system partly because that concert would keep it so, partly because of an optimistic evaluation about regimes (they would be "democratic"), economic conditions, and international legitimacy. Hence the primary responsibility for peace and security placed on the Big Five in the United Nations. Hence the famous provision of Article 2, paragraph 7, about the respect for domestic jurisdiction—a precondition for moderation in past international systems—and the procedures of chapter 6, which are traditional procedures of mediation and conciliation suitable for moderate conflicts. Hence, finally, the vague provisions about international economic affairs, inspired by "the free enterprise vision of the international economy," by the hope that there would be no fundamental imbalance between rich and poor, and by the expectation that, as in the past, economic development would be promoted essentially by private means.[2]

The bipolar world of the late 1940s did not resemble this idyll any more than the Greek world before the Peloponnesian War resembled the international system after 1815. The charter had created an international organization that was irrelevant to the revolutionary world in which two fierce ideological conflicts—East versus West and colonial versus anticolonial—seemed to destroy both the chances of any great power consensus and the chances for moderation.

Facing a choice between permanent paralysis and transformation, a majority of the members of the United Nations opted for the latter even though it meant a drastic de facto revision of the charter. Despite the legal primacy of the Security Council the United Nations, confronted with the breakdown of the great-power consensus, overhauled the system of the charter through General Assembly Resolution 377A (V) of November 3, 1950 (the "Uniting for Peace Resolution"), which appeared to reopen the road to collective security. Faced with life and

2. Ernst B. Haas, *Tangle of Hopes: American Commitments and World Order* (Englewood Cliffs, Prentice-Hall, 1969), p. 120.

death disputes, many of which originated within what the colonial powers claimed to be their domestic jurisdiction, the organs of the United Nations disregarded Article 2, paragraph 7, tried to blur the differences between colonies and trusteeships, and innovated far beyond traditional diplomatic procedures by methods of collective intervention and the establishment of UN presences. When economic development emerged as a major problem in world politics, the United Nations multiplied agencies for technical assistance and development.

This de facto transformation of the United Nations was based on an image of the world that was at least as far removed from reality as had been the image of the original United Nations. It was the image of a fictitious world community able and willing to make of the United Nations a force that would represent and expand the common interest of mankind. It could be useful as a kind of Sorelian myth thanks to which one of the superpowers would rally a majority against its rival and enlist the United Nations behind its own policies, but it was once again bound to create illusions and disillusionment. For at the basis of these changes one finds two postulates. One was majority rule — a neat reversal from the days of the great-power unanimity principle and from the sober but paralyzing realism of those who had deemed international organization incapable of imposing the will of a majority, especially against a great power or its allies, in matters such as collective security or race relations. (And yet the only powers that were explicitly charged with aggression by UN organs turned out to be the Democratic People's Republic of Korea [North Korea], the ally of the Union of Soviet Socialist Republics; then the People's Republic of China after its intervention in Korea; and later the Soviet Union after its invasion of Hungary.) The second postulate was the capacity of the Secretary-General to play a kind of executive role, carrying out mandates given to him by the General Assembly but also filling gaps, interpreting ambiguities in these delegations, taking political initiatives, enlarging, so to speak, the bridgehead toward one world, and defending the common interest of mankind.

Illusions have their virtue when they inspire action. The fiction of a world community has made it possible for the organs of the United Nations to concern themselves with most of the important political and economic issues that agitate the international system, and to promote that equalization of concern which is a rudimentary, first factor of homogenization in a highly diverse and uneven world. Yet, as a result, a gap between attempts and achievements, resolutions and resolution, motions and motion appeared — a gap no smaller nor less frustrating than the original charter's gap between legal possibilities and political aspirations. The majoritarian illusion has been short-lived. An obvious discrepancy between votes and compliance developed almost as soon as the Uniting for Peace Resolution was adopted. Thus the resolution was never to be fully put into effect insofar as collective security was concerned. Moreover, after the increase in UN membership since 1955 the art of obtaining sufficient majorities became subtle, arduous, and uncertain, and the hazards of such consensus building revealed all too often that numerical majorities in organs without weighted voting may breed as many disadvantages as the paralyzing vetoes of the Security Council. The hope for a largely autonomous Secretary-General, executor or even shaper of the majority, was crushed twice: once when Trygve Lie had to resign because of Soviet obstruction, once when Dag Hammarskjöld, who after a cautious beginning in office and behind the misty screen of deliberately fuzzy language had become a bold manager and theorist of the "new United Nations," died in the midst of the most serious constitutional crisis of the organization.

And yet the demise of fictions has not meant a verdict of complete impotence and paralysis. The United Nations has been able to play a limited role as "universal actor" in the system because of certain favorable features that reintroduced a modicum of moderation into the international system. These features were quite different from those the founding fathers had expected. They have not obliterated either the revolutionary characteristics of the elements cf the system (bipolar distribution of power; heterogeneity of the basic unit, of regimes, ideologies, and levels of development) or the revolutionary aspects of relations between units in the system (immoderate ends and means). But they have imposed certain limits on those means, thereby contained the inflation of ends within practical (if not verbal) limits, and restored some flexibility. It is the existence of these features which explains why in the United Nations in the 1950s even the minority went along (despite protests and filibusters) with the de facto revision of the charter. The reason why the search for more elastic procedures of discussion and intervention, despite its excessive ambition, has allowed the United Nations to develop is the evolution of the international system: it is still an interstate system of competing units, but it is no longer the bipolar system of the late 1940s and early 1950s—neither "tight" nor "loose"; new features have emerged.

I have analyzed elsewhere[3] the nature of the present system in terms

3. Stanley Hoffmann, *Gulliver's Troubles, or the Setting of American Foreign Policy*, Atlantic Policy Studies (New York, McGraw-Hill [for the Council on Foreign Relations], 1968), chap. 2.

of three different layers: the fundamental, latent bipolar stratum; the manifest layer of polycentrism; and an emergent layer of multipolarity. Insofar as the relations between states that develop in this system are still revolutionary, the impact of the United Nations on world affairs continues to be severely limited. Thus, on the one hand, the bipolar contest has constantly reduced UN effectiveness: the United Nations has been timid and ineffective whenever one of the Big Two was determined to act freely with force or threats of force in its sphere of domination (the Soviet Union in Hungary and Czechoslovakia, the United States in the Caribbean). Also, serious rifts between the superpowers have continued to result in UN impotence. There have been no attempts at organizing collective security in a world in which the mobilization of one camp against the other could all too easily mean World War III and in which those minor conflicts that find both superpowers determined not only to remain uninvolved but even to restore peace can be handled in less ponderous ways — in ways which also do a better job of concealing the collusion of the otherwise hostile superpowers. When serious disputes have broken out between the United States and its allies on the one side and members of the now splintered Communist world on the other, the role of the United Nations has been either nil (as during the second Berlin crisis of 1958-1962, the Vietnam war, and the Quemoy and Matsu incidents of 1955) or minimal (as during the Berlin blockade of 1948, the war in Laos, the Cuban missile crisis of 1962). When moderation was observed or restored, it was not through the United Nations (as was evident during the Yom Kippur war in October 1973). Whenever the Great Powers were at odds over a conflict that, even though it may not have involved them or their allies directly, nevertheless greatly affected their interests, the effectiveness of UN peacekeeping operations suffered an eclipse, as in the Congo in the fall of 1960 and in Cyprus in the summer of 1974, or even collapsed, as in the Middle East in May 1967. The financial crisis which has affected UN peacekeeping ever since 1961 and has never been resolved is the direct result of a continuing constitutional conflict between the superpowers.

On the other hand, quite apart from cold war situations, the prevalence of life and death conflicts between states or within states and the formidable challenge of the poor nations in the economic and social realms have left the United Nations incapable of finding remedies in the absence either of any substantive consensus of the superpowers or of any joint determination on their part to enforce such a consensus and in the presence of all the obstacles raised by state sovereignty. In major political crises the United Nations has sometimes been absent when it was obvious that intervention would meet with fierce resistance from one party (Algerian war) or else when an attempt at intervening risked escalating, rather than resolving a local conflict (Biafra). More often, the General Assembly or the Security Council have adopted resolutions that have not been effective. A considerable difference has emerged between attempts at peacekeeping (or peace restoration) — successful for reasons to be discussed below — and attempts at solving the disputes that had led to violence — unsuccessful because of the resistance of some or all parties in matters which seemed to them to affect their essential interests. Hence the long record of UN disappointments in Kashmir, Palestine, Cyprus, and in the cases of Southern Rhodesian and South African apartheid. In economic affairs there has been no massive transfer of funds from the rich to the poor through UN channels. The story of efforts at creating agencies for capital development has been depressing, and the results of the UN conference on Trade and Development (UNCTAD) have been disappointing. The bulk of aid to the underdeveloped countries continues to be handled by bilateral agreements. However huge the majority behind a resolution, if those who are asked to make a sacrifice, a gamble, or a move remain deaf, the majority will remain frustrated and the crises will stay unresolved in a world of states where the superpowers are often among the deaf and, even when they are not, where they distrust each other too much to establish a condominium.

However, there has been a dampening of the superpowers' contest and a reintroduction not only of restraints but even of cooperation in multiple forms in the international system. I have stressed two factors as the main causes for these developments; the new legitimacy of the nation-state and the new conditions of the use of force in a nuclear world. A third factor deserves equal recognition: the heterogeneity of the system, which has made it impossible for the superpowers to engulf the whole planet into their rivalry (whereas Athens and Sparta had absorbed all the Greek world into theirs). It has also made it possible for the lesser powers, protected by the legitimacy of nationalism and by the superpowers' fear of collision, to impose various restrictions on the Big Two duel. It has given to this duel and to the other contests in the system a variety of configurations depending on local and regional circumstances, and it has reintroduced — in what is the first worldwide international system in history — broad opportunities for balancing within and between regions. The second and third layers of the system — polycentrism and multipolarity — have thus appeared as a consequence of the muting of the bipolar conflict and as a reaction against the astringency of bipolarity. It is the combination of these three factors and of these changes in the international hierarchy that has given to the United

Nations its chances and its role in postwar political and economic affairs.

The United Nations has reflected those features but has also contributed to, exploited, and magnified them. Thus, the change in the balance of forces within the UN organs and the increasing need for bargaining and compromise in order to get resolutions passed reflects the shift from a bipolar world to the new, more complex system. In the bipolar one there could perhaps be thumping majorities piled up by one camp against another, but at the cost of effectiveness and with a purely symbolic meaning. In the present world, within the limits set by latent bipolarity (that is, the exclusion of those issues over which an irreconcilable rift between the superpowers still condemns the United Nations to impotence) the lesser powers can play a conspicuous role on the world stage largely because of another kind of impotence: that of the superpowers which owe their dominant position to a kind of material might which they cannot freely use (weaponry). The relative deference with which the United Nations, even in colonial affairs, has treated France and the United Kingdom, its prudence toward Communist China, and the importance of India reflect the tendency toward multipolarity, that is, the rise of secondary or potential nuclear powers. But the United Nations has also contributed to polycentrism because of the role the voting procedures give to small states, each one of which counts as much as any large power and must be courted and coaxed for the requisite majority to be attained. Thus, the new balance of forces that has emerged in the 1960s (both in a much larger General Assembly where no single bloc has any more the control of the requisite two thirds majority and, more recently, in the broadened Security Council) has allowed the United Nations to mitigate somewhat the importance of bipolarity. What matters is not the positive agreement of the Big Five but the absence of deep disagreement of the Big Two. The enlargement of the membership gives an opportunity to third parties, whose votes are indispensable to the Big Two, to appeal to the common or convergent interests of the superpowers and thus to coax through their initiatives the kind of consensus which the original charter had seemed to leave almost exclusively to the initiative of the superpowers themselves. In some instances it is the prodding of the smaller powers, dissatisfied with the gap between them and the superpowers, that produces a kind of defensive rapprochement of the Big Two qua superpowers, determined both to protect their superiority and to disarm the lesser powers' drive by occasional concessions that do not threaten their own position as top dogs (for example, the Treaty on the Nonproliferation of Nuclear Weapons, various votes on economic development, and also the recent tendency to return to the Security Council its primary role).

Similarly, the United Nations reflects — indeed is based on — the principle of state sovereignty. But it has made quite a contribution to the legitimacy and sanctification of the nation-state. The increase in the importance of the General Assembly has heightened the attraction of statehood, and the case with which the United Nations has, after 1955, given its blessing and opened its doors to new nations has been largely responsible for the huge rise in the number of new states: The United Nations, and especially its General Assembly, has been the matrix and target of new nation-states — even if, as in the case of the Palestinians, such states are likely to add to turbulence in troubled areas. Moreover, in the excolonial area as well as in economic affairs the organs of the United Nations have given a solemn endorsement to the nation-state (even to the mini-state) and have wrapped the rights and privileges of the charter around the frail and shivering new nations, thus promoting a kind of pluralist and equalitarian legitimacy which inhibits considerably the more blatant moves the superpowers could be tempted to make in their relations with weaker states.

No one will doubt that the organs of the United Nations reflect the heterogeneity of the international system: in every major crisis submitted to the organization, such as the Congo or the Middle East, the diversity of regimes, ideologies, levels of development, regional concerns, allegiances, and so on, engenders a drama of conflicting purposes and a process of painful negotiation. It is the combination of national legitimacy and fragmentation that accounts for the failure to establish an international police force and for the glaring weaknesses of past peacekeeping forces, for they have been crippled both by the nations' jealous defense of the principle of consent, as applied to the stationing and financing of those forces, and by the bloc conflicts that have shaped the composition of the forces and that led in May 1967 to the disintegration of the United Nations Emergency Force (UNEF). The more fragmented the international system, the less likely the establishment of a permanent force based on universally applicable principles and the more likely the reliance on ad hoc procedures and local balances. But the United Nations has also contributed to this fragmentation. The Sisyphean approach of its major organs, with their tendency to sacrifice precedents and legalism to flexibility and political expediency, has meant that each issue would be considered on its merits with due respect for the configuration of political forces at the moment and in the area. The attempt by Hammarskjöld and, more quietly, by his successors to engage in what the former had called "preventive diplomacy" so as to avoid the spread of the cold war to all parts of the globe has strengthened heterogeneity by reinforcing all those specific, sometimes parochial, forces that resist the absorption of local conflicts into the cold war mäelstrom. The frequent reliance on, or deference to, regional organizations has had the same effect.

Finally, the United Nations has of course reflected the new conditions of the use of force. Had the fear of nuclear war and the desire to prevent an escalation of major head-on collisions between the superpowers not dominated their policy and strategy, the United Nations would not have had the chance to become a test of coexistence. Had conquest and the subjugation of determined, well-organized peoples in revolt not become prohibitively costly, the United Nations would not have had the opportunity to intervene so often in wars of national liberation. The United Nations has been effective whenever there has been a sufficient consensus (explicit or tacit) between the superpowers to curtail third-party violence. If one examines the cases in which the Security Council or the General Assembly have been able to adopt resolutions which were put into effect by the organization or its members, one finds that they fall into three groups, all of which entailed such a consensus. First, there are the cases in which a concert of the superpowers developed for the restoration of peace in a troubled area in which they were not directly involved (Indonesia, Middle East crises of 1948 and 1956, Kashmir, Yemen). Second, there are the instances of resolutions adopted after a balancing process in which groups of states other than the two camps of "cold warriors" played a major role but succeeded in formulating an effective text only because of the explicit or tacit consent of the superpowers (Congo crisis in the summer of 1960 and after Hammarskjöld's death, Middle East crisis of 1958, Cyprus, Middle East crisis during the first week of June 1967 and later in November 1967, aftermath of the Yom Kippur war). Third, there is a case involving both a concert and a balancing process: that of the nonproliferation treaty.

But the United Nations has, once again, gone beyond this: it has skillfully exploited what I have called the upper and the lower limits of the usefulness of applying force. It has buttressed the lower limit not by simply condemning the resort to force against peoples in revolt for their independence but by actually giving its blessing to the use of force toward the acquisition of statehood—much to the indignation of the colonial powers and despite the creation thereby of an apparent double standard toward violence (for example, India's attack on Goa): wars of national liberation are legitimate, other resorts to force or threat of force are not (unless in case of self-defense). Also, the United Nations has done its best to strengthen the one barrier that is decisive for world peace—the upper limit on the use of force—through its practices of international neutralization in those military conflicts that it can handle. Its long record of cease-fires, military observers, and peacekeeping forces expressed both the determination of the superpowers not to let world peace be upset by moves of (or conflicts within) the lesser powers and the determination of the small states to maximize the restraints on great-power intervention in such disturbances. The United Nations has thus provided indispensable devices for all-round face-saving, making it possible, not only for belligerents to put an end to hostilities without humiliation, but also to install some impartial, if fragile, checks on peace once the fighting has ended. The result is original: even though the stopping of armed conflicts through international pressure (including the tacit or explicit consensus of the superpowers) is an old practice of balance-of-power systems, the fact that UN peacekeeping mechanisms have kept aside the Great Powers contributes to the atrophy of the latter's coercive power.

A final judgment on the *role* of the United Nations in the system and on the *impact* of the United Nations on the system must, once again, be balanced. Concerning its role, the change in legal practices and the emergence of new voting groups in the United Nations have increased the flexibility, maneuverability, and scope of interests of UN organs without drastically transforming the limits imposed by the international system. On the one hand, as an instrument of international cooperation and conflict resolution the United Nations appears as a kind of residual category. It is effective in the sense of having both authority and legitimacy in cases which prove to be neither too divisive (as are the cold war conflicts, substantive disagreements in the Middle East or Asia, racial issues in southern Africa, and so on), nor too huge to be handled by the limited means of the organization (as was Algeria), nor capable of being treated primarily by or shunted to a regional organization (for example, the Organization of American States for Guatemala and the Dominican Republic, the Organization of African Unity for Biafra). The only exception to this has been the Korean war, which turned out to be neither a precedent nor a model.

On the other hand, as a residual instrument the United Nations has been extraordinarily resilient. As an arena and a stake it has been useful to each of the competing groups eager to get not only a forum for their views, but also diplomatic reinforcement for their policies, in the Cold War as well as in the wars for decolonization. As an institution able to discharge various executive responsibilities in peacekeeping or technical assistance or economic development the United Nations has proven to be necessary almost to all. It has been necessary to those states that were the beneficiaries of efforts whose absence would have exposed them to greater poverty, more debilitating defeats, or more overt great-power pressure. It has also been necessary to major states which, had the

United Nations not existed, would have had a difficult choice between direct, undisguised, and trouble-making involvement on behalf of their national interests and possibly damaging abstention. What has kept the United Nations afloat in a stormy world has been, and remains, the need for all states to find some form of deterrence against the most formidable of those storms (large-scale wars, major economic disasters) and the impossibility for even the superpowers to count exclusively on their own individual efforts or on direct agreements (ruled out by their contest) for such protection.

Concerning the impact of the United Nations on the system, the United Nations has contributed to defusing it by restoring elements of moderation and management and has helped to subvert the international hierarchy. There are other, powerful reasons for this subversion, for the relative "impotence of power" of the Great Powers and the greater freedom of maneuver of the small states. But the United Nations, by its procedural practices as well as by the way in which it has exercised its legitimizing function, has reinforced the importance of the lesser powers. In this respect its contribution to world order is mixed, for while it was and remains necessary to curtail the predominance of the superpowers in a world in which force is too blunt a tool and most of the tasks have to be performed through consent, too radical a reversal of the hierarchy can be pretty unhealthy. The United Nations propels on the world scene states or statesmen whose performance rests more on showmanship than on realities and thus divorces posture from responsibility. It also prepared a potentially excessive reaction of middle powers, some collusion of the Great Powers, determined to restore or protect their supremacy, and a symbolic insurrection of the smaller powers against their own actual ineffectiveness, as shown by various resolutions of the 24th session of the General Assembly. The role played by the United Nations in legitimizing the nation-state helps safeguard national independence and integrity, but it also perpetuates all the obstacles which the traditional state of nature has accumulated on the road to peace and cooperation. The United Nations' contribution to heterogeneity has moderated and fragmented the relation of major tension between the United States and the Soviet Union, but it has also made calculations of deterrence and control more difficult and has complicated the search for worldwide solutions to major problems. The UN approach to the use of force has added to the inhibitions on conventional and nuclear war, but, combined with repeated UN failures in solving disputes and with the encouragement to wars of liberation, it has also helped the generalization of violence at lower levels, favored the "internalization" of war, and encouraged further trends toward balkanization. Success in extinguishing fires has not prevented, indeed it has facilitated, the freezing of undying conflicts and the incitation of troublemakers to resort to subversion, infiltration, psychological warfare, and so on.

Thus, one can conclude that while the United Nations has been a significant factor in establishing a world order based on the nation-state and possessing a distorted, rather equalitarian hierarchy, considerable flexibility, and severe taboos on the traditional ways of using force, it has also perpetuated the drawbacks of sovereignty and brought moderation at the cost of making the resort to limited or subliminal violence endemic and the recurrent explosion of unsolved disputes inevitable. Only utopians will find this mixed balance sheet distressing. Historians will recognize in this picture many (but not all) of the features of balance-of-power systems, in which the code of legitimacy was far less equalitarian and resort to force less inhibited but in which large conflicts used to be avoided or moderated at the cost of multiplying lesser ones.

A Query for the Future

The future relations between the United Nations and the international system and the role the United Nations could play in it depend essentially on what this system will be and this, in turn, depends much less on UN actions (given their limited effectiveness and the fact that they reflect state policies more than they affect them) than on other factors to be mentioned below.

The Evolution of the International System. We are living in what might be called the world political system, an international system which differs from past ones not only through its scope but also through features that deserve a theoretical and empirical study. The nature of this system is original, its future unclear.[4]

It is marked, in the first place, by increasing interpenetration between domestic politics and international politics. The conceptualization of the latter as a "state of war," in contrast with the ideal type of the former as a community with central power, remains valid at the level of ideal types (there is still no central power in the international system, and given its radical heterogeneity, consensus either about ends or about the means toward generally accepted ends is as far away as ever; moreover, many of the bonds that appear to have put some civil

4. For a formulation both very close to and more detailed than this one see Karl Kaiser, "Transnationale Politik," *Politische Vierteljahresschrift* (1969), special issue, pp. 80-109.

order into the state in which the nations live exist only by sufferance and result merely from the changeable calculations, of the separate states). There are however two new and important qualifications. On the one hand, there is a rapprochement in practice between the two kinds of politics. In many nations (new and old) there is little consensus, central power is more a stake than a force, and there is a potential and even endemic state of war. At the same time international politics have become more moderate. This is partly because of the new conditions of the use of force. There is another cause: for a variety of reasons (including those new conditions as well as economic enmeshment in an age dominated by the expansion of science and technology) the competition between states takes place on several chessboards in addition to the traditional military and diplomatic ones: for instance, the chessboards of world trade, of world finance, of aid and technical assistance, of space research and exploration, of military technology, and the chessboard of what has been called "informal penetration." These chessboards do not entail the resort to force. On most of them competition is based, not on the traditional kind of strategic-diplomatic interaction in which each player remains a separate unit following the logic of diversity, but on an interdependence which, to be sure, covers relations of domination and dependence and entails attempts to escape from such bonds and burdens, yet creates a logic of integration which restricts considerably the theoretical freedom of choice of each actor. Thus, "winning" presupposes the acceptance and mastery of numerous constraints. These constraints result either from the player's own entanglement in the web or (as, for instance, in the case of attempts at "playing domestic politics" abroad by manipulating foreign political movements or interest groups) from the hazardous nature of the game on this chessboard over which the actor rarely has adequate control. International politics thus becomes much more complex. Not only does each chessboard have rules of its own which have often not been adequately studied, but there are complicated and subtle relations between chessboards: for instance, depending on the national situation a state may be able to offset its weakness on one chessboard thanks to its strength on another or else be prevented from exploiting its strength on one because of its weakness on another.

On the other hand, there is a tight *interconnection* between the two kinds of political systems: while international politics still consists largely of interstate moves, a fourfold "internalization" of world politics is going on. Foreign policy entails increasingly attempts at influencing domestic affairs, that is, at operating within rather than across borders. Major changes in the system result from revolutions rather than wars:

internal upheavals and crises short of all-out war (that is, breakdowns which reflect the greater moderation of international politics) are now the two chief agents of change. Major shifts in rank in the international system result from domestic achievements or failures rather than from interstate contests. Finally, the international system of today is not one of cool, somewhat interchangeable, cabinet diplomats but one of "socially mobilized" polities which project on the world scene their domestic conceptions, experiences, and fantasies instead of following some external and objective national interest. Thus international politics becomes a kind of confrontation of domestic political systems in action (with an alternation of periods in which international politics is a frenzied clash of national designs or phobias and quieter periods in which the national systems "turn inward" and give priority to domestic demands, with a corresponding shift in priorities on and between the chessboards).

In the second place there is also a growing interpenetration between transnational society and world politics (defined as interstate politics). The logic of the "game" of world politics, so well analyzed by Raymond Aron, is shaped by the nature of the international milieu. But the scope and the specific rules of the game at any given time are determined, on the one hand, by the type of international system in existence (characterized mainly by the number of major powers, the presence or absence of major ideological cleavages, and the technology of conflicts) and, on the other hand, by the nature of the relations between state and society in the main competing units. Today, there is a world political system but no worldwide transnational society: there is still little contact between Communist China and much of the rest of the world at the level of society (whereas Communist China is definitely part of the international political system), and great discontinuities persist between the non-Communist transnational society and the Eastern world. Especially, but not only, in the latter there is — by comparison with the world of economic liberalism — a considerable politicization of transnational society, brought about by the domestic requirements and by the interdependence of advanced industrial economies. The states control, directly or indirectly, the international economy and communications, international monetary relations, the development of technology. The large so-called multinational corporations, because of their structure, size, and wealth, cannot be considered either purely private or genuinely cosmopolitan. Their unfettered establishment and operations abroad often are a foreign policy objective of the parent state. Their activities do affect the chips with which states play on several of the chessboards of international politics, hence the frequent resistance of states to their penetration by "private" foreign companies. For in a world in which the demand for technology and capital is insatiable, the parent state can exploit the assets which these companies represent, whereas the host states, deprived of control on often vital resources or "commanding heights" of their economies, find their freedom of foreign policy maneuver mutilated.

But, conversely, despite such politicization there is in much of the world a semiautonomous transnational society in the sense that it too has rules of its own, determined by its functions, which the state players must respect or can disregard only at prohibitive costs given the degree of interdependence. Indeed, they are partly constrained to accept those rules by the fact that they must compete or cooperate with actors other than states, over which their controls are often limited and indirect. One can speak of additional chessboards such as that of industrial technology, on which the actors are both states (either as clients or as initiators) and private groups (corporations, banks), or that of scientific research, on which the actors are states, universities (public or private), foundations, industries, and so on, or the geographically fragmented chessboard of transnational financial transactions, on which governments, multinational and national business enterprises, banks, individuals, and so on, compete for capital. Thus the interstate competition of today, while it has reached an unprecedented scope geographically and functionally, must observe a variety of restraints which contribute to making the world political system look more like domestic polities (a term which refers both to the narrow political sector, that is, the state, and to the state's relations to society).

In what direction is this world political system going? It is easy to predict that the two interpenetrations will persist. But, far from limiting the number of possibilities, this prediction actually increases them. If one examines the international system of today, one can state that some of its features are irrevocable. Nuclear weapons will not be disinvented, "social mobilization" (or the decline of apathy, or the growth of communications) will continue, and technological innovation will probably be accelerated. Other features are likely to persist but not with the same degree of certainty: the nuclear stalemate between the superpowers (yet who can be sure that there will never be any unilateral breakthrough?), the military gap between the superpowers and other states, the relative fragmentation of the system and its basic heterogeneity. All the rest—including the present balance between its three layers and its ad hoc restraints on force—is dubious. Moreover, the irrevocable or likely features are all ambiguous in their effects from the viewpoint of world order, that is, cooperation and the moderation of conflict. Nuclear weapons have so far had a stabilizing and restraining impact. But in the long run the very fear of nuclear war may increasingly force the superpowers to do battle through proxies and thus to play Russian roulette with their interests. This could be destabilizing, as one observes in the Middle East. The other powers are caught between the unsettling attraction of nuclear diffusion and the recurrent crises which the freeze on the large-scale use of force engenders. Social mobilization has also had a stabilizing impact by making foreign penetration into internal political systems more difficult and total domestic concentration on foreign policy less likely; but it can be disruptive by making foreign policy too rigidly bureaucratic or on the contrary by exposing it to internal instability and passions. The fragmentation of the international system makes it possible to isolate local conflicts and limits the scope and significance of superpower gains or losses. But it also makes for more uncertainty in the mechanism of escalation and complicates the superpowers' dilemmas in maintaining world order. As for technological and economic interdependence, not only will it continue to conceal complex relations of command and dependence shaped by the power relations of national economies and by the connections between the traditional chessboard of interstate politics and the newer chessboards described above, but the ties woven by interdependence will remain suspended to and dependent on the ultimate issues of war and peace — unless one endorses the optimistic and unproven deterministic thesis which foresees the taming of violent conflict by commerce and industry and celebrates the conquest of all other passions by greed.

Thus there is a broad range of choices for the future. One can only say that international relations in the world political system will be the manipulation of interdependence by the separate, competing units. This formula suggests the growing awareness by states of the limits of their freedom of action and of its risks on the military as well as on the other chessboards. That is, it suggests the new dimensions of prudence, the triple safety net of nuclear deterrence, economic solidarity, and domestic priorities under the tightrope of competition. But it also suggests that world order remains precarious, since the name of the game is still manipulation and contest. The desire to preserve *a* world system is not synonymous with a desire to preserve any existing system or exclusive of the desire to establish a radically different one on the ruins of the present one. The economic revolution performed by the oil-producing nations in 1973-74 bears witness to this. And if the manipulation of interdependence should lead to a breakdown of the latter — through economic disruption or a return to economic fragmentation or warfare — the current moderation on the traditional chessboard of diplomatic-strategic interaction may well be strained to the point of collapse. There will therefore remain a tension between, on the one hand, the states' tendency to manipulate interdependence for their own benefit, as well as the explosive consequences of big internal disruptions, and, on the other hand, the need to turn the world political system into more of a society, that is, to tame the independence of its members, to provide for more cooperation, and to keep violence within limits.

In a world which knows no political and psychological mutations (and short of the kind of mutation that might take place if there were a holocaust large enough to convert those not directly affected, yet not so huge as to annihilate us all) the establishment of world order means the achievement of a moderate international system. This rules out a return to an intense bipolar conflict. It does not rule out either a bipolarity of condominium (or collusion) or the prolongation of the present international system; yet I do not believe (for reasons described elsewhere) that either formula is likely to assure moderation or capable of it.[5] A moderate system will have to be a "multihierarchical" one. It is impossible to predict whether the latter will emerge sooner rather than later. (there is considerable resilience in the present international system); nor is it possible to predict whether a multihierarchical system will be moderate or not. The answer to both questions depends essentially on three factors. First, there is the behavior of the superpowers, their degree of competition and cooperation and their degree of involvement in other parts of the world (on those factors depend, in turn, the degree of autonomy of subsystems and the degree of superpower resignation to domestic changes abroad). Second, there is the behavior of the present and potential middle powers, with its impact on the relations between the superpowers as well as on the degree of moderation, coherence, and autonomy of the subsystems. Third, there is the scope, rate, and location of nuclear diffusion (and, perhaps, nuclear control). It is obvious that there are countless configurations, and it would be depressing to try to list them all or to give degrees of probability to each.[6] Let us therefore abandon empirical forecasting for normative political analysis and see what role international organization *ought* to play if a moderate international system is to prevail, that is, if the present world political system were to become a true society.

The Role of International Organization in a Moderate International System. My assumption—which will not be accepted by all—is that

5. Hoffmann, *Gulliver's Troubles,* chap. 10.

6. For a sobering example of what happens when one tries, see Herman Kahn and Anthony J. Wiener, *The Year 2000: A Framework for Speculation on the Next Thirty-Three Years* (New York, Macmillan Co., 1967), chaps. 5, 7, and 9.

there will be no institutional mutation; that is, sovereignty, anything but absolute and probably emptied of much of its erstwhile meaning and sting, will remain a claim and a foundation for the states' foreign policies. Even though there may be a considerable development of international and regional institutions, including a successful pursuit of integrative policies in some parts of the world, there will be no "superseding of the nation-state" (whatever its devaluation) at the global level. It is my contention, first, that such a mutation is unlikely; second, that a world political system based on the nation-state can procure world order as long as (and as soon as) its most important members adopt certain kinds of attitudes and policies and, as long as the traditional state insistence on total freedom of decision and from outside interference is curbed on behalf of international institutions and procedures. In other words, a moderate world political system will require an expansion and strengthening of international organization, but, in my opinion, it does not require the kind of centralization of power that world federalists have envisaged. It requires that international organizations, while continuing to be arenas and stakes, be allowed to develop greater autonomy, not in the sense of ceasing to be "expressions of the interests of particular states or other international actors," but in the sense of also expressing what might be called systemic interests, those long- and short-term interests of states which aim, if not at maintaining the system (for it is futile to hope for a world of status quo powers), at least at maintaining moderation.[7]

It is necessary to examine separately the conditions for the establishment of a moderate international system and the conditions of its maintenance. In each instance I will try to list the tasks which international organization ought to perform as well as its limits.

The establishment of a moderate international system requires three broad sets of conditions. First, such a system will emerge (or, if one prefers, continue to develop out of the original bipolar cold war) only if certain kinds of crises are avoided. There ought to be no resort to nuclear weapons. The taboo that has prevailed since Nagasaki has become psychologically and politically essential (even though tactical nuclear weapons might conceivably be used without political and military disaster, the psychological effects could well prove deeply disruptive). In this respect the role of international organization will probably remain modest yet useful in a variety of ways: by providing what one might call a code of illegitimacy through resolutions and

---

7. See Robert Keohane, "Institutionalization in the United Nations General Assembly," *International Organization,* 23.4 (Autumn 1969), 862.

treaties; by establishing a legal framework for measures to restrict or slow down nuclear proliferation (which, if it became too widespread and especially if it reached certain countries with pressing grievances or fears, would strain the present taboo intolerably); by giving an international sanction to superpower agreements on arms control in the field of nuclear weapons and missiles; by lending the appearance of an international mandate to what might otherwise look like superpower collusion with respect to guarantees to third powers; by creating sufficiently objective or depoliticized mechanisms of inspection as soon as the refusal of one superpower has vanished (for internal as well as external reasons) and thus has ceased to justify the reticence of other states. To be sure, one can argue that a small nuclear war between lesser powers could take place without destabilizing the whole system; only a nuclear war involving a superpower or middle state would disrupt it. However, any violation of the nuclear taboo, even if it is restricted and contained when it first occurs, could have repercussions in the subterranean world of attitudes and expectations. The same considerations apply to biological and chemical warfare.

For similar reasons there ought to be no large-scale conventional war. The imperative of limitation—in geographical area (the number of states participating in a conflict) and in intensity—must be maintained, both because of the danger of escalation if a superpower is or becomes involved and because of the fact that the control of violence requires a kind of progressive "ritualization" or routinization of strictly limited wars. Here the United Nations will have to play a very important role. It will have to put pressure on the industrial powers, whose suicidal drive to sell arms abroad for a mix of economic and political reasons ignore all the lessons of history. It will have to continue to practice "preventive diplomacy" and preventive peace restoration so as to keep local conflicts between nations (other than those between superpowers and their allies) from becoming superpower confrontations; the United Nations may well be aided here by the superpowers' increasingly strong unwillingness to be dragged into such confrontations by third parties. Also, in the future the United Nations will have to find more effective ways than it has found in the past of limiting conflicts in which a superpower or a middle power (such as Communist China) is or becomes involved. Even though—as before—the capacity to resolve such a dispute may be lacking, the willingness to apply some of the techniques of peace restoration and peacekeeping to these kinds of conflicts will have to develop; for whereas there can be no world order that fails to recognize the special position and responsibilities of the superpowers, there can also be no world political society if these states, while playing an important role in defining political legitimacy and the rules of the game, nevertheless insist on being above the latter and outside the former. To be more precise and blunt, in the long run there can be no moderate international system with a United Nations and a United States behaving as they have done during the war in Vietnam.

However, it will be impossible to curtail violence if its causes and opportunities remain unchecked. Despite past failures the United Nations (and regional organizations) have no alternative to trying even more persistently to solve or attenuate those disputes between states which the restraints on force have perpetuated and brought to periodic bloodshed. What is needed is a permanent engagement of all these organizations in diplomacy. This is the area in which the greatest efforts of imagination on the part of these agencies' secretariats will be needed and the most constant amount of gentle pressure by their bodies on states engaged in potentially destructive conflicts will have to be maintained. It would be wrong to say that past fiascoes were due to the sporadic, sputtering quality of the efforts made: the reasons go much deeper. It would also be wrong to believe that more persistent efforts could ever succeed if the member states, particularly the major powers, fail to provide support and pressure on behalf of such attempts. But moderation will require, here again, ritualization. Such disputes should be under constant mediation, not merely under occasional mediation combined with preventive yet superficial or belated injunctions against force; international agencies often appear better centers for such mediation than specific groups of states. In a world in which, for many reasons, there may not be a permanent police force the development of diplomatic techniques may be the best hope and greatest challenge. (In this respect, as in few others, one might look back at the practices of the League of Nations.)

Since explosions remain nevertheless likely, a last contribution of international organization in this area should be helping to make the costs of military operations prohibitive, although the greatest obstacle to successful wars will undoubtedly remain the solidity and resistance of each party to a conflict. To the extent to which international agencies can participate in what has been called "nation building" (an ugly expression for a muddy concept) they will strengthen the two current limits to the usefulness of the resort to force.

This brings me to the last kind of crisis that will have to be avoided: large-scale economic disruptions, either in the relations between the rich and the poor or, more generally, in international financial mechanisms and through balance-of-payments problems. This is an area in which the chances for order and the development of international organization—as the framework of interstate cooperation, as a center for executive action on behalf of the states, and as the place in which a code of conduct for multinational corporations can be defined—are synonymous. There have been remarkable beginnings among the industrial nations (primarily in the non-Communist world). But enormous progress remains to be made both with respect to the regulation of transnational activity there and in relations between advanced, "rich" developing and "poor" underdeveloped countries, particularly in order to protect each group from balance-of-payments and commodity price fluctuations.[8] Here, international organization provides the only alternative to disastrous confrontation, and the best way of taming or regulating the moves of the players and their frequently reckless effects.

Such progress requires a change of attitude among the industrial nations. Otherwise, the developing nations with assets such as oil will continue to resort to a kind of economic warfare. Here we come to a second set of conditions for the establishment of a moderate international system: superpower restraint. This is not the place to describe in detail the perils of superpower activism; the experiences of Nikita Khrushchev and Lyndon Johnson are eloquent enough. The more active and involved the superpowers, the greater the perils of imbalance— through confrontation or disequilibrium between the superpowers and their protégés or tension between their external commitments and their internal troubles. Now, restraint will be incompatible with the pursuit and protection of their policies and interests and therefore acceptable to the superpowers only under certain circumstances; here again, international and regional agencies will have a role to play. There will have to be a restraint on arms races that could lead to superpower confrontations. This means, of course, first of all, a limitation of their own arms race. Such a limitation is beginning to appear to them as being in their own interest despite their security fears. Also contributing to this new sense of urgency is the superpowers' fear of nuclear arms race contagion to middle powers, a contagion inspired by the superpowers' example and by their determination not to be immediately outdistanced by the Big Two. If the superpowers want to stop their challengers, they will have to make concessions to them. Reciprocity operates here, as the long negotiations over the nuclear nonproliferation treaty have shown, and a cumulative mechanism (somewhat comparable to that which, within limits, works in the European Communities) may have been set in motion—in an area in which the prohibitive economic and financial

8. The writings of Charles P. Kindleberger and Raymond Vernon ought to be consulted for suggestions on these issues.

imperatives of the arms race may fortunately overtake and overturn the traditional logic of competition and diversity. The United Nations and regional organizations provide the best framework (and face-saving facade) for such bargaining and balancing. Restraint also means curbing arms races among third parties whose conflicts might engulf the superpowers in their role as providers of weapons and supporter of clients. Here again, international and regional organizations can serve as arenas for negotiation, sources of inspection, and concealers of super-power collusion.

Restraint will also mean adopting a kind of residual, or reserve, position with respect to peacekeeping. The enforcement of peace by the superpowers in every conflict between third parties could only either exacerbate their differences or also lead to a breakdown due either to third-party resistance or to opposition within the superpowers' own political systems. And yet, the Great Powers will continue to want local armistices and settlements to reflect their own views and to satisfy their own ambitions. Again, in a world in which traditional military alliances have lost much of their advantage, both for the superpowers, scared of being too deeply entangled, and for their allies, afraid of being either abandoned or subjugated, only international and regional organizations can perform at the same time three important functions. They can provide the procedural battlefield in which the Great Power's views and ambitions can be expressed and pressed; they can offer the channels of bargaining in which the lesser powers (without whose participation there can be no world order other than the dangerously activist one of superpower imperialism) can both amend the designs of the superpowers and be courted by them; and they can be the source of legitimacy once a solution has been adopted. In other words, insofar as crises break out in various parts of the world (whether they involve a superpower or not), the large states, in order to establish a moderate international system, will have to resort to international and regional agencies, first so as to end hostilities and restore peace, second so as to supervise and execute settlements (whether those settlements will have been negotiated directly by the parties, achieved through the efforts of the international or regional agencies themselves, or obtained through other procedures of mediation).

Finally, restraint by superpowers will mean a considerable change in their attitudes toward underdeveloped countries — both a willingness to separate economic aid from expectations of political advantage in the Great Powers' contest and, in the case of the United States, a resignation to inevitable manifestations of economic nationalism at the expense of American private interests deemed nefarious for the development of a national economy. Once more, recourse to international and regional agencies will be essential. The shift from bilateral to multilateral aid and the settlement of disputes arising out of expropriations through the efforts of such agencies and according to guidelines laid down by them (instead of a vicious cycle of mutual reprisals) should allow for the kind of superpower restraint that would not amount to neglect of the needs of the poorer nations and for the sort of superpower retreats that would not amount to a dangerous humiliation of the rich.

Global and regional agencies will be able to play such roles, however, only if a third condition of moderation is met: the gradual ending of quarantines in the world political system. This system will obviously be moderate only if it is worldwide. States excluded or quarantined remain the most dangerous sources of crises because of their very psychological or ideological isolation. They are least likely to accept as impartial international or regional agencies which either do not admit them as members or treat them as pariahs within their organs and which can therefore not expect to be allowed to play any significant role in peace-keeping, in the working out or in the carrying out of settlements involving such states. At this time, the very code of legitimacy developed by international organizations justifies the quarantine of states which refuse to conform to their code and whose ideological aggressiveness or racial policies are repugnant to a great majority of nations. But moral indignation and political or even economic boycotts are not the most effective forms of disapproval, the most likely ways of influencing behavior, nor the kinds of practices most capable of creating a moderate world political system. Those who have disapproved of the isolation of Communist China are often supporters of the quarantine of South Africa or Southern Rhodesia; but, on balance, and for the purpose of establishing a system of cooperation and management of conflict among interdependent but drastically diverse states, no quarantine ought to be perpetuated. For if one wants all states to adopt certain rules of conduct, they all have to be brought into the game and caught in its grip.

This does not mean that they will immediately accept those rules and play by them or be caught in the web at once. But the chance that this will eventually happen is greater if they are in than if they are out. The decision not to play, the decision to stay in splendid isolation, ought to be theirs. There are different ways of achieving moderation. The best is that which results from ideological homogeneity, from the convergence of parallelism of national practices and policies. But given the nature of the present world this remains a utopian vision. An international organization that would try to achieve it by verbal thunderbolts would only get farther away from it. Diversity would be inflamed instead of being made manageable. There remains only one other way to moderation. It consists of combining (regretfully perhaps) the toleration of, or resignation to, repugnant internal religions and relations with the prevention and repression of efforts by such regimes to spread their gospels and export their venom. Changes in their domestic beliefs and behavior will have to result from the frustration of such efforts, from domestic upheavals, and from the gradual effects of entanglement in the world political system.

This brings us to the conditions for maintaining a moderate international system, established thanks to the observance of the imperatives discussed above. Some of these conditions concern the elements that make up the system, others concern relations between the actors. A moderate system will have to be endowed with a fairly complex hierarchy of superpowers, middle powers, and small states or rather with a number of functional hierarchies that will overlap but much more diversified than the traditional hierarchy based essentially on military might. It will also, given the complexity and continuing heterogeneity of the world, require considerable regional decentralization. Despite (or because of) the multiplicity of regimes it will need an attitude of competitive coexistence on their part instead of one of mutual exclusiveness. And it will require strong transnational links, that is, a broad transnational society that will provide the states with new areas of cooperative goals or with goals that cannot be reached through violent conflict. Thus, the elements of the system will by themselves require, and allow for, a multiplicity of regional as well as universal organizations (the latter consisting largely of functional agencies). Each one will have its own bargaining process and its own balancing mechanism, based on the specific hierarchy of power that corresponds to its region or to its function. Each one will contribute therefore to decentralization and functional specialization in the system and to the diversification of power; each one will come close to what Ernst Haas has called a self-contained negotiating universe.

The relations within the world political society, or the rules of the game, will consist both of the imperatives for the establishment of a moderate system, which will continue to be indispensable, and of further developments in two directions. First, a new international legitimacy will have to emerge, as in every past moderate system. The world political society of the future, if it wants to avoid becoming a jungle, will have to meet two requirements. On the one hand, even though there appears at first sight to be a contradiction between the interpenetration of domestic and world politics, as well as that of transnational society and international politics, and a gradual extinction of foreign policy efforts at manipulating domestic politics in other countries, such a withdrawal from manipulation will have to take place. It would be facilitated by the increasing impermeability of consolidated societies to foreign intervention in a world in which the overt use of force becomes the exception and by statesmen becoming increasingly aware of the risks and uncertainties of such attempts at controlling others. This does not mean that the old principle of nonintervention will become more sacred than in the past. It means that the scale and scope of interventions must shrink and that attempts at influencing the behavior of a state must aim primarily at its external behavior on the various old and new chessboards of international affairs instead of being aimed at *internal* control. This will require on the part of international and regional agencies both continuity and change. They would continue to defend their members' sovereignty against outside intrusion and to be prudently ready to intervene through "preventive diplomacy" or for humanitarian reasons in large-scale civil wars so as to deter more interested and selfish interventions by cunning or greedy powers. But they would change, insofar as it would become more difficult for certain states to utilize regional or international agencies as a cloak behind which they resort to the manipulation of domestic affairs, under the pretext provided by collective statements condemning certain kinds of regimes or endorsing certain kinds of domestic practices. Such a change will occur only if the elements of the system meet the requirements listed, that is, if the international hierarchy and the panoply of power available to any given state are sufficiently complex and diversified to allow for the types of balancing and bargaining that would curtail such instrumental uses of regional or international bodies by a handful of dominant actors.

On the other hand, the nature of the new chessboards and the need to dampen conflict on the old ones will require in a shrinking world, if not an increasing transfer of sovereignty to international organization (which would gradually receive some of the attributes of statehood), at least an increasing pooling of sovereignties for the exercise of cooperation in the various economic, monetary, and technical fields; in communications; in scientific research and exploration, and so on; and even in peacekeeping. Thus, progressively, overt conflict and all-out competition would be replaced, not by harmony, but by competition in a framework of cooperation and by muted conflict, that is, by bargaining (which is not at all, as labor negotiators know, necessarily a mild, easy, and brotherly activity). It is obvious that only regional and universal institutions can provide the framework, incentives, expertise, and rules of security and predictability required.

Second, along with the new legitimacy of nonmanipulation and competitive cooperation, the procedures for the maintenance of order will have to be fortified in two areas discussed in connection with the emergence of a moderate system. Insofar as peacekeeping is concerned, there is obviously in the long run no substitute for international measures of arms control with a growing network of supervision, inspection, and enforcement. Transfers of sovereignty of the kind envisaged once by the Baruch plan or by the Clark-Sohn scheme remain improbable; but complex third-party procedures and balanced (one dare hardly say objective or impartial) safeguards going beyond unilateral limitations and contractual promises will be necessary. And even if no permanent world police force emerges, ad hoc forces in readiness for the policing of violent conflicts other than those involving major powers will be needed (even if the deterrence of nuclear war or of conventional aggression by secondary nuclear powers remains the preserve of the superpowers themselves). On the other hand, beyond the strengthening of the techniques of diplomacy for the settlement of disputes, international and regional bodies will have to develop regular procedures of peaceful change if the avoidance or limitation of the resort to force is to become a ritual; for there will always be tensions and pressures for change, and the more one insists on keeping them under control, the more one will need to develop mechanisms of review and nonviolent adjustment. This is the realm in which the outlines of the future are dimmest and in which the role of international organization may be greatest, especially by comparison with its past failure and present pallor.

A moderate world society will have to be based on three principles. One is the universalization of concern. This does not mean that (as in the theory of collective security) every conflict should be escalated to the world level rather than localized. Universal concern does not require universal involvement. Actual participation in the management of troubles ought often to remain within the boundaries of subsystems, and the need for superpower restraint has been stressed before. But in a worldwide political system the real alternative to universal concern is unilateral action, especially by a superpower within or even outside its self-proclaimed sphere of vital interests. If this recipe for immoderation is to be discarded, and although (or because) there can be no ironclad guarantees of security and there neither is nor should be any possibility for constant, worldwide policing by the superpowers, there will have to be collective intervention for peacekeeping and settlement so as to increase the disutility of the resort to force. Superpowers at the world level and middle powers in their regions will themselves find it necessary to obtain collective sanction for their interventions in interstate disputes or collective participation in the enforcement of peace or of settlements. The second principle is the gradual reduction of the most extreme inequalities—material as well as political, that is, the cases of extreme domination and dependence. The capacity of the international system to deal with these in a world in which the resort to force in order to fight injustice is too risky will be limited and complex. But in the long run moderation and a modicum of equalization are inseparable. The third principle is the need for safety valves for change, the more the uses of force are repressed. Hence, the requirement that states stop manipulating internal affairs and accept broad, even violent, domestic change and regimes hostile to their own conceptions or to private foreign interests, as long as the external behavior of these regimes or revolutionary forces is nonviolent and nondisruptive; hence also the necessary development of collective procedures of peaceful change for interstate relations.

At this stage in world affairs it is difficult to foresee whether a world society built on those principles will emerge. The listing of conditions and requirements provides a better critique of the present than a prophecy of the future. Thus, it helps us see how extraordinarily far we still are from a moderate system of world order, despite the wishful thinking of those who believe in the demise of force or in the compelling impact of "modernization." In any case, international organization will essentially remain a forum in which a consensus of states (and of the other players of world politics) may be forged, as well as the executor of the agreements and the framework for the cooperation which a moderate world society would engage in. Whether such a society emerges depends only for a very modest part on what international organization initiates, even though international organization will have these many important roles to play if states allow this society to emerge. What can be stated is that such a society would afford the greatest opportunities and the widest need for international and regional organizations without which it would be crippled. It has been noted earlier that not every moderate system has a procedural consensus that makes of such agencies the legitimate channels for controlling conflict and for promoting cooperation; but it is obvious that a worldwide international system with a complex hierarchy of power and a formidable range of tasks and chessboards can have no other legitimate channels. The scope and intensity of interstate and transnational relations leave no alternative. It can also be stated, in turn, that such organizations—which today remain epiphenomena rather than prime movers—will not develop fully as long as the international system has not found more organic forms of moderation than the rather mechanical or tactical ones which have appeared in recent years. And it is perfectly possible to conceive of a diversified world society with a network of such agencies even though a (much tamer) nation-state would still, in theory and practice, be the highest form of social organization and center of allegiance.

10. The Fragile Sanity of States: A Theoretical Analysis

Karl Deutsch and Dieter Senghaas

It has been a tradition in much of political theory to describe the behavior of states as rational. Indeed, the "reason of state" often has been pictured as embodying a logic more profound and more constant than the reasoning of individuals and lesser groups.[1] In addition to their overriding importance, the logic of this reason of state is sometimes described as inherently realistic. The political realist, as described by Hans Morgenthau, must give precedence to the interests of his nation over the personal wishes and values of its statesmen, and, of course, over those of its less influential citizens. This "concept of interest defined in terms of power . . . provides the link between reason . . . and the facts . . . On the side of the actor it . . . creates that astounding continuity in foreign policy which makes American, British, or Russian foreign policy appear as an intelligible, rational continuum, by and large consistent within itself, regardless of the different motives, preferences, and intellectual and moral qualities of successive statesmen."[2]

The Limited Rationality of Governments and Nations

We propose an alternative approach. The "reasons of state" model seems to us inadequate for two reasons. First, it asserts a higher degree of *continuity* in the foreign policy of major powers than can actually be observed. In the four decades between 1930 and 1970 the United States, Britain, and the Soviet Union have all changed their major foreign policies, both in regard to major methods and strategies, and in regard to particular objectives. The United States and Britain have changed major foreign policy goals, and the Soviet Union, too, has changed its avowed policy goals by the official acceptance of the doctrine of peaceful coexistence, including the assertion that world wars are no longer inevitable even though two thirds of mankind live under capitalist economic systems.

1. Classic formulations of the "reason of state" are found in N. Machiavelli, *The Prince;* and Karl von Clausewitz, *Vom Kriege*, 17th ed. (Bonn, Dummlers Verlag, 1965), trans. Col. J. J. Graham, *On War* (New York, Barnes & Noble, 1966), selections, ed. Anatol Rapoport, *On War* (Baltimore, Penguin Books, 1968), with an important critical introduction. A major critical survey is Friedrich Meinecke, *Die Idee der Staatsraison in der Neueren Geschichte,* vol. I (Munich, 1957); and a recent restatement is Hans Morgenthau, *Politics among Nations,* 4th ed. (New York, Knopf, 1967), pp. 4-11.
2. Morgenthau, *Politics among Nations,* p. 5.

There is a second objection which seems to us still more farreaching in its implications: states act much less *rationally* than the theory asserts. The rationalist model suggests a higher frequency of correct predictions on the part of governments, in regard to the consequences of their own major foreign policy actions than can be observed in practice. The *frequency of errors* and misperceptions has been particularly high in those decisions by which governments initiated or deliberately escalated major warlike actions. Of all governmental decisions initiating major wars since 1910, about three fifths appeared to be mistaken, both in terms of the appraisal of the capabilities and intentions of other major governments, at the time when war was started, and in terms of the eventual consequences at its end.[3]

Thus, the decision in 1914 of Austria-Hungary to make war on Serbia, the decision of Russia to make war on Austria-Hungary, the decision of Germany to make war on Russia and France and to invade Belgium, the decision of the Ottoman empire to enter the war on the side of the Central Powers rather than to remain neutral, and the decision of Austria-Hungary to fight for Trieste and the Alto-Adige territory rather than to cede these so as to keep Italy neutral — all these turned out to be mistakes which contributed substantially to the destruction of the governments that made them. The German decision to attack Poland in 1939 and Russia in 1941, the Russian decision not to expect a German attack in July 1941, and the Japanese decision to attack the United States in September 1941, all proved to be similar mistakes. In the case of Japan and Germany they led to the destruction of the governments, and in the case of Russia Stalin's error exacted an additional heavy price for the eventual survival of that state.

The Search for Rational Models of Irrational Behavior

Purposive rationality seems to be significantly rarer in the major decisions of governments than a rationalistic theory of interests would lead us to expect.[4] Something similar has long been observed in the life of

3. Computed from data on 50 international wars, 1815-1965, collected by J. David Singer and Melvin Small, in their book, *The Wages of War* (New York, John Wiley, 1973). We are indebted to Professors Singer and Small, and to Mrs. Susan Jones, for making these data available before publication and to Professor Small for help in identifying the initiators and losers in each war. The responsibility for the final coding decisions, however, remains our own.

4. Purposive rationality refers to behavior which in fact has a high probability of leading to the outcome desired by the actor. His desire for this outcome is, of course, subjective, but the probability that his behavior will actually lead to this outcome is a question of objective fact. Following Max Weber and Karl

individuals. They, too, act in moments of critical decisions far less often in accordance with objective purposive rationality and far more often in a manner damaging or destructive to themselves or to their own major values, than one would expect on the basis of any rationalist theory of enlightened self-interest. Moreover, it is notorious in the case of individuals that, if they are supplied with additional cognitive information about the expectable consequences of their behavior, they often disbelieve it or reject it on other grounds. Cognitive inputs, in short, notoriously play a much smaller role in actual decisions made by individuals at critical moments than any rationalistic interest theory would predict.

Conventional wisdom labels the gap between what purposively rational people would do and what real people actually do as the "irrationality" of human nature; it tends to treat irrationality as a label for counterproductive behavior and as an uncaused cause. Modern depth psychology and psychiatry try to retrace, step by step, the processes that lead people to act so as to produce outcomes that they themselves do not consciously desire and which they even may wish strongly to avoid. Psychiatrists, like Sigmund Freud, have tried to develop formally rational models for the purposively irrational, counter-productive behavior of their patients in the hope that these models will lead the physicians eventually to therapeutic procedures by which the self-damaging behavior of their patients may be cured or mitigated.

More recently, something similar has been attempted by students of decision making in large organizations. Studies of modern business organizations show that the purposive rationality of their behavior cannot always be taken for granted. Business organizations are less often steered by market forces, government agencies are less often steered by the approval of voters or congressional majorities, and political parties

---

Mannheim this purposive rationality should be distinguished from formal rationality which consists in the retraceability of the sequence of steps by which a result or a decision has been reached. The procedures of formal logic, mathematics, and accountancy, are examples of formal rationality. If each step in such a procedure can only lead to a unique result, we call such a procedure not only formally rational but rigorous.

Purposively rational procedures need not be formally rational. They may get the desired results even if the steps leading to them cannot be retraced. Formally rational procedures need not be purposive; though retraceable in every step, they may fail to lead to the desired outcome, particularly when they started from incomplete or unrealistic premises. The coincidence of formal and purposive rationality is thus again a question of empirical fact in every case. The simple everyday notion of rationality leads us to expect it, but experience shows that it cannot be taken for granted.

are less often steered by the response of voters, than any simple rationalistic interest theory would lead us to expect. Recent studies have tried to understand and retrace the processes by which such organizations behave in a purposively irrational manner, so as to produce outcomes opposite to the mission of the organization, as well as to the desires of its leading personnel.

Comparable problems may occur in the design of large computers and of complex self-steering mechanical or electronic systems. In such cases the designers have in mind a specific class of outcomes which they desire; and they try to design overall control circuits operating on the feedback principle, which are to steer the system to the desired goals or outcomes. Such complex systems include, however, a multiplicity of feedback circuits, often arranged in subsystems and in hierarchies. Such subsystems and lower level feedbacks may then produce decisions which may prevent the overall system from reaching its goals; or else, even in the absence of such internal difficulties, the overall system may receive insufficient or misleading information from the still larger suprasystem within which it has to operate. The result in each case may be behavior which is counterproductive in terms of the goals of the original overall design. Problems of this kind are being studied by specialists in communication and control, and in many cases they have proved capable of being solved.

Individual human personalities, large human organizations, and certain nonhuman communication and control systems thus seem to have certain problems in common. Each of them may show a gap between expected purposive rationality and actual behavior; and each of them may show a difficulty of coordination among feedback processes on the level of an entire self-steering system, and on the level of its constitutive subsystems and of its surrounding suprasystem.

In the field of research on war and peace, studies of this kind are needed to account for the frequency and the causes of purposively irrational behavior of governments and nations in decisions that may critically affect their stability and survival.

A Structural Interpretation of Freud's Three-Level Model of the Decision System of Individuals

Freud's basic theories are the result of his attempt to derive generally applicable abstract patterns from his clinical experiences. Though his subject matter was complex and though he was much concerned with the questions of biological foundations and developmental sequences both in individuals and in the species, the basic model at which he arrived has a relatively simple structure. It is this structure of Freud's model of the human personality system, rather than Freud's ideas about its possible genesis, that will concern us here.

The structural comparison whcih we propose will be based on the deliberate use of incomplete analogies. Analogies that have proved useful in scientific thought often have been radically incomplete, in the sense that they omitted many important aspects of the two systems which they were comparing, but that the very limited aspects in which the two systems were comparable were important within each system, and that their comparison proved fruitful for further work. Thus Harvey's comparison of the circulation of the blood with a system of mechanical valves and pumps omitted very much that was essential for the actual functioning of the blood supply of the human body. In comparing the structure of our circulatory system with the strueture of a hydraulic system, Harvey omitted — or indeed was ignorant of — the role of red and white blood corpuscles and their chemical and biological characteristics, the mechanisms maintaining the temperature of the blood, the processes preventing or producing its coagulation, the existence of blood groups, and many other things. In all these respects and many others, human blood in a living body indeed was "not comparable" to water in a pump. But in its response to the actions of valves and pumps it was comparable. To see this real though limited comparability, and to develop this comparison effectively, was an important part of Harvey's scientific contribution.[5]

We propose to explore a similarly limited comparison of certain structural properties of Freud's model of the individual human psyche with certain structural properties of national governments, intranational interest groups, and the international system. In so doing, we shall often be moving back and forth between the levels of the individual and the state without losing sight of the limits of the similarities we are seeking to exploit. Readers are urged to bear in mind that all such comparisons will disregard many important aspects of Freud's model, such as his views of the development of personality from childhood, and that they will treat others only in part, such as Freud's concept of the libido and its distribution among different activities and objects in the mind. All we hope to do is to suggest that the limited structures which we do compare will prove comparable within their relatively narrow limits, and that their comparison may turn out to be illuminating and potentially fruitful.

Freud himself might have found such an undertaking perhaps not

5. James B. Conant, *Science and Common Sense* (New Haven, Yale University Press, 1951), pp. 221-222.

wholly contrary to the spirit of some of his works. In 1915 Freud published an article on "Timely Reflections about War and Death" in which he wrote of "the human individuals on a large scale, the nations and states."[6] There he discussed how these "individuals on a large scale" in time of war had "dropped the restraints of morality towards one another" and were using this as an opportunity "to escape for a while the existing pressure of culture and to permit temporary satisfaction to their pent-up instincts," probably without injuring, he added, the relatively high level of morality within the national community of each.[7] "The peoples," he concluded, "at present obey their passions far more than their interests. At most they use their interests in order to rationalize their passions; they pretend their interests in order to find reasons for the satisfaction of their passions."[8]

In passages like these, Freud clearly treated large-scale human collectivities as social systems, and he compared limited but important aspects of their behavior with that of the small-scale systems of individual human personalities. In order to pursue further the possibilities of such comparisons, we shall first outline what seemed to us the relevant aspects of the structure of Freud's model of the individual personality, and later compare it with relevant aspects of nation-state behavior.

Instincts and the Id. Starting from the behavior of young children, Freud saw human behavior motivated by a number of basic drives which he called *instinctual,* that is, inborn rather than learned, and based on the physical, neurological, and biochemical constitution of the human organism. Breathing, thirst, hunger, and love — of which sex was not the only form — seemed to him examples of such basic drives. A plurality of such drives existed in the human organism and gave rise, through the human nervous system, to sequences of behavior leading to some temporary state of satisfaction, or at least aiming in its direction.

The "region" or "mental province" of the human personality which included all such drives Freud called the id. For Freud the id was thus a

6. Sigmund Freud, "Zeitgemässes über Krieg und Tod," in *Gesammelte Schriften* (Leipzig: Internationaler Psychoanalytischer Verlag, 1924), X, 315-346, esp. pp. 316, 319, 320, 327, 330 (translated by the authors).
    7. Ibid., p. 327.
    8. Ibid., p. 331. Freud might have found some food for thought in President Richard M. Nixon's television address in May 1970 with its statement, "I would rather be a one-term President . . . than a two-term President at the cost of seeing America become a second-rate power and see this nation accept the first defeat in its proud 190-year history," *Chicago Daily News,* May 13, 1970, p. 13.

collection or class of nervous and mental processes. He explicitly stated that it was not an organization; that it had no requirements of consistency and was not subject to the law of excluded contradictions as it is known in the classic form of logic. The id knew neither logic, nor morality, nor fear. Its component instincts or subsystems only blindly pressed or called for satisfaction. This satisfaction, however, was felt as pleasure by the organism and the search for such pleasure — which Freud called the pleasure principle — was the only principle the id obeyed. The id in its totality, as the aggregate of all these instincts, seemed to Freud the source of all "psychic energy," and thus at bottom of all human motivation, and particularly of all human spontaneous behavior.[9]

Although Freud defined the id in principle as a collection of a plurality of different and potentially contradictory instincts, he actually paid most attention throughout his writings to one of these, which he called libido. In his own words, Freud chose to call "by that name the energy, regarded as a quantitative magnitude (though not at present actually measurable), of those instincts which have to do with all that may be comprised under the word 'love.' "[10]

Nonetheless, Freud never denied the importance of other basic instincts in man, even though he paid less explicit attention to them — perhaps because their satisfaction seemed to him less often neglected and repressed in the milieu of middle-class Vienna of his time. A present-day psychiatrist, Dr. Roy F. Grinker, has communicated a case study of his, in which he found that extreme food deprivation in childhood had led in the later life of a patient to a series of symptoms closely

9. Freud's model at this point appears both more simple and more subtle than that of Jeremy Bentham who had seen human behavior as steered by two sources of motivation, the attainment of pleasure and the avoidance of pain. From his clinical experience as a psychiatrist and perhaps also from his anti-authoritarian predisposition, Freud gave little weight to the avoidance of pain as a general motive for human behavior. Nonetheless Freud's model accounted for a wider variety of human actions and often with greater precision, than Bentham's model could.

10. Sigmund Freud, *Group Psychology and the Analysis of the Ego* (New York, Bantam Books, 1965), p. 29. Freud continued: "The nucleus of what we mean by love naturally consists (and this is what is commonly called love and what the poets sing of) in sexual love with sexual union as its aim. But we do not separate from this . . . on the one hand self-love, and on the other, love for parents and children, friendship and love for humanity in general, and also devotion to concrete objects and abstract ideas . . . all these tendencies are an expression of the same instinctual impulses . . . In its origin, function, and relation to sexual love the 'eros' of the philosopher Plato coincides exactly with the love force, the libido of psychoanalysis," ibid., pp. 29-30.

paralleling the symptoms found by Freud in patients who in childhood have been deprived of love.[11]

Reality and the Ego. At the other extreme of Freud's model was his largest and most comprehensive system, which he called reality or the real world. This included not only the physical world of sticks and stones and day and night but also the entire human and social environment of the individual, such as his family, his neighbors, his government, and his entire society and culture. Each man had to seek the satisfaction of his diverse instincts in that real world, which existed for the most part outside his own body and independent of his own preferences and perceptions; but even his own body, such as a broken leg, could function as part of this reality. Man could operate upon this reality and change it somewhat in order to satisfy some need of his instincts; he could, as Freud pointed out, till a field [to grow] food to still his hunger. Whether as a limitation or an opportunity, however, reality confronted man with the reality principle, which demands from each individual that he take into account the conditions imposed by the outer world and the consequences of his actions in it.

The id, however, as well as any and all of the instincts included within it, was blind to most of this reality. A particular instinct might respond to some particular signal relevant to it, much as a suffocating man may gasp for air or a thirsty man might reach for water. But the great preponderance of a man's perception of the outside world was not part of his id. Rather, perceptions belonged to the perceptual system, through which alone the id received information from the outside world and which therefore in a sense mediated between the instincts and reality.

In the course of human evolution, Freud thought, this perceptual system and its mediating functions had developed a great deal. It had become enriched by memories and elaborated in its capacities for coordination and decision. Eventually it had become a full-fledged system of its own, intermediate between the large system of the outside world and the poorly organized pluralistic system of the id, which was largely blind to it, having only "its own world of perception," obeying "the inexorable pleasure principle" but lacking the internal organization to ensure consistency among its component and competing drives.

This intermediate organization, Freud called the ego. It was indeed an organization as he described it:

> The principal characteristics of the ego are these. In consequence of the relation which was already established between sensory perception and muscular action, the ego is in control of voluntary move-

---

11. Personal communication by Dr. Roy F. Grinker, Chicago, 1954.

ment. It has the task of self-preservation. As regards *external* events, it performs that task by becoming aware of the stimuli from without, by storing up experiences of them (in the memory), by avoiding excessive stimuli (through flight), by dealing with moderate stimuli (through adaption) and, finally, by learning to bring about appropriate modifications in the external world to its own advantage (through activity). As regards *internal* events, in relation to the id, it performs that task by gaining control over the demands of the instincts, by deciding whether they shall be allowed to obtain satisfaction, by postponing that satisfaction to times and circumstances favorable in the external world or by suppressing their excitations completely. Its activities are governed by considerations of the tensions produced by stimuli present within it or introduced into it. The raising of these tensions is in general felt as *unpleasure* and their lowering as *pleasure*. It is probable, however, that what is felt as pleasure or unpleasure is not the *absolute* degree of the tensions, but something in the rhythm of their changes. The ego pursues pleasure and seeks to avoid unpleasure. An increase in unpleasure which is expected and foreseen is met by a *signal of anxiety*; the occasion of this increase, whether it threatens from without or within, is called a danger. From time to time the ego gives up its connection with the external world and withdraws into the state of sleep in which its organization undergoes far-reaching changes.[12]

For every individual, his ego was that organized part of his personality that permitted him to adapt to the outside world and at the same time to maintain some compatibility and consistency in his behavior. No person, however, was born with a fully developed ego of this kind. Most of the elements of the ego were derived from the experiences of the individuals and built up into an organized system in the course of his development as a person. Many of these experiences differ from person to person; many indeed are accidental. From such different elements acquired in different sequences, every individual builds up his own ego which is in some ways different from any other.

Society, Morality, and the Superego. One class of experiences which enter the ego of almost every person, according to Freud, is the prescriptions and prohibitions which he receives in infancy from his parents and from other persons who have a part in his upbringing. Many of these do's and don't's are standardized in the particular culture, religion, or ideology in which the individual has been raised. Associated with these are his loving or painful memories of his parents, his memor-

12. Sigmund Freud, *An Outline of Psychoanalysis,* quoted after *Freud Dictionary of Psychoanalysis,* eds. N. Fodor and F. Gaynor (Greenwich, Conn., Fawcett Publications, Inc., 1966), pp. 55-56.

ies of his childhood fears and of the authority figures who gave protection or else aggravated them. The collection of these commands and prohibitions, and the feelings of love and fear connected with them, according to Freud, become a coherent special subsystem within the ego. This part Freud called the superego, or the ego ideal. Its commands then constitute what we commonly call the voice of conscience.

Though a part of the ego, the superego could separate from it and, so to speak, confront it. Its commands could contradict those actions chosen by the ego; and actions which the ego had directed could incur the severe disapproval of the superego which then would symbolize the disapproval which the parents and authority figures, remembered from the individual's past, would have expressed of this behavior if they had learned of it.

Although most of the attention of Freud's contemporaries was attracted to his view of the id, and of the unconscious manner in which it operated, *it is the ego that occupies a central position in the structure of his model.* In recent decades the ego has attracted more attention from psychiatrists; and it is the ego and its functions which made Freud's general model, from a structural point of view, particularly relevant for the analysis of international politics.

The Tasks of the Ego: Perception, Mediation, and Control. For the relation of the ego to the id, Freud's descriptions are suggestive:

> For the ego, perception plays the part which in the id falls to instinct. The ego represents what may be called reason and common sense, in contrast to the id, which contains the passions . . .
>
> The functional importance of the ego is manifested in the fact that normally control over the approaches to motility devolves upon it. Thus in its relation to the id it is like a man on horseback, who has to hold in check the superior strength of the horse; with this difference, that the rider tries to do so with his own strength while the ego uses borrowed forces. The analogy may be carried a little further. Often a rider, if he is not to be parted from his horse, is obliged to guide it where it wants to go; so in the same way the ego is in the habit of transforming the id's will into action as if it were its own.[13]

In its relation to the outside world, the ego has the task of perception and adjustment. In taking account of its dangers and obstacles, its performance criteria may include prudence and expediency, as well as foresight and decisiveness.

In its relation to the superego, however, prudence and expediency toward the present outside world may clash with the commands of

13. Sigmund Freud, *The Ego and the Id* (New York, Norton, 1960), p. 15.

tradition and authority figures remembered from the past. These commands of the superego may be the more formidable in their effects, since both they and their sources are likely to have become unconscious and thus inaccessible to any countermessages from the ego. In most people, the superego speaks but cannot be spoken to.

Something similar applies to the id. Most of its contents, too, is unconscious. Much of our basic drives is unconscious, and so are most of their elaborations and the memories and responses which have become associated with them in the course of our mental and emotional development. They are usually inaccessible, therefore, to the criticism of the ego in regard to their possible inappropriateness or inconsistency with one another, or, with any of the other systems. Ordinarily, they cannot be reasoned with at their sources. They can only be heeded or resisted, accepted or repressed—and since the id is the source of all psychic energy and spontaneous motivation, the costs to the ego of resisting it are serious indeed.

Freud describes the conflict between the ego and the id in these words:

> There are two paths by which the contents of the id can penetrate into the ego. The one is direct, the other leads by way of the ego ideal; which of these two paths they take may, for some mental activities, be of decisive importance: The ego develops from perceiving instincts to controlling them, from obeying instincts to inhibiting them. In this achievement a large share is taken by the ego ideal, which indeed is partly a reaction-formation against the instinctual processes of the id . . .

> From the other point of view, however, we see this same ego as a poor creature owing service to three masters and consequently menaced by three dangers: from the external world, from the libido of the id, and from the severity of the super-ego. Three kinds of anxiety correspond to these three dangers, since anxiety is the expression of a retreat from danger. As a frontier-creature, the ego tries to mediate between the world and the id, to make the id pliable to the world and, by means of its muscular activity, to make the world fall in with the wishes of the id. In point of fact it behaves like the physician during an analytic treatment: it offers itself with the attention it pays to the real world, as a libidinal object to the id, and aims at attaching the id's libido to itself. It is not only a helper to the id; it is also a submissive slave who courts his master's love. Whenever possible, it tries to remain on good terms with the id; it clothes the id's unconscious commands with its preconscious rationalizations; it pretends that the id is showing obedience to the admonitions of reality, even when in

fact it is remaining obstinate and unyielding; it disguises the id's conflicts with reality and, if possible, its conflicts with the super-ego too. In its position midway between the id and reality, it only too often yields to the temptation to become sycophantic, opportunist and lying, like a politician who sees the truth but wants to keep his place in popular favour.[14]

As this passage shows, Freud emphasized the perpetual possibility of three kinds of conflict: between the ego and reality, between the ego and the id, and between the ego and the superego. In another passage he discusses a fourth kind of conflict, that between reality and the id. In such a conflict, he says the ego must side with reality, but if it does so in an inappropriate manner the result in the case of an individual will be the formation of a neurosis. Such a neurosis, according to Freud, arises from a conflict between

an ego, prevented in its synthetizing activity . . . and an id in which individual instincts have made themselves independent, pursuing their own aims without regard for the interest of the whole personality . . . the ego has made an attempt to suppress certain parts of the id by an *inappropriate method* . . . and the id has taken its revenge. Neurosis is thus a consequence of a conflict between ego and id, on which the ego centers because . . . it insists throughout on retaining its adaptability towards the outer world. The opposition lies between outer world and id, and because the ego, true to its inmost nature, takes sides with the outer world, it becomes involved in conflict with its own id. But mark well that it is not the fact of this conflict which brings about the illness—for such opposition between reality and id is unavoidable, and the ego's constant task is to mediate between them. It is the fact that the ego, for settling the conflict, has employed the inadequate method of repression. But this in turn arises from the fact that at the time when this task was presented to it the ego was undeveloped and weak.[15]

Other types of conflict receive attention elsewhere in Freud's writings. If one orders systematically the major types of possible conflicts, implicit in Freud's scheme, ten possible conflict types result; and it is these ten types which may have their counterparts in types of potential political conflicts at the subnational, national, and international level.

14. Ibid., pp. 45-46. For a recent discussion of similar problems facing advisers to the President of the United States and advisers and officials generally, see Albert O. Hirschman, *Exit, Voice and Loyalty* (Cambridge, Mass., Harvard University Press, 1970).

15. Sigmund Freud, *The Question of Lay Analysis,* quoted after *Freud Dictionary of Psychoanalysis,* n. 12, pp. 102-103.

A Simple Typology of Possible Conflict in Freud's Structural Model

In much of his own writing, Freud paid particular attention to conflicts between the id and the other three system levels in his model.
These were id and reality, id and superego, and id and ego, as well as
conflicts within the id, that is to say, among some of the subsystems
composing it. In addition to these four potential conflict types, there
can be a fifth type of conflict between the ego and the superego; to such
conflicts, too, Freud paid a good deal of attention.

There is also a possibility, however, of a sixth type of conflict between
the ego and reality. The physical or social reality may be so complex, so
fast changing or so threatening, that the ego cannot form an adequate
image of its environment, or else that it cannot find an adequate set of
behavioral responses to cope with it. The first of these possibilities was
touched upon by Karl Mannheim in his concept of the "opacity" of
modern industrial societies.[16] The second possibility, that of overwhelming cognitive emotional and behavioral demands by an unbear-
able environment, is one of the aspects discussed by Bruno Bettelheim
in his work on the behavior of prisoners in Nazi concentration camps,
and it plays a role in the research on the psychological responses of individuals to disaster situations.[17]

A seventh type of conflict situation could occur between the superego
and reality — if the superego fails to be relevant to reality, or if reality is
such that the commands of the superego cannot be followed under its
conditions. In such situations, either reality or the superego may have to
be changed. But until this happens, conflict may well be severe. Conflicts of this type play a role in much of contemporary youth unrest and
also in the case of social and political leaders who reorient both their
own superegos and some of the value patterns of their own time, as occurred in the cases of Martin Luther and Mahatma Gandhi, studied by
Erik Erikson.[18] Freud himself paid relatively less attention to such conflicts of the sixth and seventh type, but some of the more sociologically
oriented psychiatrists and psychologists of our time have done so.[19]

16. Karl Mannheim, *Man and Society in an Age of Reconstruction* (New
York, Harcourt, Brace, 1950).

17. See Bruno Bettelheim, *The Informed Heart: Autonomy in a Mass Age*
(Glencoe, The Free Press, 1960); and Allen H. Barton, *Communities in Disas-
ter: A Sociological Analysis of Collective Stress Situations* (New York, Anchor
Books, 1970).

18. Erik Erikson, *Young Man Luther* (New York, Norton, 1958), and
Gandhi's Truth (New York, Norton, 1969).

19. See particularly Alexander Mitscherlich, *The Fatherless Society* (Boston,
Schocken, 1970); Alexander and Margarete Mitscherlich, *Über die Unfähigkeit*

Three other types of conflict also received less of Freud's attention, although they are logically implicit in his scheme. First of all, reality itself is not free of serious conflicts, contradictions, and incompatibilities. In regard to social reality in particular there is no culture, nor is there any political or economic system, that does not contain some internal conflicts and contradictions involving some of its human components, its prevailing practices, or the conditions of its physical environment. The history of social conflicts, of population growth, and resource conservation or depletion is too rich in examples to require their recounting here.

In the second place, the memories and commands, which constitute the superego are unlikely to be free from contradictions and internal conflicts. It is difficult to construct any complex system of commands, or of logical propositions, or of electric switches, or of synapses among nerve cells, in such a manner as to make it completely free from contradictions and paradoxes, even over the short run. For the long-run operation of any such system, according to the mathematician Kurt Goedel, its immunity to such contradictions can never be proved.[20] The history of philosophic and religious systems shows that each of them, sooner or later, has given rise to mutually contradictory commands. The resulting conflict of conscience, or of loyalties and obligations, have formed a perennial theme in literature, philosophy, and politics.

Finally, by the same reasoning, the ego system itself is unlikely to be free from contradictions and conflicts within itself. To be sure, its task is the search for consistency and synthesis; but it is itself still a system. No matter how logical his own structure, it is still subject to Goedel's theorem. Here, too, experience confirms deduction. Inner conflicts within the ego — the conscious part of a personality — have occupied researchers in psychology and psychiatry, and writers and thinkers throughout the ages.[21]

zu trauern (Munich, Piper, 1968); Theodor W. Adorno, "Zum Verhältnis von Soziologie und Psychologie," in *Sociologica,* 1 (Frankfurt, Europäische Verlagsanstalt, 1955), 11-45; Klaus Horn, "Politische Psychologie" in G. Kress and D. Senghaas, eds., *Politikwissenschaft* (Frankfurt, Europäische Verlagsanstalt, 1969), pp. 215-268. See also Kenneth Keniston, *The Uncommitted: Alienated Youth in American Society* (New York, Harcourt, 1965), and by the same author, *Young Radicals: Notes on Committed Youth* (New York, Harcourt, 1968).

20. On the Goedel theorem see Ernst Nagel and James R. Newman, "Goedel's Proof," in James R. Newman, ed., *The World of Mathematics,* III (New York, Simon and Schuster, 1956), 1668-1695.

21. For recent examples of studies of conflict within the ego system, see Corbett Thigpen and Hervey Cleckley, *Three Faces of Eve* (New York, McGraw-Hill, 1957); and Gregory Bateson, D. D. Jackson, J. Haley, and J.

Freud himself paid less attention to these conflicts within each of the system levels in his model: the conflicts within reality, within the super-ego and within the ego system. Philosophic traditions on the other hand, from Kant, Hegel, and Marx to the modern existentialists, have long emphasized their importance.

Altogether, Freud's model thus generates ten types of possible conflict, as shown in Table 1. Four of these are conflicts within system levels, while six involve cross-level conflicts. It is assumed here that the sequence of initiating and responding unit within each unit pair is irrelevant so that a conflict between ego and id is treated as equivalent to a conflict between id and ego. If this simplifying assumption is dropped — for instance, if we should wish to distinguish between the subsystem in which a conflict producing change is initiated, and the subsystem in which its effects arise later — then the number of possible intersystem conflict types would rise to twelve, and the total number of potential conflict types to sixteen.

Ego Burden and Ego Performance. Each of the ten types of potential conflicts represents a potential burden to the ego. According to Freud, the human personality has no other mechanism that the ego system for coping with any kind of conflict. Even in regard to its own inner conflicts, the ego must work out its own stability.

Freud's model thus inescapably suggests the great size and seriousness of the burden of communication and decision making with which any ego has to cope if it is to fulfill its burden of control. The concept of such an ego burden is not explicitly formulated by Freud, but it is implicit in the concepts of ego strength and ego performance (*Ichleistung*) which occurs in his writings and which has received continuing attention from present-day psychiatrists.[22]

As man's relevant environment becomes larger and more complex and the social systems within which he lives become more complex and contradictory, the burdens upon his ego necessarily increase, and so does the ego performance which life demands of him. As success in his ego performance becomes more difficult, failure becomes more frequent and more dangerous.

Weakland, "Toward a Theory of Schizophrenia," *Behavioral Science* (October 1956), pp. 251-264.

22. See references in note 19. For another approach to the problem of ego performance, see David Riesman, *The Lonely Crowd* (New Haven, Yale University Press, 1952), particularly in regard to Riesman's concept of the autonomous personality.

Table 1.   A Scheme of Possible Conflicts in Freud's Model

	Reality	Superego	Ego	Id	Types of conflict
Reality	Conflict among reality components	Reality vs. superego	Reality vs. ego	Reality vs. id	Reality conflicts (frustrations)
Superego	Superego vs. reality (e.g., indignation)	Conflicts among superego components (e.g., conflict of loyalties)	Superego vs. ego (e.g., guilt feelings)	Superego vs. id (e.g., repression)	Superego conflicts
Ego	Ego vs. reality (e.g., denial)	Ego vs. superego	Conflicts among ego components	Ego vs. id (e.g., repression, or rationalization)	Ego conflicts
Id	Id vs. reality (e.g., projection or autism)	Id vs. superego	Id vs. ego	Conflicts among id components	Id conflicts

Defenses of the Ego: Repression, Projection, Denial, and Autism

It seems clear from this scheme that the burdens of the ego may be great and that the ego performance demanded from the individual may be high indeed. Often, as Freud points out, the overburdened ego will fail its task. In its failure it may become the blind servant of one system level at the cost of the profound frustration of impairment of another. The ego may then become wholly subservient to the superego, repressing or penalizing the needs of the id, and depriving the individual of essential sources of pleasure and motivation. In the service of the superego it may blindly defy reality to the point of self-destruction. Or the ego may become, on the contrary, an abject servant of the id, obeying its demands for pleasure and "rationalizing" each demand in language borrowed from reality or from the superego but without paying serious attention to either.

Even where the ego puts itself fully in the service of one subsystem, the other subsystems do not disappear. Evaded or repressed, their messages have been denied access to the consciousness of the ego, but they will remain within the system, unconscious but at work, with indirect but far-reaching effects.[23]

The repressed wishes of the id may become associated with other messages acceptable to the ego and the superego, but they may add to these seemingly more innocuous or objective messages some powerful additional charge of pleasure or unpleasure stemming from the hidden strivings of the id. Thoughts of stern morality and punishment well endorsed by the superego, as Freud has pointed out, may thus become endowed with hidden but powerful associations of self-punishment, neurotic quilt feelings, expectations of disaster, and even a hidden desire for it.

Repression is only one of the defenses of the ego against the seductions of pleasure and the prohibitions of reality and conscience. Another one of its defense mechanisms — or defense procedures — is called projection. Here the ego does not seriously admit the thought that some prohibited wish from the id could be present in one's own personality. Since the wish is felt so vividly, however, that its existence cannot be denied, it is projected on some other actor who is clearly not the self and against whom the repressive fury of the superego can now safely be directed. Thus, as Freud has shown, one's own repressed wishes for spontaneity, laziness, disorder, uncleanliness, sexual license, and the like, are often

23. On the relation of Freud's general theories to the analysis of war and peace, see Alix Strachey, *The Unconscious Motives of War* (London, Allen, Unwin, 1957).

projected upon the images of one's subordinates in society, or upon the members of foreign nations and other races. The poor, the workers, the ethnic minorities, the Negroes, or the foreigners are then endowed in one's imagination with a particular propensity and prowess for this type of forbidden behavior. Once our perceptions have been distorted in this manner, our superego and ego may drive us with a mixture of moral indignation, hate, and hidden envy to persecute, oppress, and even kill the persons or groups upon whom the repressed wishes of our id have been projected. Psychic processes of this kind occur, automatically, according to Freud, in many individuals, and they could do so in all individuals, given the appropriate conditions.[24] Political movements and national governments often deliberately strive to create such conditions for purposes of politics and war. Their use of the mechanisms of governments and the mass media for the deliberate propagation of hate may then amplify and intensify the effects of projection to a vast degree.[25]

Still another defense procedure of the ego is directed against reality. Reality may clash with valuation. Messages from the real world which are incompatible with strong wishes from the id or with strong prohibitions from the superego — or with a favorable, narcissistic self-image of the ego — may simply be denied. By means of such denial, the ego pretends to itself that these unacceptable messages from reality did not arrive, or that the real world conditions which they describe do not exist, or that they are irrelevant.

Similar processes of denial may occur in response to clashes of cognition. Here they may serve to eliminate messages about the real world which seem incompatible with other cognitive memories and images held by the ego. While Freudian psychiatrists have tended to emphasize people's tendency to deny messages incompatible with the strong feelings generated by the id and the superego, or with their pleasure-associated self-image, other psychologists have stressed the propensity to deny information which is incompatible with the cognitive consonance of what we think we know.[26] In practice, emotional and cognitive elements in the process of denial are often intermingled in the case of

24. See Daniel J. Levinson, "Authoritarian Personality and Foreign Policy," *Journal of Conflict Resolution,* 1 (1957), 37-47; and for a summary report, William Eckhardt and Theo Lentz, "Factors of War/Peace Attitudes," *Peace Research Review,* 1.5 (October 1967), special issue.

25. See Gordon Allport, "The Role of Expectancy," in Hadley Cantril, ed., *Tensions that Cause Wars* (Urbana, University of Illinois Press, 1950), pp. 43-78.

26. A collection of these theories can be found in Robert Abelson et. al., eds., *Theories of Cognitive Consistency* (Chicago, Rand McNally, 1969).

individuals, and even more so in the similar processes that occur on the level of governments and nations. For example, the Nazi government in 1944 denied the relevance and truth of the allied plans for the invasion of Normandy which Ambassador Franz von Papen had forwarded from Ankara after they had been captured there from the British embassy by Nazi agents. The information which these plans revealed about allied strength and capabilities were incompatible with earlier estimates by the Nazi leaders, and with the self-image of those leaders as prudent and foresighted. Accordingly they disregarded the new information, with disastrous consequences for their side.[27] Generally, denial and the defense of cognitive consonance and consistency seem to play a major part in most of the major intelligence failures by governments in peace and war.

It is common to the processes of repression, projection, and denial that they tend to weaken or eliminate the control of messages from reality over the actions of the ego. To the extent that effective control by the reality principle has been eliminated the ego comes to act in an autistic manner. Autism is a state of communication patterns in which messages from within the self prevail decisively over messages from the larger environment of the individual. A related response is psychism—to use Robert J. Lifton's term—where the actor pretends to himself that the outside world can be transformed by a mere effort of the psyche or the will.[28] In either case, messages from the environment are then rejected outright, or formally accepted but disregarded in the decision processes of the ego. The actor then becomes blind and deaf to his environment, and listens increasingly only to the outcome of his inner voices.[29]

Autism is a last desperate defense of the overburdened ego against the intolerable conflict between the general reality of the outside world and the partial inner realities of his own id and superego. As the outside reality becomes actually more hostile, intractable, or unresponsive, its conflicts with man's inner needs from his id and superego are likely to become less tolerable, and thus the likelihood of autistic behavior will increase. Part of this autistic behavior itself, however, may consist in picturing reality as more hostile than it actually is and projecting the

27. L. C. Moyzish, *Operation: Cicero,* with an introduction by Franz Von Paven (New York: Universal Publishing Distributing, 1969).

28. See Robert J. Lifton, *Revolutionary Immortality: Mao Tse Tung and the Chinese Cultural Revolution* (New York, Random House, 1968).

29. For an earlier discussion on autism, see Theodore M. Newcomb, "Autistic Hostility and Social Reality," *Human Relations,* 1 (1947), 69-86.

individual's own feelings of fear, anger, and aggression upon other individuals and groups. Autistic behavior will then acquire a momentum of its own. As a self-aggravating process, it may lead in individuals or in groups into increasing isolation from reality and from other actors, and into increasingly severe conflicts with them.[30]

Against the pressures that impinge upon them, national governments resort to defenses which in their communication aspects resemble many of the ego defenses of the individual. Defending their cognitive consonance, they use the mechanisms of projection, repression, denial, and particularly autism. The process of increasingly autistic behavior in individuals as described by Freud and his followers has striking parallels in the processes of imperialism as described by Joseph Schumpeter.[31] According to Schumpeter, peoples or states may experience some real but limited or temporary military threat from their environment. They are then likely to respond to this threat by developing warlike skills and warlike social institutions, castes, and social classes which may help them to overcome the threat. Having overcome the outside threat, however, they are now left with strong warlike social classes, institutions, interest groups, and culture traits within their own society. Persons and groups habituated to expectations and acts of war will tend to continue to act out their habits, or to seek opportunities to do so. Classes and interest groups rewarded by war in the past will continue to seek similar rewards. Messages from the outside world indicating the need for continuing war preparations and wars will be eagerly sought out, accepted, reinforced, and rewarded by such "defense-oriented" or "war-habituated" individuals and groups. Other messages about the outside world, indicating the opposite will be rejected or disbelieved, or acting on them will be penalized in various ways. As a result, warlike behavior will come to be determined increasingly by processes from within the warlike state. Its rulers and soldiers will discover ever new reasons why new precautions must be taken, additional weapons acquired, alliances made, bases established, allies turned into subjects, foreign governments overthrown, and new border provinces added.

The expansion of empires in Schumpeter's view is thus largely driven from within, by a sociologically based process of cognitive distortion, and it was followed in some cases by the conquest of the "entire world,"

---

30. For an interpretation of deterrence policy within the model of autistic behavior, see Dieter Senghaas, *Abschreckung und Frieden: Studien zur Kritik organisierter Friedlosigkeit* (Frankfurt, Europäischer Verlagsanstalt, 1969).

31. Joseph Schumpeter, "The Sociology of Imperialisms," pt. I in *Imperialism and Social Classes* (New York, Meridian Books, 1955), pp.3-98 (first published in 1919).

as it was then effectively attainable to the conquerors by their contemporary means. Schumpeter's study was written in 1918, and his historical examples ranged from ancient Egypt and Rome to World War I. More recent empirical research has added support to Schumpeter's general thesis, though not necessarily to his special corollary, according to which such autistic warlike behavior was supposed to be limited mainly to aristocratic and land-owning societies and was ultimately to decline and disappear with the growth of commercial and capitalistic economies and societies, which in Schumpeter's view were more likely to be oriented to reality, rationality, and peace. Recent research shows autistic perception of hostility clearly at work in the foreign policy of a much wider variety of major modern powers both before 1914 and in the 1950s and 1960s.[32]

Freud's Notion of the "Death Wish": The Pain and Failure of Control Performance

Ego processes ordinarily involve reality testing. As such they imply self-criticism, self-correction, and the frequent reversal of earlier impulses and earlier behavior. Opposing and reversing one's own earlier behavior often involves temporary increases in internal disequilibrium, which we call inner tension. Such increases are felt as unpleasure, similar to the unpleasure caused by pain.

Other ego processes involving mediation in our sixteen kinds of conflicts also are likely to bring about temporary increases in internal disequilibrium. These increases in inner tensions, too, are felt as unpleasure and this unpleasure may reach levels of intensity as hard to bear as pain. The less the ego can cope with any such conflicts, the more the ego burden will become aggravated, and the more often will the ego performance become associated with unpleasure.

According to Freud, however, mental processes automatically seek pathways ending in a relaxation of tension and thus with a production of pleasure or with a reduction or avoidance of pain.[33] If this is so, then pathways will be sought which will lead away from the full ego burden and its concomitant nagging or painful self-awareness. At the same time, images of those actions and states of the personality which are perceived as in some sense opposite to the ego burden will become associated with pleasure. In Freud's terms they may become charged with

32. For a review of this literature see Robert Jervis, "Hypotheses on Misperception," *World Politics,* 20 (1968), 454-479.

33. Sigmund Freud, *Beyond the Pleasure Principle* (New York, Bantam Books, 1967), pp. 21-28.

libido. Under such conditions, images of intoxication, sleep, and even death, all may become pleasurable or libidinous. They will become the more inviting and attractive — sometimes almost overwhelmingly so — the greater and more frustrating the ego burden has become.

What Freud has called the death wish, the death urge, or the death instinct, will grow, according to our hypothesis, with growing ego overload. This hypothesis predicts an increase in the frequency and/or intensity of death symbols in the communications and dream reports of persons suffering from ego overload. It also predicts that social conditions posing intolerable demands for ego performance and subjecting the ego to extreme inner tensions will produce many death-oriented symbols of this kind, as well as many death-oriented patterns of behavior. Finally, death-oriented works of art and literature, as well as death-oriented cultural and political symbols will have a widespread appeal, particularly among those persons to whom such conditions apply. The first prediction can be tested by content analysis of relevant materials; the second by the frequency of acts of homicide, suicide, and other kinds of destructive or self-destructive behavior; and third by observing the frequency of appearance and circulation of death-oriented artistic, political, and cultural expressions.[34]

If we accept this argument provisionally as a working hypothesis, it follows that the death urge is not an innate tendency or instinct, as Freud primarily saw it.[35] Rather it appears now as a function of a system, and perhaps more specifically as a concomitant of system overload. In moving toward death, the ego burden — the burden of painful or frustrating decisions, anxieties, and inner conflicts — is cast off. A single determinant of behavior may become predominant over all others in a

---

34. Some example of death-oriented political symbols are cited in a somewhat different context in Karl W. Deutsch, *Nationalism and Social Communication* (Cambridge, MIT Press, 2nd ed., 1968), pp. 182-183, 306. Such an internally generated interest in death — internal from the viewpoint of the actor — should be distinguished from responses to death symbols which have been made salient by external events, such as after the Black Death in the Middle Ages, or the nuclear explosions at Hiroshima and Nagasaki. For the latter, see Robert J. Lifton, *Death in Life* (New York, Random House, 1967). For internally generated preoccupation with death as a splendid alternative to unending decision problems and frustrations, see the treatment of death in Friedrich Hebbel's *Die Nibelungen* and in Richard Wagner's musical tetralogy, *Der Ring des Nibelungen*, with its enormous popularity which lasted from the 1870s throughout the Nazi period. See also Robert J. Lifton, *History and Human Survival* (New York, Random House, 1970), pt. 2, pp. 114-207.

35. Freud, *The Ego and the Id*, pp. 30-37, and Freud, *Beyond the Pleasure Principle*, passim.

magnificent disregard of the multiple demands and restrictions of reality: the heros of the Eddic poems or of the *Nibelungenlied* go calmly to their deaths, and centuries later, Oswald Spengler advises Western nations to adopt similarly heroic attitudes toward their inevitable doom. Or else, all determinants of behavior are equally reduced to insignificance, and life ends in the Nirvana of the Buddhists or in the ultimate resignation sought for by Schopenhauer.[36]

Freud's own notion of a death instinct was labeled by himself as "only a hypothesis; I have no proof to offer; this hypothesis was developed," said Freud, "on the basis of theoretical considerations, supported by biology."[37] Yet this instinct differed from other instincts as these were understood by other behavioral scientists and often by Freud himself. Unlike hunger or sex, this "death instinct" had no specific biochemical basis. Like Eros, the "death instinct" was supposed to be "active in every part of living substance"; but while Eros was supposed to be concentrated in unequal proportions "so that some one substance might be the principal representative of Eros," Freud made no suggestions that any one identifiable substance might be the main carrier of the death instinct. Nor did the "death instinct" appear to have any survival value for the species. Unlike other instincts, therefore, it would not be preserved or favored by natural selection.

In short, Freud's "death instinct" was an abstract principle, the reduction of differences and tensions toward a conceptual zero point. Freud's Eros was more concrete in conception, but in juxtaposing it to the death instinct, it, too, was defined as a general principle "which by bringing about a more and more far-reaching combination of the particles into which living substances dispersed, aims at complicating life and at the same time, of course, at preserving it."[38] This concept of the death instinct comes close to becoming another name for the general principle of entropy, the tendency for all differences of form and energy to even out toward a state of faintly lukewarm random noise; and Eros here comes close to representing the opposite principle, negative entropy or the building up of increasing information and order, as applied to living substances.

Despite its abstractness, Freud's notion of the "death instinct" and of its turning outward from the actor in the form of an instinct of aggression, contains an important element of insight from the viewpoint of general systems theory. Freud's approach suggests to us that behavior

36. Freud, *Beyond the Pleasure Principle,* p. 88.
37. Freud, *The Ego and the Id,* pp. 30 and 34.
38. Ibid., p. 30.

patterns tending toward death and toward aggressiveness can be understood as the result of the dismantling of more complex patterns of order. In the most striking cases of death seeking or destructive behavior, it seems to us that the patterns which are so dismantled are the patterns of control and of ego performance.

In our view, the death wish belongs among the phenomena of regression, associated with the loss of ego performances or with the flight from them. In this manner the exhausted victim of a snowstorm finally sits down to fall asleep and never to awake again; and the suicide makes the last decision that is to save him from all others. In all such cases it is the painful task of continuing reality-oriented self-control that is abandoned.

Freud's basic system model is suggestive for many aspects of nation-state behavior. Before we can explore its applicability at the nation-state level, however, one specific intellectual task must be performed. Freud's simple concept of aggression must be replaced by a more differentiated analysis of approach-behavior and of the various constructive and destructive functions which it may acquire in various contexts. This task will be attempted in the next section of this discussion. We shall then turn to inquire which processes on the level of the nation-state correspond to the conflicts of the pleasure principle, the reality principle, and the superego in Freud's model, in what ways governmental performance in the nation may resemble ego performance in the ego, and how nation-states, like mentally ill individuals, may regress to destructive and self-destructive action.

Ego Performance and Aggression: A Typology of Approach Behavior

The concept of aggression has played a large role in the study of international politics, as well as in the study of the psychology of groups and individuals and also in studies of animal behavior.[39] Despite its im-

---

39. On the literature about theories and research on aggression see the bibliography compiled by Eva Knobloch and Dieter Senghaas, "Ausgewählte Bibliographie zur Friedensforschung," in Ekkehart Krippendorff, ed., *Friedensforschung* (Cologne, Kiepenheuer and Witsch, 1968), pp. 559-589, esp. pp. 584-586. For an early trend report see Elton McNeil, "Psychology and Aggression," *Journal of Conflict Resolution,* 1 (1957), 195-293; and for a later trend report see Leonard Berkovitz, *Aggression* (New York, John Wiley, 1962). Among most recent publications see Leonard Berkovitz, ed., *Roots of Aggression: A Re-examination of the Frustration-Aggression Hypothesis* (New York, Atherton Press, 1969); Johan Galtung, "Violence, Peace and Peace Research," *Journal of Peace Research,* 6 (1969), 167-192; Herbert Marcuse et al., *Aggression und Anpassung in der industriellen Gesellschaft* (Frankfurt, Suhrkamp

portance, however, this concept of aggression usually has been defined only loosely. In general there has been an agreement that aggression always involves approach behavior, as the latin word *aggredi* to approach, to attack—literally to step toward—suggests. To this day many writers, particularly in the USA, are likely to call any vigorous approach "aggressive," and the corresponding attitude is often positively valued in many social roles, from suitors to salesmen. Many psychologists, too, including Freud himself, have pointed out the positive aspect of such aggressive behavior and of the attitudes and instincts which are supposed to lie behind it. Only in certain contexts, or above certain levels of intensity, aggression is then said to be bad, or aggressiveness is negatively valued. Much as a weed is only a plant in the wrong place, so aggression in this view is held to be bad only when it occurs in the wrong context.

Such a view sounds inviting in words but it is awkward to apply in research. What classes of contexts are the wrong ones for aggressive behavior to occur in? And is there nothing intrinsic about some subclasses of approach behavior, which will make their consequences destructive or self-destructive over a very wide class of contexts, while other subclasses of approach behavior may rarely or ever prove thus damaging? And is there any kind of approach behavior which includes no element of aggressiveness?

According to Freud, there is indeed none. He supposed aggression to be some kind of pure instinct, similar to an element in chemistry. All observable human behavior, he thought, was produced by mixtures of this aggressive-destructive element or instinct with other instincts, particularly the instinct of love, and the varying proportions of these admixtures were then held to account for the vast variety of human actions and their models. Unfortunately this supposed pure and simple element, the instinct of aggression or destruction, remained an abstract mental construct, and it remained itself unanalyzed. Here psychologists and psychiatrists seemed to have followed a pattern familiar from the history of chemistry and physics. In these sciences, various elements and particles had been treated for a time as unanalyzable and indivisible, mere primitive building blocks of more complex structures. As knowl-

Verlag, 1968); Alexander Mitcherlich, *Die Idee des Friedens und die menschliche Aggressivität* (Frankfurt, Suhrkamp Verlag, 1969); Alexander Mitcherlich, ed., *Bis hierher und nicht weiter. Ist die menschliche Aggression unbefriedbar?* (Munich, Piler Verlag, 1969); Anthony Storr, *Human Aggression* (New York, Bantam Books, 1970). The views of Konrad Lorenz, as set forth in his book *On Aggression,* trans. Marjorie K. Wilson (New York, Bantam, 1970), are controversial.

edge grew, however, these supposedly primitive units became accessible to analysis. Elements were found to be composed of atoms, and atoms turned out to be constructed of still smaller subatomic particles and processes.

Perhaps the time is ripe to find out whether something similar could not happen to the seemingly primitive concept of aggressiveness as the essential ingredient in all approach behavior. A possible tool for such an analysis is the distinction among the different operations involved in approach behavior, each with its own operational purposes and consequences. Another tool is the distinction developed by modern information theory between processes which are primarily matter-energy-oriented on the one hand and processes which are predominantly information-oriented on the other. A third tool is the distinction, familiar from the modern theory of communication and control, between primarily autonomous, self-determined systems on the one hand and primarily non-autonomous outside-determined or past-determined systems on the other.

With the aid of these distinctions, it should be possible to construct a typology of six operational varieties of approach behavior each of which has been included by some writer in the concept of aggression.

Elimination or Destruction. The most clear-cut type of aggression are those kinds of behavior which aim directly at the destruction or elimination of the object which the actor is approaching. Obstacles are to be destroyed, barriers to be broken through, sources of threat or pain to be eliminated, and incompatibilities, obstructions, and frustrations to be swept away. Land is to be cleared of forests, native tribes or obsolescent buildings and their inhabitants. In each case, the effector subsystems of the actor are to be enabled to operate more freely.

In pure cases of this kind the actor does not aim to take anything away from those he is attacking, except the space they occupy, the resources they use, and the communication channels which they fill or contaminate with the distracting noise of their messages. The objects of this kind of aggression are not to be exploited nor indoctrinated or enslaved; they are merely to be got out of the actor's way. Their removal is to be his liberation. Such behavior resembles a kind of vector, indicating a direction. The actual behavior may aim at moving the obstacle only a short distance, no more than seems needed to ensure the actor's opportunity to carry out his own program or to do so more freely or more conveniently.

Whether we shall welcome or condemn such behavior will depend first of all on the positive or negative value we impute to the actor and to his program, and on the negative or positive value we impute to the target of his attack. We deplore the destruction of a forest but hope for the wiping out of a disease. We may oppose the disturbance of order and tradition, and of institutions and practices we value, but we may hope for the destruction of oppression, including sometimes the oppressors. To say in the 1850s of a man in the United States that he was an abolitionist — that he wanted to abolish human slavery — was to praise him in much of the North but to insult him in much of the South.

Eliminative and destructive aggression thus derives some of its significance from its social context but not all of it. Even justified rage, Berthold Brecht wrote, makes one's voice hoarse.[40] Eliminative or destructive attacks not only reduce the autonomy of the target and its autonomous level of information. They usually add little or nothing to the autonomous information level of the actor except that they may permit him to work out with less hindrance some of the combinatorial implications of his program and thus perhaps to derive new information from real new combinations in his own behavior — information which he could not have obtained so long as external obstacles prevented him from turning these potential combinations into real ones. To that extent, the greater freedom of action may help an actor to greater self-knowledge. At the same time, however, eliminative or destructive attacks have their own costs for the actor. If they persist for a long time they will involve him in cumulative opportunity costs — the value of alternative actions he had to forego in favor of the aggressive behavior he adopted — that may seriously reduce his own autonomy.

Aggression of this type may sometimes be rational in the service of some other goal which may be promoted by the purposive clearing of obstacles. In this manner, revolutionaries or counterrevolutionaries may try to exile or even "liquidate" their opponents. More frequent are its irrational aspects. In rare cases destructive behavior may acquire an additional evaluative aspect and appear as an end in itself. The slogan of some extreme adherents of Generalissimo Franco in the Spanish civil war — *viva la muerte* ("long live death") may be a case in point. Other possible examples are the worship of symbols of destruction in certain aspects of Hindu religion, such as Shiva's dance of destruction, and the cult of the death goddess Kali. The elaborate symbols of black flags, skulls, and crossbones, death heads, insignia on black uniforms and the like, used in Germany in the Napoleonic Wars, and prominently in the 1930s, also may indicate a positive value attributed to symbols of death and destruction.

40. Berthold Brecht, "An die Nachgeborenen," in *Hundert Gedichte* (Frankfurt, Suhrkamp Verlag, various editions).

Most often, however, elimination and destruction may serve a cathectic function. They aid a discharge of inner tension, or a reduction of inner disequilibrium in the actual elimination of frustrating realities or at least of symbols of frustration. This aspect can be sensed weakly in the emotional appeal of such words as "breakthrough" and "liberation" and more strongly in such political slogans as the Horst Wessel song, *Die Strasse frei* ("Clear the road"), and the poet Bertold Brecht's image of a proletarian mother who sees her unborn child as "unstoppable" when grown.

Exploitation and Compellence. This is the most frequent and natural form of aggressive behavior. A material object is approached in order to extract matter or energy from it. This is what any living creature will do in regard to its food and environment. It is what any child does when seeking food from his mother. It is also what any man does who approaches and changes a tree for firewood or a cave for habitation. In all these cases, the autonomous information of the target of the attack is reduced; its autonomous patterns are partly destroyed or modified and are replaced by those corresponding more nearly to the needs of the aggressor. As a result of the same process, however, the autonomous information patterns of the aggressor are preserved or increased. His life is sustained; his body or his possessions are enhanced or elaborated. In general the entropy or disorder of the object he attacks is increased, and the negative entropy or order of the attacker and his works is preserved or made larger.

A similar process may occur in the exploitation of autonomous creatures, such as animals or people. Here the attacker seeks to break down some of the autonomous pattens of the attacked and to substitute for them other behavior patterns conforming to his own needs. This behavior may be called compellence: it compels the attacked to perform the action which the attacker wants. Aggressive behavior of this kind is involved in the taming of animals, and in subjecting subordinates in armies, industries, or governments to the commands of their superiors. In international relations, this type of approach behavior is found in the conquest of a country, or in the subjugation of a population to the commands or interests of some conquering or otherwise predominant nation, class, business organization, or ethnic group.

Exploitation or compellent behavior is usually rational, at least in the short run. It is usually purposive from the viewpoint of the attacker. It becomes irrational when evaluative or cathectic elements come to outweigh its purposive aspects. Individuals for whom acquisitiveness has become an end in itself are ridiculed as misers. According to Joseph Schumpeter, nations tend to succumb to a similar irrational behavior pattern of "objectless expansion" when they adopt the social structures and military policies of imperialism. In these cases, according to Schumpeter, their efforts to acquire and conquer territories eventually go far beyond any economic advantages that can be derived from it.[41] Imperial conquest in such cases becomes a value in itself, and to a still greater extent it may come to resemble a cathectic process; a mere acting out of psychological patterns or sociological structures which the attacking society acquired at an earlier stage.

Information Acquisition. Approach behavior may be directed not at the acquisition of matter or energy but at the acquisition of information. Curiosity, or the "investigatory reflex," is inborn, according to Pavlov, in man and many animals. Societies may make organized efforts to acquire information from nature or from other societies. Already Francis Bacon suggested this in his *New Atlantis*, and modern governments carry on both scientific research and foreign intelligence operations on a large scale.

Approach behavior, in order to acquire information, need not necessarily reduce or destroy the autonomous information pattern of the target object, individual, or population. It is a key property of information that, in principle, it can be multiplied or copied without significant loss. The attacking or approaching actor thus can acquire information and with its aid build up his own autonomous information pattern — he can increase his own negative entropy — without necessarily increasing the disorder or positive entropy of his target. Only if his approach is intrusive and disrupts some of the autonomous patterns of the target will the acquisition of information become an exploitative process. The distinction between intrusive and nonintrusive methods of observation and experiment is thus of fundamental importance.[42]

This difference is related to the actor's valuation of the autonomous information patterns of the object of his approach or his attention. If he values them little or negatively, his approach may be intrusive, as in vivisection, or in Francis Bacon's reference to experimentation as "putting nature the question," that is, torture. If the observer values the autonomous information patterns of the object very highly, however, and as not subject to manipulation, they may be for him a source of experiences of awe, respect, or beauty.

Information acquisition is often purposively rational. The information is to be acquired as a tool for some specific purpose, or for a

41. Joseph Schumpeter, "The Sociology of Imperialism."
42. Eugene Webb et al., *Unobtrusive Measures: Nonreactive Research in Social Sciences* (Chicago, Rand McNally, 1966).

broader class of purposes. Military intelligence, overflights, and acts of "armed reconnaissance" are obvious examples. Nonetheless, curiosity and evaluation of information is a value in itself. The value of "enlightenment," as Harold Lasswell calls it, is characteristic of man's nature, as well as of the practice of all the world's highly developed countries. Curiosity may become charged with libido, as it did, according to Freud, in the case of Leonardo da Vinci.[43] (Otherwise, it is difficult to imagine information acquisition as a cathectic act, except as an effort to relieve the inner tension known as boredom. The latter, however, may differ from the usual concept of a cathectic situation in that boredom may be more similar to a deficiency disease following upon deprivation of information relevant to the actor.)

Assistance to Autonomy. It is possible for an actor to value the autonomous information patterns of the object of his attention far more highly than he values his own self. If he then approaches such an object with the aim to help or assist it in preserving its own autonomous patterns, or to help to unfold and develop it further in continuing freedom and autonomy, then we may speak of love.[44] Love in this sense is selfless. It puts the good and the freedom of the beloved higher than one's own. The traditional marriage formula "to cherish and comfort" describes such a relationship. In rendering assistance to the beloved object, person or group, the actor preserves and enhances its autonomous information patterns. In the process he may also increase his own autonomous information patterns, either through information acquisition from the beloved or through his own autonomous learning in the process of assisting.

A love relation of this kind usually cannot be called rational. Purposive elements are rarely prevalent. As Machiavelli noted, love is notoriously hard to control or to subject to other purposes; Machiavelli preferred to base governments on the supposedly more reliable elements of fear and deception. Socrates came close to the opposite view when he claimed that politics in the last analysis was based on friendship.[45] Modern statesmen and nations, too, have sometimes suspected that they might benefit more from friends and allies than from serfs and satellites.

In the approach behavior which we call love, the evaluative aspect is

43. Sigmund Freud, *Leonardo da Vinci: A Study in Psychosexuality* (New York, Vintage Books, 1961).

44. See also Karl W. Deutsch, *The Nerves of Government* (New York, Free Press, 2nd ed., 1966), p. 233.

45. Werner Jaeger, *Paidaia* (New York, Oxford University Press, 1945), II, chap. 2, "The Memory of Socrates."

predominant. By definition, the specific beloved object is treated as a value in itself. Beyond this, the entire class of love relationships may be treated as a value, regardless of wide variations in the particular objects to be loved. Individuals may then "fall in love with love," and national leaders and publics may find altruism an attractive role. If such genuinely unselfish patterns of approach behavior should increase in international relations, the chances for world peace should grow. Love, or the assistance to someone else's autonomy, only rarely serves a cathectic function for the actor. It may help him sometimes to escape from preoccupation with a self which he has come to find frustrating, and it may aid him to sublimate some of his inner conflicts.

Even the most selfless effort to assist the autonomy of another actor or object involves an approach to them, in actual behavior or at least in terms of observation and attention. In this sense, even the most selfless efforts at assistance may become aggressive and intrusive. They may then mar the process of assistance, which is based on the coordination of behavior. If they are accompanied by cognitive inadequacies or failures or by failures of self-control, they may engender severe conflicts on the level of individuals as well as of nations or other large political units. Cases range from clumsy, tactless, or possessive lovers among individuals to overpowering protectors in international affairs. On the latter level, failures of political integration may result from such prolonged protracted failures of coordinative behavior.

Demands for Response. It is rare for love relationships to be as selfless as the model just discussed. Ordinarily they are apt to include persistent demands for responses from one's partner. Such responses may be valued more highly than one's own self; they may themselves become an object of solicitous assistance; and they may be needed by the actor as a means to strengthen his own personality, by meeting some of the needs of his id, his ego, or his super ego, or of all of them together.

In principle, however, demands for response represent a different dimension of approach behavior. By definition they imply the placing of a lower value upon the autonomous information patterns of one's partner. If these autonomous patterns will not yield a response, or not the response desired, they are to be modified, perhaps even disrupted, until the desired response is being elicited. Demands for response thus can be insistent and intrusive. In the extreme case they can become destructive, wholly or in part, of the autonomous patterns of the object of approach.

Demands for response are thus essentially ambivalent. They are aggressive like all approach behavior. The more insistent the demands, the more urgent the needs that drive them, and the more frustrating the failure to get a desired response, the closer the relationship may come to turning into cruelty and hate. Just as mere curiosity can come close to cruelty in vivisection, so overwhelming demands for a response from an unresponsive object may turn into genuine cruelty. Sadism from this viewpoint appears as a pathological desire to force a response from an object that has still some remnants of autonomy.

Demands for responses are often rational, since such responses often may serve other purposes of the actor. Most frequently, however, they are primarily evaluative. There seems good reason to think that responsiveness from one's environment and particularly from other persons, is a major human need from infancy. To deprive individuals or whole disadvantaged groups of such responses may mean to do serious damage to them.

It is possible that something similar holds even in international politics. Individuals in many countries look to other nations for cues about the status of their own people and country and indirectly about their own worth as persons. This may hold even more strongly for disadvantaged minorities within a country: subject to status deprivation both as individuals and as a group, they may look to a contest between their group and others as a source for increasing their self-respect. Beyond any other rational purpose, ethnic politics and world politics may turn into status politics. Those who feel themselves deprived of status turn aggressive in their demands for response. Echoes of this theme could be heard in the German demand for "a place in the sun" on the eve of World War I, and the Nazis claimed to have "restored German prestige" on the eve of World War II; in the expression of joy by the then Soviet minister V. M. Molotov in San Francisco in 1945 that the beautiful Russian language was at last resounding from the international tribune of the United Nations; and in the persistent concern of many Americans for the "image" of the United States in international opinion, in competition with the image of the Soviet Union.

Demands for response sometimes may serve a cathectic function as an escape from loneliness, or as an escape from the tensions and sufferings by sensory or social deprivation.

Information Imposition. The last form of aggression is that kind of approach behavior which aims at the imposition of some of the autonomous patterns of the actor upon the object of his approach. The imposition may be physical, as in the child who rushes to put his footprints into the fresh snow, or the young man who cuts his initials into a tree. Or the imposition may be abstract, cultural, and on a large scale, as in the case of a nation that sends religious or ideological missionaries into other countries to convert their populations to its own ways or that sends them teachers to induce them to accept its own language or culture, or both, as English and French were imposed from the eighteenth to the twentieth century upon the elites of many countries in Asia and Africa, and as a Western style of clothing was imposed — more often by example than by command or exhortation — upon most of the population of the world.

Information imposition usually reduces the autonomous information pattern of the target upon which the information is imposed; and it does nothing to increase the autonomous information patterns of the actor, since it merely copies them for imposition in new places. If information imposition is nonintrusive, however, and if it remains modest in scale, then it may increase the opportunities at a later stage for new combinations between the autonomous information patterns of the recipient system and the patterns that have been imposed by the actor. In this case information imposition may lead indirectly to a gain in the autonomous information patterns of the recipient. On the level of individuals, indoctrination may give way to education. Indoctrination reduces the autonomy of the recipient; education helps him increase it. On the level of international relations, there is a similar contrast between "cultural imperialism" and genuine technical or cultural assistance.

Information imposition is often rational. Frequently it imposes upon the environment some pattern of order favorable to some purposes of the actor. Or else, it may make the environment more generally familiar, predictable, and manageable. Teaching or culture to other peoples may make them more receptive to the goods we seek to sell and to the policies for which we seek support.

Still more often perhaps, information imposition may be a value in itself. It is an affirmation of one's own self in individuals as well as collectivities. It serves as a reinforcing feedback to the narcissism which plays an important role in Freud's model.[46] Information imposition upon the environment may also meet another important need; the need of the self for feedback from self-produced traces which it has imposed on the environment. Dogs and other animals put their marks on the environment and use these later for orientation. Since men began to labor, they have received feedback information from the traces of their work. To have "written in sand," to have "ploughed the sea," or to have merely performed what Alexander and Margarete Mitcherlich called "traceless labor" is felt to be frustrating and a genuine deprivation.[47] If such frustration creates serious inner tensions, information imposition

46. Sigmund Freud, *Leonardo da Vinci*, chap. 3.
47. Alexander and Margarete Mistscherlich, *Über die Unfähigkeit zu trauern*, pp. 348, 351.

may serve as a cathectic process. Goethe's Faust rejoices at the thought that the trace of his days on earth "cannot perish in eons"; in a darker mood, Orwell's oppressor O'Brien in 1984 is thrilled at the thought of impressing a footprint on a human face.

A similar pattern may apply at the level of international relations. Members of a nation may find it frustrating to live in a world to which they can make no difference outside their borders and in which their efforts will leave no traces. They may desire to leave their mark on foreign countries and on history, and they may support policies designed to this end.

Combinations of These Types. The preceding six types of aggressive or approach behavior may rarely be found in practice in their pure form. Rather, aggressive behavior in the real world may involve a mixture of two or more of these dimensions. One example of such mixtures may suffice.

An actor may feel the need to impose some information on the outside world as well as the need to obtain some response from it, but he may lack sufficient information of his own. He may use elimination as a substitute for information imposition, and for the eliciting of a response he then may use acts of *destruction* as a substitute in order to gain a sense of effectiveness and power. He may impress the marks of his destructive acts upon his physical environment, as in the case of vandalism, or upon the memory of future generations, as in the classic story of the crime of Herostratus who destroyed the great temple of Diana in order to have his name remembered. Even without a strong desire for information imposition, the frustration of an actor's desire for response may lead him to destroy the unresponsive or frustrating object or arrangement. The act of destruction then eliminates the immediate source or symbol of his frustrations, or else it serves as a substitute for the missing response from the environment and perhaps also as a substitute for the actor's failure to impose its own information pattern on the outside world. In the novel, *The Temple of the Golden Pavilion* (1959), based on an actual incident, the Japanese novelist Yukio Mishima tells the story of a young Japanese Zen monk who destroyed in 1947 the most beautiful temple in Japan, apparently for reasons of this kind. Similar examples of destructive rage have been reported as a response to extreme frustration in the case of Hitler in the last days of World War II, from the Spanish Civil War, and of "black rage" in some Negro psychiatric patients in the United States.[48]

48. Yukio Mishima, *The Temple of the Golden Pavilion* (Tokyo, Charles Tuttle Company, 1959); Hugh Trever-Roper, *The Last Days of Hitler* (New York, Macmillan, 1947); W. H. Grier and P. M. Cobbs, *Black Rage* (New York, Basic Books, 1968).

Neglected Aspects of Aggression in the Theory of International Politics. Most of the traditional theories of international politics have only emphasized elimination and exploitation, the first two of our six types of aggressive behavior. According to the classic theory of the balance of power, states will act chiefly so as to restrict or eliminate any dangerously powerful competitors, or to exploit them, suitably weakened, as future allies. According to Marxist theories, the main source of aggression is the search for human objects of exploitation; and only strongly class-divided states are expected to engage in it. But conflicts stemming from aggressive efforts of information acquisition, information imposition, demands for response, or poorly steered or coordinated efforts at nurturance and information assistance—all occur in international politics and have produced wars or warlike crisis situations during recent decades. Nonetheless, they have remained largely ignored by theorists of international politics and neglected or underrepresented in simulation exercises.

These omissions impose a serious distortion upon our understanding of the origins of war and peace in our time. The first two types of aggressive behavior—elimination and exploitation— are *purposively* rational, and it has been these aspects of war which have been conventionally studied. But, as reported in an earlier section of this discussion, the purposive functions of wars have been manifestly declining in recent decades with the increasing destructiveness of weapons and the increasing participation of masses of the population in politics and wars, both international and civil. If we recall that since 1911, wars have been counterproductive for the purpose of the initiators in about three fifths of all the cases, in contrast to the period from 1815 to 1910 where about four fifths of the wars were still rewarding for those who started them, we must conclude that for more than half a century, wars have, in effect, ceased to be rational instruments of policy. Yet their frequency has not declined. For the period from 1815 to 1910 one international war broke out every three years, and just about the same average holds for the periods from 1911 to 1945 and in 1945 to 1965, not counting for this last period the wars in Algeria and Vietnam. Most of these wars are no longer rational in any *objective* sense, even though they may not have appeared so to the leaders and peoples deluded enough to start them.

Theories of international politics which mainly stress rational and purposive motives for resorting to war cannot account for these developments. Nor can they bridge the gap between theories of state behavior in foreign policy, which are rationalistic, and studies of nationalism, which stress its irrational and potentially counterproductive aspects.[49] At most they could lead to a counsel of despair, ascribing the persistence of wars to some vague general "irrationality" of individuals and nations. We need something better than that; we need a theory that can account in *rational* terms for the frequency and kind of such irrational behavior on the part of individuals, groups, and states, and which can be tested by observable data and eventually repeatable experiments and simulation exercises. Such a theory may not be developed soon, but it is time to aim our efforts in this direction.

Interest Groups, Reality Testing and Supranational Morality at the Level of the Nation-State

As our discussion thus far has suggested, the basic structure of Freud's model may be more generally applicable to the analysis of the behavior of states and nations. Some limited but specific similarities can be identified (see Table 2, in comparison with Table 1, above). Many modern interest groups behave somewhat like the partial mechanisms within the id: each interest group behaves in ways designed to approach its own particular goal or to promote its own particular demands, with little or no regard to the efforts of other groups. Somewhat as no act is pleasurable to an individual unless it is rewarding to his id, so no political act is likely to find strong backing unless it wins the support of some interest group. In this sense interests are the pleasure principle of politics.

In terms of interest group politics, moves toward higher armament levels and even limited warfare are likely to be politically pleasurable. In many localities and regions, new weapons installations, defense production facilities, or defense orders are likely to be popular as sources of increased employment, business sales, and real estate values. Closing a government arsenal or navy yard, no matter how obsolete, almost invariably causes protest. Senators and congressmen from states and districts with the highest level of specific defense contracts are in the forefront as general spokesmen for higher levels of armament expenditure. Specific interest groups, such as the aerospace industry, and particular firms, such as the Boeing Company, are actively working to promote defense consciousness among the public. In some ways such companies move as

49. For rationalistic theories see references in note 1, as well as Morton A. Kaplan, *System and Process in International Politics* (New York, John Wiley, 1957); and William Riker, *The Theory of Political Coalition* (New Haven, Yale University Press, 1965). For stress on irrational aspects of nationalism, see Hans Kohn, *Force or Reason* (Cambridge, Harvard University Press, 1937); and also Rupert Emerson, *From Empire to Nation* (Cambridge, Harvard University Press, 1960).

Table 2.   A Scheme of Possible Conflicts in the National and the International Political System

	World System	Ethical Values and Tradition	Governmental System	Interest Groups	Types of Conflict
World system	Conflicts within the world system	World system vs. ethical values and tradition	World system vs. governmental system	World system vs. interest groups	World system conflicts
Ethical values and tradition	Ethical values and tradition vs. world system	Conflicts among ethical values and tradition components	Ethical values and tradition vs. governmental system	Ethical values and tradition vs. interest groups	Ethical values and tradition conflicts
Governmental system	Governmental system vs. world system	Governmental system vs. ethical values and tradition	Conflicts within governmental system	Governmental system vs. interest groups	Governmental system conflicts
Interest groups	Interest groups vs. world system	Interest groups vs. ethical values and tradition	Interest groups vs. governmental system	Conflicts among interest groups components	Interest group conflicts

blindly and mindlessly toward higher defense appropriations as the hunger reflex in the human body moves toward stabilizing our blood sugar level.[50]

Somewhat as messages from the world of external reality may counteract the drives of the id and of the various subsystems within it, so information about the larger international systems may tend to limit and counteract the blind strivings of interest groups for enlarging the military and industrial defense establishment. Such outside information might deal with the technical limits of a nation's own weapons system and with the capability of rival nations. Or they may refer to the risks of arms races and escalation processes in the international arena, or to the likelihood that a prospective minor war might prove larger and more frustrating. Or they might point to social and political limitations upon an expansionistic foreign policy: the probable loss of international sympathies, the erosion of alliances, the overcommitment of national manpower and financial resources, the possible decline in the purchasing power of the nation's currency. If so, messages from external reality will clash with interest group pressures.

National communication systems, similar to individual personalities, also may contain elements fulfilling the functions of a superego. Abraham Lincoln urged his countrymen to be less concerned whether God was on their side but whether they were on His. A century later in October 1962, John and Robert Kennedy opposed the urging of some top ranking advisers for an American first strike against Cuba which would have cost an estimated 25,000 lives in that country and brought the risk of larger war. "My brother has no desire to become the Tojo of World War III," said Robert Kennedy on that occasion.[51] Until now, something like a superego has retained a measure of effectiveness in the American political tradition. Comparable elements of a superego are observable in the decision processes of most other nations, including Communist-ruled nations such as Russia and China, where the internalized commands may be couched in Marxist-Leninist language. The deliberate rejection of any superego beyond the nation-state was a characteristic of the fascist regimes of Hitler and Mussolini, which proved short-lived.

50. For a recent discussion, see Senator William Proxmire, *Report from Wasteland* (New York, Praeger, 1970); and George Thayer, *The War Business* (New York, Avon, 1970). For relevant recent research on determinants of armament spending, see Bruce M. Russett, *What Price Vigilance?* (New Haven, Yale University Press, 1970) and Emile Benoit and Kenneth Boulding, eds., *Disarmament and the Economy* (New York, Harper and Row, 1963).

51. See Robert Kennedy, *Thirteen Days* (New York, Norton, 1969).

On the national level the superego is not only carried by individuals. It may be embodied to a greater or lesser extent in the communication structures and memories of social groups and institutions, such as churches, universities, humanitarian societies, sometimes even the medical profession, and some ideologically oriented political parties. As the experiences of the past wars have shown, every one of these groups can be swayed by national enthusiasm and special interests, but some elements, akin to a superego or world conscience, are likely to survive. Such memory-directed group values of the superego type should not be simply equated with the behavior of economic, sociological, or power oriented interest groups, all of which are steered more largely by feedback signals from current changes in rewards. The confusion of these two types in much of conventional interest group research has been detrimental to analysis.

Somewhat as in the case of the individual the ego has to carry on the three-way task of mediation between id, superego, and reality, so in the case of nation-states the government has to mediate between the day-to-day demands of interest groups, the internalized demands of the national and supranational culture, and the reality constraints of the outside world with rival actors in the international system.

The Ego Weakness of the Nation-State. The ego performance demanded of a national government by this situation is at least as difficult as the comparable ego performance demanded of most individuals, but most national governments are far less well equipped to cope with these demands. In adult individuals, the ego is usually well established; it is rare of it to lose self-control or to be split. Governments, by contrast, can be turned out of office relatively easily, and they often are. For 87 countries between 1945 and 1961 the average tenure of a chief executive was three years, and the situation may have worsened in the 1960s. Nothing like this degree of instability is found in individuals. Further analysis should, however, determine precisely whether this apparent increase of instability of governments is due to an increasing democratization of politics and the extent to which democratically and nondemocratically caused changes of government correlate with actual warlike behavior.

Moreover, the amount of attention paid to external reality, as against the attention paid to internal processes, is much higher in individuals than it is in the case of nation-states. This is true of national executives and even more so of national legislatures, mass media, and the electorate. Even where a government action is defined as a foreign policy move and as a necessary response to the international situation, closer investigation often shows that its major determinants have been domestic interests.

For all these reasons, the behavior of nation-states, in particular of large ones, is far more likely to become autistic than the behavior of individuals. In the case of individuals the process of reality testing is carried on constantly and simultaneously through many different sensory channels. We not only hear some food described as eatable, but we can also see, smell, touch, and taste it. The feedback cycles in the reality testing by individuals are short as well as multiple, reporting back to the actor additional data about reality as well as about the results of his own earlier actions. Self-correction is therefore quick and relatively dependable. In the foreign and military policies of nation-states, on the contrary, reality testing is intermittent, more circular than interactive, slow and rare. It is carried on through very few channels and sometimes only a single one. Moreover it tells relatively little about the results of earlier steps in the same policy. The self-correction of a national foreign policy is therefore far more difficult.

Finally, misperceptions of reality are not often rewarding to the individual, even though they do occur in the cases of id-influenced perceptions as discussed by Freud, as well as in the relatively infrequent cases of pure chemical or physiological addiction and in the cases of reality distortions where addictive and Freudian processes are combined. In contrast to individuals, nation-states are far more prone to addictive behavior, particularly in international politics. Misperceptions of international reality can easily become rewarding to particular interest groups and even to governments and entire national systems. Thus repetitively reinforced, they may then become entrenched in memory, communication practices, and social institutions. For all these reasons, the mental health of nation-states is far more fragile and precarious than that of individuals.

If there is truth in these propositions, and if the basic structure of the Freudian model is relevant to the analysis of nation-states, then certain predictions about the real world would follow. In international politics we should expect nations to act irrationally, in the sense of nonpurposively or counterproductively, more often than would be expected from chance. And we should expect rivalries and conflicts to escalate beyond the interests of each participating nation as a whole. Moreover, we should expect the frequency and severity of such failures to increase whenever the ego burdens upon national governments increase faster than their capabilities for ego performance. Increases in mass participation in politics, and increases in the strength of political interest groups within a country, ought to increase in this manner the burden upon its governments. Another increase of the burden upon a government should arise from any increase in the severity of the reality constraints upon its actions.

All these processes have characterized international politics in the twentieth century. In many countries there has been a large increase in mass participation and interest group pressures, and during the same decades large increases in the effectiveness of modern weapons and delivery systems have increased the real dangers and constraints in relation to the foreign policy of governments. There is no evidence of any corresponding increase in the "intelligence quotient" of national governments or political systems, that is, in their information evaluation and decision-making capabilities. We should expect therefore an increased frequency of intelligence and decision failures and of foreign policy moves proving counterproductive in the international arena.

It would be interesting to test these propositions also by means of simulation experiments. Unfortunately most of the simulation procedures up to now have not been designed to isolate these variables. And even where they did so, the relevant data often have been poorly coded and reported. Many of the current simulation procedures, similar to traditional international relations theory, seem to be modeled on the international system of the nineteenth century. But it is an error to think that such models will come at all close to the reality of international politics since 1910. Secondary analyses of some past simulation experiments, and the design and operation of more appropriate new ones, may help us overcome in time these deficiencies.

War Proneness and Overdetermination: Some Quantitative Implications of the Systems Model

The simple three-level model which we have extracted from Freud's ideas permits us to approach the problems of proneness to war and overdetermination. The concept of overdetermination may help us account for the frequency and ease of escalation in international conflicts and for the remarkable resistance of national political systems against sectoral reforms and limited political efforts aimed at reversing trends toward wars or arms competition.

If we analyze the outbreak of a specific war, such as that of World War I, we may separate for purposes of analysis the relatively blind interest group pressures within each nation, which taken together in some ways parallel Freud's id. We may distinguish these from the ego-like efforts of the various governments to make rational decisions or else, like weak egos supply mere surface rationalizations for the blind demands of some of the interest groups. These processes in turn can be separated from the effects of the traditions, images, memories, and values which have become established in the political decision system and in the minds of the crucial decision-making groups and individuals, in a manner resembling the superego in Freud's model. Finally, there are the effects of the larger reality—the international environment—which includes the cumulative effects of the acts of many nation-states as well as the effects of the weapons systems and technologies employed in regard to such matters as transport and communication.

Each of these processes may tend to promote one of three possible outcomes: it may make the outbreak of war more likely, or less likely, or leave its probability unchanged. If the processes at one system level are very powerful in promoting the outbreak of war, they may do so almost regardless of what happens at the other system levels. Events at any one system level may then be likely to produce war.

If events at several system levels or at all system levels are pushing toward war, we may call the outbreak of war *overdetermined*. That is to say, if interest group pressures alone should produce a probability of war of .9, and a corresponding probability of peace of only .1, and if the effects of the decisions of the government should have an independent effect of the same size and the same direction; then the resulting probability of peace would only be .01 or one chance in one hundred. If the same independent effects as on the first two system levels should also be found to prevail on the level of superego-like memories, images, and values, and once again independently on the larger international system level, then the probability of peace would decline to .0001, or to one chance in ten thousand. If similar independent effects should exist on all levels of a six-level decision system, the chances will decline to 10^6 which is one chance in a million. Generally for an n-level system in which each level contributes an independent probability of p for the outbreak of war, and $(1-p)$ for the preservation of peace, the overall probability of peace will be $(1-p)^n$, or q^n if we call q the probability of peace and set it equal to $(1-p)$.

The distribution of the p's and q's will follow the well-known binomial theorem, but we assume here that a preponderance of war-promoting conditions on any one system level will suffice to push the system into war. Hence the mixed terms, containing both p and q, (such as $2pq$, for $n=2$) must be counted as promoting war, and only the pure probability of peace, q^n, remains relevant.

In a system that is overdetermined in this manner, the elimination of all war-promoting conditions on any one system level alone would have only very weak effects in increasing the likelihood of peace. If we eliminated all war-promoting processes from one of the levels of our four-level model, while leaving the other three levels undisturbed, the chances for peace would only improve from one in ten thousand to one in a thousand. In a system with a larger number of levels, the effects of eliminating all causes of war from a single level would be still smaller. If we had to use limited resources for reducing the likelihood of war in a system that is overdetermined in this manner, our most promising strategy would be to spread our efforts over as many system levels as possible, so as to reduce moderately the probability of war produced at each of these levels.

To clarify our notion of overdetermination in terms of cumulative probability, let us give another illustration. Let us suppose that for some country actual conditions at each of six system levels—world and regional system, nation-state, large interest groups, small decision-making groups, individual decision makers, and intrapersonal psychic substructures and memories—were such that the state of affairs at each level would make for a 90 percent probability of war as against only a 10 percent probability of a nonwar outcome. The cumulative likelihood of peace would then be 0.1 to the sixth power, or one chance in a million. If it were then possible by a large effort for peace to eliminate wholly the war-promoting conditions on four of these system levels (no matter which ones) this composite probability of war would be reduced to 10 to the second power, and the chances for peace would rise to a still desperate one in one hundred. So long as conditions at even one single level should remain unchanged in our example, the chances for peace could not be better than one in ten.

If, however, the same effort for peace were spread over all system levels, so as to reduce the likelihood of war resulting from the state of each, then the chances for peace could be improved much more. Concentrating on eliminating prowar conditions at two thirds of our system levels under the assumptions of our example does not raise the chances for peace higher than the low level of 1 percent. If we should, instead of this, use our efforts to reduce at every level the chances for war by two thirds, that is, from 0.9 down to 0.3 for each level, then we might do more than ten times better: the cumulative chances for peace would be 0.7 to the sixth power, or 0.117649, which amounts to almost one chance in eight for peace.

In all these examples we have assumed, for the sake of simplicity rather than of realism, that the probabilities at the various system levels are independent from each other. In real life, the probability of an outcome produced jointly by the interaction of several favoring conditions may be larger or smaller than the probability accounted for by each of them in isolation. Interaction effects of this kind, like threshold effects, require for their adequate representation more complex models, often of the "nonlinear" type.

One point, however, may be touched upon briefly. Since wars usually are resorted to by relatively well-organized states, we should expect that, more often than not, the direction and strengths of war-promoting or else war-inhibiting conditions and steps should be fairly similar or conform at all system levels. If this were not the case, the nation-state ordinarily would be less well organized and adjusted within itself and with its international environment. Some degree of such adjustment, although imperfect, seems to be found in most of the states that endure. If the relatively consonant probabilities at all system levels tend more strongly toward peace, then resort to war is unlikely, insofar as the initiatives of this particular nation are concerned (although it still could fall victim to an unprovoked attack).

If, on the contrary, conditions and events at all levels tend more or less in parallel toward war, then the transition to war will be relatively smooth and easy — as easy as the ancient Romans saw the descent to hell. There will be little sense of discontinuity or inner conflict. Most system levels, institutions, and persons will function as before, often spontaneously and "naturally," that is, in accord with the earlier probabilities of their own behavior, while their nation is moving to the brink of war. There may be a sense of national unity, sometimes even of elation. The currents of national opinion may look smooth like the waters above Niagara, speeding their flow to the abyss. This may be one of the reasons why so many collision courses and crises among nations have tended to develop a momentum of their own, beyond control by the decision makers caught up in them; why incipient wars have been so rarely stopped; and why wars, once started, have tended to spread to other countries.

The argument presented here has been carried on with dummy figures. What would be needed for the next steps would be better empirical estimates, based on real world date of the likelihood of war-promoting and of war-precipitating behavior at different system levels. An important alternative approach would be to obtain such estimates from simulation procedures, appropriately designed, coded, and analyzed for this purpose.

Summary and Conclusions

Our inquiry began with an empirical fact: the increasingly frequent failure of national governments in decisions leading to the escalation of conflicts, to war, and to the defeat of the governments which initiated large-scale war. Seeking a rational model to account for such counterproductive and hence irrational behavior, we found a structural model of a decision system in the theories of Sigmund Freud, accounting for ten types of conflict within or among information streams, and for a resulting high frequency of irrational, destructive, and self-destructive behavior in the case of individuals. This Freudian model of the individual personality system turned out to have several significant analogies with the decision system of nation states, even after ecological fallacies are avoided.[52]

An operational analysis of types of aggressive behavior then identified six types of approach behavior mainly in terms of the role played in each case by information processes as against matter-energy processes. Each type of approach behavior can give rise to serious conflict at whatever system level it occurs, and it demands at each level a high degree of information processing and control performances.

National governments must meet these high standards of performance but are poorly equipped for this task. They must mediate between the pressures of domestic interest groups and the outside world of ecology, technology, and international politics as well as between each of these two worlds and the world of supranational ethical values and memories. In these respects, their tasks resemble the performance demanded from the ego of the individual which must mediate between the pleasure of the id, the constraining reality principle of the outside world, and the demands of the internalized supraindividual morality embodied in the superego. Relative to their tasks, however, governments at the level of the nation-states tend to be poorer and more unbalanced in information, and weaker in resources than the ego of the individual. Changes in twentieth century national and world politics have increased these imbalances. Irrational behavior, decision failures, and resort to destructive and self-destructive behavior all now are likely to be more frequent, therefore, at the level of nation-states than they are at the level of the individual. Under the conditions of the late twentieth century, the mental health of nation-states — non-Communist and Communist alike — is more precarious than that of individuals.

52. On the general problem of ecological fallacies, see Mattei Dogan and Stein Rokkan, eds., *Quantitative Ecological Analysis in the Social Sciences* (Cambridge, MIT Press, 1969), and especially the chapter by Hayward R. Alker, Jr., "A Typology of Ecological Fallacies," ibid., pp. 69-86.

Appendix

Bibliography of Works by Rupert Emerson

Books

State and Sovereignty in Modern Germany. New Haven, Yale University Press, 1928.
Malaysia: A Study in Direct and Indirect Rule. New York, Macmillan, 1937.
The Netherlands Indies and the United States. Boston, World Peace Foundation, 1942.
With Lennox A. Mills and Virginia Thompson, *Government and Nationalism in Southeast Asia.* New York, Institute of Pacific Relations, 1942.
Representative Government in Southeast Asia. Cambridge, Harvard University Press, 1955.
From Empire to Nation. Cambridge, Harvard University Press, 1960.
With Norman J. Padelford, eds. *Africa and World Order.* New York, Praeger, 1963.
Self-Determination Revisited in the Era of Decolonization. Cambridge, Harvard University Center for International Affairs, 1964.
With Martin Kilson, eds. *The Political Awakening of Africa.* New York, Prentice-Hall, 1965.
Africa and United States Policy. New York, Prentice-Hall, 1967.

Articles

"Iraq: The End of a Mandate." *Foreign Affairs,* January 1933.
"The Chinese in Malaysia." *Pacific Affairs,* September 1934.
"The Dutch and British in the Eastern Tropics." *Koloniaal Tijdschrift,* The Hague, no. 6. 27e Jaargang.
"The Outlook in Southeast Asia." *Foreign Policy Reports,* November 15, 1939.
"The Dutch East Indies Adrift." *Foreign Affairs,* 18.4, July 1940.
"The Future Role of the Former Colonial Peoples." *Beyond Victory.* Ed. Ruth Nanda Anshen. New York, Harcourt Brace, 1943.
"An Analysis of Nationalism in Southeast Asia." *Far Eastern Quarterly,* February 1946.
"Trusteeship Takes Shape." *The Nation,* December, 7, 1946.
"Nationalist Movements in Southeast Asia." *America's Future in the Pacific.* New Brunswick, N. J., Rutgers University Press, 1947.
"American Policy toward Pacific Dependencies." *Pacific Affairs,* September 1947.
"Reflections on the Indonesian Case." *World Politics,* 1.1, October 1948.
"American Policy toward Pacific Dependencies" and "The United States and Trusteeship in the Pacific." *America's Pacific Dependencies.* New York, American Institute of Pacific Relations, 1949.
"Problems of Colonialism." *World Politics,* 1.4, July 1949.
"Point Four and Dependent Areas." *Annals of the American Academy of Political and Social Science,* March 1950.
"Education in the Netherlands East Indies." *Journal of Negro Education,* Summer 1946.
"American Policy in Southeast Asia." *Social Research,* December 1950.

"The Soviet Union and the United Nations: An Essay in Interpretation," with I. L. Claude, Jr. *International Organization,* February 1952.

"Progress in Asia: A Pessimistic View." *Far Eastern Survey,* August 27, 1952.

"Puerto Rico and American Policy toward Dependent Areas." *Annals of the American Academy of Political and Social Science,* January 1953.

"Our Responsibilities in Southeast Asia." *Southeast Asia in the Coming World.* Ed. Philip W. Thayer. Baltimore, 1953.

"Problems of Representative Government in Southeast Asia." *Pacific Affairs,* December 1953.

"Paradoxes of Asian Nationalism." *Far Eastern Quarterly,* February 1954.

"Indo-China." *Yale Review,* Autumn 1954.

"Colonialism and the Cold War." *Nation,* January 1, 1955.

"The Progress of Nationalism." *Nationalism and Progress in Free Asia.* Ed. Philip W. Thayer. Baltimore, 1956.

"U. S. — For or Against Colonialism?" *Headline Series: Foreign Policy Association.* January-February 1957.

Foreword in Frank H. H. King, *The New Malayan Nation,* IPR, 1957.

"The Character of American Interests in Africa." *The US and Africa,* for the 13th American Assembly, June 1958.

"Nationalism and Political Development." *Journal of Politics,* 22, March 1960.

"American Interest in Africa." *The Centennial Review,* 4.4, Fall 1960.

"The Erosion of Democracy." *Journal of Asian Studies,* 20.1, November 1960.

"Some Crucial Problems Involved in Nation-Building in Africa." *Journal of Negro Education,* Summer 1961.

"American Policy in Africa." *Foreign Affairs,* January 1962.

"Pan-Africanism." *International Organization,* Spring 1962.

Foreword to Thomas Okuma, *Angola in Ferment.* Boston, Beacon Press, 1962.

Foreword to Saadia Touval, *Somali Nationalism.* Cambridge, Harvard University Press, 1963.

"Nation-Building in Africa." *Nation-Building.* Ed. Karl W. Deutsch and William J. Foltz. New York, Atherton Press, 1963.

"The Atlantic Community and the Emerging Countries." *International Organization,* 17.3, 1963. This article was published in *The Atlantic Community: Progress and Prospects.* Ed. Francis O. Wilcox and H. Field Haviland, Jr. New York, Praeger, 1963.

"Colonialism Yesterday and Today." *New Nations in a Divided World.* Ed. Kurt London. New York, Praeger, 1964.

Political Modernization: The Single-Party System. Denver, Social Science Foundation and Department of International Relations, 1964.

"Nationalism and Political Development." *Journal of Politics,* March 1960. Reprinted in *Development: For What?* Ed. John H. Hallowell. Durham, N. C., Duke University Press, 1964.

"Colonialism, Political Development, and the UN." *International Organization,* 19.3, Summer 1965.

With Martin Kilson, "The American Dilemma in a Changing World: The Rise of Africa and the Negro American." *Daedalus,* Fall 1965.

"Dilemmas of American Policy in Africa." *Transition,* Kampala, Uganda, no. 25, 1966.

"Parties and National Integration in Africa." *Political Parties and Political Development.* Ed. Joseph LaPalombara and Myron Weiner. Princeton, N. J., Princeton University Press, 1966.

"Colonialism." *International Encyclopedia of the Social Sciences,* Vol. III, New York, Macmillan, 1968.

"Colonialism." *Journal of Contemporary History,* 4.1, January 1969.

"The Problem of Identity, Selfhood, and Image in the New Nations: The Situation in Africa." *Comparative Politics,* 1, April 1969.

"American Influence in Developed and Underdeveloped Countries." *Foreign Policy and the Developing Nation.* Ed. Richard Butwell. Lexington, Ky., University of Kentucky Press, 1969.

"The United Nations and Colonialism." *International Relations,* London, 3.10, November 1970. Also reprinted in *The Evolving United Nations: A Prospect for Peace?* Ed. Kenneth J. Twitchett. London, Europe Publications, 1971.

"Self-Determination." *American Journal of International Law,* Vol. 65.3, July 1971.

"Post-Independence Nationalism in South and Southeast Asia: A Reconsideration." *Pacific Affairs,* 44.2, Summer 1971.

"The Prospects for Democracy in Africa." *The State of the Nations: Constraints on Development in Independent Africa.* Ed. Michael F. Lofchie. Berkeley, University of California Press, 1971.

"Race in Africa: United States Foreign Policy." *Racial Influences on Foreign Policy.* Ed. George W. Shephard. New York, Basic Books, 1970.

"Nations, Nationalism, and the Third World." *The African Review,* Dar es Salaam, 1.2, September 1971.

"Reflections on Leadership in the Third World." *Essays on Modernization of Underdeveloped Societies.* Ed. A. R. Desai. Vol. II. Bombay, Thacker and Co., Ltd., 1972.

Contributors

Inis L. Claude, Jr., Edward R. Stettinius Professor of Government and Foreign Affairs, University of Virginia

James S. Coleman, formerly Professor of Political Science, University of California, Los Angeles

Karl Deutsch, Stanfield Professor of International Peace, Harvard University

Leo Gross, Professor of International Law, Fletcher School of Law and Diplomacy, Tufts University

Stanley Hoffmann, Professor of Government and Director of West European Studies Program, Harvard University

Willard R. Johnson, Associate Professor of Political Science, Massachusetts Institute of Technology

Martin Kilson, Professor of Government, Harvard University

Joseph S. Nye, Professor of Government, Harvard University

Nadav Safran, Professor of Government, Harvard University

Dieter Senghass, Professor of Political Science, Institute for Political Studies, Frankfurt, West Germany

M. Crawford Young, Professor of Political Science, University of Wisconsin

Index

249

Publications Written under the Auspices of the Center for International Affairs, Harvard University

Created in 1958, the Center for International Affairs fosters advanced study of basic world problems by scholars from various disciplines and senior officials from many countries. The research of the Center focuses on economic, social, and political development, the management of force in the modern world, and the evolving roles of Western Europe and the Communist nations, and the conditions of international order.

The Soviet Bloc, Zbigniew K. Brzezinski (sponsored jointly with the Russian Research Center), 1960. Harvard University Press. Revised edition, 1967.

The Necessity for Choice, by Henry A. Kissinger, 1961. Harper & Bros.

Rift and Revolt in Hungary, by Ferenc A. Váli, 1961. Harvard University Press.

Strategy and Arms Control, by Thomas C. Schelling and Morton H. Halperin, 1961. Twentieth Century Fund.

United States Manufacturing Investment in Brazil, by Lincoln Gordon and Engelbert L. Grommers, 1962. Harvard Business School.

The Economy of Cyprus, by A. J. Meyer, with Simos Vassiliou (sponsored jointly with the Center for Middle Eastern Studies), 1962. Harvard University Press.

Entrepreneurs of Lebanon, by Yusif A. Sayigh (sponsored jointly with the Center for Middle Eastern Studies), 1962. Harvard University Press.

Communist China 1955-1959: Policy Documents with Analysis, with a foreword by Robert R. Bowie and John K. Fairbank (sponsored jointly with the East Asian Research Center), 1962. Harvard University Press.

Somali Nationalism, by Saadia Touval, 1963. Harvard University Press.

The Dilemma of Mexico's Development, by Raymond Vernon, 1963. Harvard University Press.

Limited War in the Nuclear Age, by Morton H. Halperin, 1963. John Wiley & Sons.

In Search of France, by Stanley Hoffmann *et al.,* 1963. Harvard University Press.

The Arms Debate, by Robert A. Levine, 1963. Harvard University Press.

Africans on the Land, by Montague Yudelman, 1964. Harvard University Press.

Counterinsurgency Warfare, by David Galula, 1964. Frederick A. Praeger, Inc.

People and Policy in the Middle East, by Max Weston Thornburg, 1964. W. W. Norton & Co.

Shaping the Future, by Robert R. Bowie, 1964. Columbia University Press.

Foreign Aid and Foreign Policy, by Edward S. Mason (sponsored jointly with the Council on Foreign Relations), 1964. Harper & Row.

How Nations Negotiate, by Fred Charles Iklé, 1964. Harper & Row.

Public Policy and Private Enterprise in Mexico, edited by Raymond Vernon, 1964. Harvard University Press.

China and the Bomb, by Morton H. Halperin (sponsored jointly with the East Asian Research Center), 1965. Frederick A. Praeger, Inc.

Democracy in Germany, by Fritz Erler (Jodidi Lectures), 1965. Harvard University Press.

The Troubled Partnership, by Henry A. Kissinger (sponsored jointly with the Council on Foreign Relations), 1965. McGraw-Hill Book Co.

The Rise of Nationalism in Central Africa, by Robert I. Rotberg, 1965. Harvard University Press.

Pan-Africanism and East African Integration, by Joseph S. Nye, Jr., 1965. Harvard University Press.

Communist China and Arms Control, by Morton H. Halperin and Dwight H. Perkins (sponsored jointly with the East Asian Research Center), 1965. Frederick A. Praeger, Inc.

Problems of National Strategy, ed. Henry Kissinger, 1965. Frederick A. Praeger, Inc.

Deterrence before Hiroshima: The Airpower Background of Modern Strategy, by George H. Quester, 1966. John Wiley & Sons.

Containing the Arms Race, by Jeremy J. Stone, 1966. M.I.T. Press.

Germany and the Atlantic Alliance: The Interaction of Strategy and Politics, by James L. Richardson, 1966. Harvard University Press.

Arms and Influence, by Thomas C. Schelling, 1966. Yale University Press.

Political Change in a West African State, by Martin Kilson, 1966. Harvard University Press.

Planning without Facts: Lessons in Resource Allocation from Nigeria's Development, by Wolfgang F. Stolper, 1966. Harvard University Press.

Export Instability and Economic Development, by Alasdair I. MacBean, 1966. Harvard University Press.

Foreign Policy and Democratic Politics, by Kenneth N. Waltz (sponsored jointly with the Institute of War and Peace Studies, Columbia University), 1967. Little, Brown & Co.

Contemporary Military Strategy, by Morton H. Halperin, 1967. Little, Brown & Co.

Sino-Soviet Relations and Arms Control, ed. Morton H. Halperin (sponsored jointly with the East Asian Research Center), 1967. M.I.T. Press.

Africa and United States Policy, by Rupert Emerson, 1967. Prentice-Hall.

Elites in Latin America, edited by Seymour M. Lipset and Aldo Solari, 1967. Oxford University Press.

Europe's Postwar Growth, by Charles P. Kindleberger, 1967. Harvard University Press.

The Rise and Decline of the Cold War, by Paul Seabury, 1967. Basic Books.

Student Politics, ed. S.M. Lipset, 1967. Basic Books.

Pakistan's Development: Social Goals and Private Incentives, by Gustav F. Papanek, 1967. Harvard University Press.

Strike a Blow and Die: A Narrative of Race Relations in Colonial Africa, by George Simeon Mwase, ed. Robert I. Rotberg, 1967. Harvard University Press.

Party Systems and Voter Alignments, edited by Seymour M. Lipset and Stein Rokkan, 1967. Free Press.

Agrarian Socialism, by Seymour M. Lipset, revised edition, 1968. Doubleday Anchor.

Aid, Influence, and Foreign Policy, by Joan M. Nelson, 1968. The Macmillan Company.

Development Policy: Theory and Practice, edited by Gustav F. Papanek, 1968. Harvard University Press.

International Regionalism, by Joseph S. Nye, 1968. Little, Brown, & Co.

Revolution and Counterrevolution, by Seymour M. Lipset, 1968. Basic Books.

Political Order in Changing Societies, by Samuel P. Huntington, 1968. Yale University Press.

The TFX Decision: McNamara and the Military, by Robert J. Art, 1968. Little, Brown & Co.

Korea: The Politics of the Vortex, by Gregory Henderson, 1968. Harvard University Press.

Political Development in Latin America, by Martin Needler, 1968. Random House.

The Precarious Republic, by Michael Hudson, 1968. Random House.

The Brazilian Capital Goods Industry, 1929-1964 (sponsored jointly with the Center for Studies in Education and Development), by Nathaniel H. Leff, 1968. Harvard University Press.

Economic Policy-Making and Development in Brazil, 1947-1964, by Nathaniel H. Leff, 1968. John Wiley & Sons.

Turmoil and Transition: Higher Education and Student Politics in India, edited by Philip G. Altbach, 1968. Lalvani Publishing House (Bombay).

German Foreign Policy in Transition, by Karl Kaiser, 1968. Oxford University Press.

Protest and Power in Black Africa, edited by Robert I. Rotberg, 1969. Oxford University Press.

Peace in Europe, by Karl E. Birnbaum, 1969. Oxford University Press.

The Process of Modernization: An Annotated Bibliography on the Sociocultural Aspects of Development, by John Brode, 1969. Harvard University Press.

Students in Revolt, edited by Seymour M. Lipset and Philip G. Altbach, 1969. Houghton Mifflin.

Agricultural Development in India's Districts: The Intensive Agricultural Districts Programme, by Dorris D. Brown, 1970. Harvard University Press.

Authoritarian Politics in Modern Society: The Dynamics of Established One-Party Systems, edited by Samuel P. Huntington and Clement H. Moore, 1970. Basic Books.

Nuclear Diplomacy, by George H. Quester, 1970. Dunellen.

The Logic of Images in International Relations, by Robert Jervis, 1970. Princeton University Press.

Europe's Would-Be Polity, by Leon Lindberg and Stuart A. Scheingold, 1970. Prentice-Hall.

Taxation and Development: Lessons from Colombian Experience, by Richard M. Bird, 1970. Harvard University Press.

Lord and Peasant in Peru: A Paradigm of Political and Social Change, by F. LaMond Tullis, 1970. Harvard University Press.

The Kennedy Round in American Trade Policy: The Twilight of the GATT? by John W. Evans, 1971. Harvard University Press.

Korean Development: The Interplay of Politics and Economics, by David C. Cole and Princeton N. Lyman, 1971. Harvard University Press.

Development Policy II—The Pakistan Experience, edited by Walter P. Falcon and Gustav F. Papanek, 1971. Harvard University Press.

Higher Education in a Transitional Society, by Philip G. Altbach, 1971. Sindhu Publications (Bombay).

Studies in Development Planning, edited by Hollis B. Chenery, 1971. Harvard University Press.

Passion and Politics, by Seymour M. Lipset with Gerald Schaflander, 1971. Little, Brown, & Co.

Political Mobilization of the Venezuelan Peasant, by John D. Powell, 1971. Harvard University Press.

Higher Education in India, edited by Amrik Singh and Philip Altbach, 1971. Oxford University Press (Delhi).

The Myth of the Guerrilla, by J. Bowyer Bell, 1971. Blond (London) and Knopf (New York).

International Norms and War between States: Three Studies in International Politics, by Kjell Goldmann, 1971. Published jointly by Läromedelsförlagen (Sweden) and the Swedish Institute of International Affairs.

Peace in Parts: Integration and Conflict in Regional Organization, by Joseph S. Nye, Jr., 1971. Little, Brown & Co.

Sovereignty at Bay: The Multinational Spread of U.S. Enterprise, by Raymond Vernon, 1971. Basic Books.

Defense Strategy for the Seventies (revision of *Contemporary Military Strategy*), by Morton H. Halperin, 1971. Little, Brown & Co.

Peasants Against Politics: Rural Organization in Brittany, 1911-1967, by Suzanne Berger, 1972. Harvard University Press.

Transnational Relations and World Politics, edited by Robert O. Keohane and Joseph S. Nye, Jr., 1972. Harvard University Press.

Latin American University Students: A Six Nation Study, by Arthur Liebman, Kenneth N. Walker, and Myron Glazer, 1972. Harvard University Press.

The Politics of Land Reform in Chile, 1950-1970: Public Policy, Political Institutions, and Social Change, by Robert R. Kaufman, 1972. Harvard University Press.

The Boundary Politics of Independent Africa, by Saadia Touval, 1972. Harvard University Press.

The Politics of Nonviolent Action, by Gene E. Sharp, 1973. Porter Sargent.

System 37 Viggen: Arms, Technology, and the Domestication of Glory, by Ingemar Dorfer, 1973. Universitetsforlaget (Oslo).

University Students and African Politics, by William John Hanna. 1974. Africana Publishing Company.

Organizing the Transnational: The Experience with Transnational Enterprise in Advanced Technology, by M. S. Hochmuth, 1974. Sijthoff (Leiden).

Becoming Modern, by Alex Inkeles and David H. Smith, 1974. Harvard University Press.

Multinational Corporations and the Politics of Dependence: Copper in Chile, 1945-1973, by Theodore Moran, 1974. Princeton University Press.

The Andean Group: A Case Study in Economic Integration among Developing Countries, by David Morawetz, 1974. M.I.T. Press.

Kenya: The Politics of Participation and Control, by Henry Bienen, 1974. Princeton University Press.

Land Reform and Politics: A Comparative Analysis, by Hung-chao Tai, 1974. University of California Press.

Big Business and the State: Changing Relations in Western Europe, edited by Raymond Vernon, 1974. Harvard University Press.

Economic Policymaking in a Conflict Society: The Argentine Case, by Richard D. Mallon and Juan V. Sourrouille, 1975. Harvard University Press.

Harvard Studies in International Affairs*

[formerly Occasional Papers in International Affairs]

† 1. *A Plan for Planning: The Need for a Better Method of Assisting Underdeveloped Countries on Their Economic Policies,* by Gustav F. Papanek, 1961.

† 2. *The Flow of Resources from Rich to Poor,* by Alan D. Neale, 1961.

† 3. *Limited War: An Essay on the Development of the Theory and an Annotated Bibliography,* by Morton H. Halperin, 1962.

† 4. *Reflections on the Failure of the First West Indian Federation,* by Hugh W. Springer, 1962.

  5. *On the Interaction of Opposing Forces under Possible Arms Agreements,* by Glenn A. Kent, 1963. 36 pp. $1.25.

† 6. *Europe's Northern Cap and the Soviet Union,* by Nils Orvik, 1963.

  7. *Civil Administration in the Punjab: An Analysis of a State Government in India,* by E. N. Mangat Rai, 1963. 82 pp. $1.75.

  8. *On the Appropriate Size of a Development Program,* by Edward S. Mason, 1964. 24 pp. $1.00.

  9. *Self-Determination Revisited in the Era of Decolonization,* by Rupert Emerson, 1964. 64 pp. $1.75.

 10. *The Planning and Execution of Economic Development in Southeast Asia,* by Clair Wilcox, 1965. 37 pp. $1.25.

 11. *Pan-Africanism in Action,* by Albert Tevoedjre, 1965. 88 pp. $2.50.

 12. *Is China Turning In?,* by Morton Halperin, 1965. 34 pp. $1.25.

†13. *Economic Development in India and Pakistan,* by Edward S. Mason, 1966.

 14. *The Role of the Military in Recent Turkish Politics,* by Ergun Özbudun, 1966. 54 pp. $1.75.

†15. *Economic Development and Individual Change: A Social-Psychological Study of the Comilla Experiment in Pakistan,* by Howard Schuman, 1967.

 16. *A Select Bibliography on Students, Politics, and Higher Education,* by Philip G. Altbach, UMHE Revised Edition, 1970. 65 pp. $2.75.

 17. *Europe's Political Puzzle: A Study of the Fouchet Negotiations and the 1963 Veto,* by Alessandro Silj, 1967. 178 pp. $3.50.

 18. *The Cap and the Straits: Problems of Nordic Security,* by Jan Klenberg, 1968. 19 pp. $1.25.

 19. *Cyprus: The Law and Politics of Civil Strife,* by Linda B. Miller, 1968. 97 pp. $3.00.

†20. *East and West Pakistan: A Problem in the Political Economy of Regional Planning,* by Md. Anisur Rahman, 1968.

†21. *Internal War and International Systems: Perspectives on Method,* by George A. Kelley and Linda B. Miller, 1969.

*Available from Harvard University Center for International Affairs, 6 Divinity Avenue, Cambridge, Massachusetts 02138
†Out of print. May be ordered from AMS Press, Inc., 56 East 13th Street, New York, N.Y. 10003